# Planning and Evaluating Library Networked Services and Resources

# Planning and Evaluating Library Networked Services and Resources

Edited by John Carlo Bertot and
Denise M. Davis

**LIBRARIES**
U N L I M I T E D
A Member of the Greenwood Publishing Group

Westport, Connecticut • London

**Library of Congress Cataloging-in-Publication Data**

Planning and evaluating library networked services and resources / edited by John
  Carlo Bertot and Denise M. Davis.
      p.   cm.
      ISBN 1–56308–964–5 (pbk. : alk. paper)
    1. Library information networks. 2. Libraries–Special collections–Computer
  network resources.   3. Electronic information resources–Use studies. 4. Library
  administration–Decision making. 5. Library planning. 6. Library statistics. I. Bertot,
  John Carlo. II. Davis, Denise.
  Z674.7.P52   2004
  021.6'5—dc22       2004061539

British Library Cataloguing in Publication Data is available.

Library of Congress Catalog Card Number: 2004061539
ISBN: 1–56308–964–5

First published in 2004

Libraries Unlimited, 88 Post Road West, Westport, CT 06881
A Member of the Greenwood Publishing Group, Inc.
www.lu.com

Printed in the United States of America

The paper used in this book complies with the
Permanent Paper Standard issued by the National
Information Standards Organization (Z39.48–1984).

10   9   8   7   6   5   4   3   2   1

# Contents

# Illustrations

**Figures**

# Preface

John Carlo Bertot and Denise M. Davis

The roles, issues, considerations, services, and resources that libraries face and provide in the networked environment continue to evolve. Libraries offer more network services and resources than ever before, and expenditures for electronic material are on the rise (ARL, 2003; PLDS, 2003). At the same time, however, library evaluation approaches, techniques, and data reporting systems still favor traditional building-based services. Indeed, many libraries continue struggling to determine what evaluation approaches best assess a library's planning and decision making needs, given a library's organizational and situational factors; what measures or indicators of network services and resources are available; and how to conduct network service and resource evaluation efforts within a library (Bertot, 2004; Davis, 2004). As a result, libraries in general do not assess their network services and resources; incorporate network service and resource assessment into larger organizational evaluation efforts; or report the actual use, uses, and value of libraries in an increasingly networked society. This leads to two significant problems for library managers and staff: 1) They do not have access to critical data that can assist them in making key decisions regarding services and resources; and 2) They do not have data that can demonstrate to the communities that they serve the true nature of library use and value, one that reflects both building-based and network services and resources.

This book attempts to address the foregoing issues. In particular, the goals and objectives of the book are to:

- Provide a foundational understanding of the networked environment in which libraries offer services and resources;

- Guide librarians in the evaluation of and planning for library network services and resources;
- Prepare students enrolled in professional library degree programs for the evaluation of library network services and resources;
- Describe selected evaluation frameworks and provide an understanding of which evaluation approaches may offer libraries the best data regarding their network services and resources, given a library's organizational and situational factors;
- Offer techniques, tools, and methods that assist librarians in evaluating their library's network services and resources;
- Demonstrate the relationship between library evaluation needs, the implementation of library technology infrastructure, and service and/or resource use data;
- Identify specific e-metrics, performance indicators, standards, and other measures that can assist librarians in assessing their library's network services and resources;
- Describe the use of e-metrics and performance indicators for resource allocation and other decision making purposes;
- Offer approaches to and strategies for using vendor-provided database usage data;
- Provide a vendor perspective on the importance of usage data, standards development, and library data reporting needs;
- Identify policy issues for libraries associated with providing network services and resources; and
- Identify issues that are on the horizon for the provision of library network services and resources.

The 11 chapters and the appendices, supporting Web site, and other material strive to meet the book's overall goals and objectives.

The book has two parts. Part I contains five chapters that address overall evaluation, planning, and measurement issues associated with library network services and resources. Part II contains six chapters that provide guidance on specific aspects of library network services, such as developing requests for proposals and policies that govern the use of network services and resources, using vendor data for collections development and other decision making purposes, and understanding the vendor perspective on vendor data usage and reporting standards.

## Part I

In Chapter 1, John Carlo Bertot addresses library network services and resources evaluation and planning issues, activities, and processes.

The author describes an evaluation planning approach and establishes the context for library evaluation efforts regarding network services and resources. The chapter focuses on network-based evaluation planning, though in the context of larger evaluation efforts in which the library may engage.

John Carlo Bertot and J.T. Snead describe in Chapter 2 selected key evaluation frameworks and the types of evaluation data that such frameworks can provide library managers and staff regarding their library's network services and resources. In addition, the chapter provides guidance concerning which evaluation frameworks may provide the best data for library managers and staff, given their evaluation needs. The chapter also discusses issues that library managers and staff should consider with the various evaluation approaches.

Chapter 3, by John Carlo Bertot, focuses on the actual methods, tools, and techniques associated with evaluating library network services and resources. The chapter details various methodological considerations, approaches, and implementations that enable library managers and staff to assess their network services and resources. The chapter also provides sample surveys, questions, and other documentation that can assist library managers and staff in their evaluation efforts.

Chapter 4 details the latest standards and research efforts that provide various e-metrics (statistics and data elements) and performance indicators (measures of efficiency and effectiveness) for library network services and resources. In the chapter, John Carlo Bertot describes efforts by the National Information Standards Organization (NISO), International Standards Organization (ISO), Project COUNTER, International Coalition of Library Consortia (ICOLC), Florida State University's Information Use Management and Policy Institute, and others to identify, develop, field test, and implement e-metrics and performance indicators throughout libraries. The chapter also describes how libraries can use such e-metrics and performance indicators for various decision making, resource allocation, and external reporting purposes. In addition, the chapter assists library managers and staff in identifying evaluation preparation that the library will need to undergo as it engages in network service and resource assessment efforts.

Denise M. Davis describes, details, and discusses the needs assessment process regarding a library's provision of network services and resources in Chapter 5. Included in this chapter is a "tool kit" of assessment resources offering a range of baseline methods and models. The combined value of continued improvement of such methods and analysis, and the integration of e-metrics into regularized surveys of libraries, contribute to more reliable data reporting and replicable assessment models in the future.

# Part II

Chapter 6 offers library managers and staff a detailed discussion of the development of requests for proposals (RFPs) for vendor-based library network services and resources. In the chapter, Denise M. Davis identifies issues, provides guidance, and offers sample language that assists libraries to develop and engage in an RFP process. The chapter also provides examples of procurement models at the state, regional, and multiregional levels, and suggests an evaluation process that integrates e-metrics and traditional cost assessment measures.

In Chapter 7, Denise M. Davis and John Carlo Bertot describe selectively the policy environment in which libraries operate as they provide network services and resources. The legal framework created by the Children's Internet Protection Act and the USA Patriot Act, for example, has implications for libraries in general and network-based services and resources in particular. The chapter provides suggestions, identifies issues, and offers approaches that library managers and staff should consider as they plan for and offer network services and resources.

Judith Hiott and Syma Zerkow of the Houston Public Library provide in Chapter 8 a number of ways in which library managers and staff can use various e-metrics and performance indicators, techniques, and approaches for resource allocation and collection development decisions in libraries. The chapter offers worksheets, decision rules, and various other useful documentation that facilitate the resource allocation decision process. In addition, the chapter assists library managers and staff to rethink collection development policies and procedures as increasing amounts of material become available in digital format.

Chapter 9, by Wonsik "Jeff" Shim, offers libraries a number of useful strategies, solutions, and techniques for using database and aggregator vendor data. In particular, the chapter offers librarians various ways in which to access, analyze, report, and use vendor data for a number of decision making purposes. The chapter also provides library managers and staff with a decision making context in which vendor data resides, and suggests a number of options that libraries have at their disposal when using vendor data.

A key stakeholder in evaluating library network services and resources is the vendor community. In Chapter 10, Oliver Pesch of EBSCO Information Services identifies and describes issues in practice and future preparation that vendors face regarding vendor service and resource usage data that libraries so strongly desire. The chapter provides a vendor perspective on the key e-metric and standards initiatives (e.g., NISO, ISO, Project COUNTER, ICOLC, and others), including the importance of such efforts to both internal and external practices of the vendor community. The chapter also identifies future issues associated with emerging technologies that vendors and libraries will face.

The book concludes with a chapter by Charles R. McClure that summarizes key themes and issues presented in the book and looks forward as libraries measure, plan, and evaluate their network services and resources. The chapter considers the work and progress to date regarding the evaluation of library network services and resources, but also identifies issues in research and practice that still require attention as researchers, practitioners, and members of the vendor and publisher communities work together in the networked environment.

Collectively, these chapters provide broad coverage of a number of issues, considerations, strategies, approaches, and techniques in the assessment of library network services and resources. The book offers higher-level planning and evaluation content through approaches and techniques in assessment and in using specific data in library decision making activities. The book also includes policies, procedures, and other content that libraries should consider as they implement publicly accessible network services and resources.

## Additional Resources

In addition to the book's print content, there are four key Web-based resources that support the book:

- **Supporting Web site.** The authors established a Web site that contains supplemental and other useful material that enhances the contents of the book. The Web site, located at http://www.ii.fsu.edu/neteval/, includes tutorials, worksheets, and other items that readers of the book may find helpful. Various chapters in the book reference specific content on the Web site.
- **E-metrics instructional Web site.** The Information Use Management and Policy Institute, through a National Leadership Grant from the Institute of Museum and Library Services (IMLS), developed the E-Metrics Instructional System (EMIS) to assist librarians in using and reporting selected e-metrics. The interactive site is located at http://www.ii.fsu.edu/emis/ and is accessible to all who desire to use the tutorials, modules, and other site content.
- **NISO *Z39.7 Library Statistics* standard Web site.** Beginning in 2002, NISO engaged in a revision of its library statistics standard that includes a number of e-metrics adopted from ISO, various research

efforts, and input by the standards planning committee (which Denise M. Davis chaired and John Carlo Bertot served as a member). The standard is available at http://www.niso.org/emetrics and contains the latest data elements (e-metrics) and definitions.

- **Outcomes assessment Web site.** In collaboration with the Florida Division of Library and Information Services, the Information Use Management and Policy Institute developed an online instructional site designed to assist public libraries in assessing the outcomes of their Library Services and Technology Act (LSTA) grants. The project, funded in part through a grant from IMLS, offers substantial material that assists libraries in developing outcomes assessment plans, methodological approaches, data collection efforts, and presentation of findings in an LSTA context. The site is located at http://www.lstatoolkit.com/.

The book also references numerous additional sources throughout the content that readers may find useful.

## Limitations of the Book

As readers will soon discover, the topic area that this book addresses is large and complex. Each topic addressed in this book could certainly include additional discussion, presentation, and content. This required that the authors select key content and discussion items, which provides substantive discussion, but also identifies other resources for those readers who desire a more in-depth understanding of a particular issue.

Perhaps the most significant limitation to the book is that it focuses only on library network services and resources planning, and evaluation activities. This is by design. The authors readily agree that library network planning and evaluation efforts should occur in the larger context of library service and resource evaluation practices. Though we acknowledge this need throughout the book, space does not permit a discussion of overall planning and evaluation. Moreover, there are a number of resources that address library evaluation strategies. Most notably, the Public Library Association's *Planning for Results* and *Managing for Results* series (see http://www.pla.org) provide an excellent planning and evaluation framework for library services. As librarians use this book, they should consider ways in which to link the evaluation of network services and resources to larger library evaluation efforts.

In addition, the book touches on different evaluation frameworks–outputs and performance indicators, service quality, outcomes assessment, and balanced scorecard–from a network services and resources assessment perspective. The book presents these evaluation perspectives in the context of which evaluation approaches may yield the *best* data for management decision making, resource allocation, and other purposes. The book does not advocate one particular evaluation framework, but rather identifies which type of data each approach would provide in determining the quality and outcomes, for example, of network services and resources. Library managers and staff will need to consider the limitations, strengths, and potential of each approach, as well as various organizational and situational factors, as they evaluate their network services and resources.

## Moving Forward

Network service and resource e-metrics, performance indicators, methodologies, issues, and trends will continue to evolve even as this book is being read. This is the nature of the networked environment–new technologies will continue to emerge and find their place in the provision of library network services and resources. This will inevitably lead to the need for new metrics, indicators, and methods–and all the issues associated with planning and evaluating network services and resources.

The result is that libraries will need to be in a continual state of assessment and reassessment of their network service and resource evaluation efforts. While this will undoubtedly lead to short-term pain for libraries as they map out their evaluation strategies, the long-term gains will be substantial, as libraries are better able to describe the ways in which they contribute and add value to the communities that they serve.

# CHAPTER 1

# Network Service and Resource Evaluation Planning

## John Carlo Bertot

## Introduction

The evaluation process regarding library services and resources should not be something in which libraries engage as an afterthought, or after service and resource implementation. Rather, librarians should strive to build in evaluation opportunities, strategies, and efforts as a part of the service and resource planning, development, and implementation efforts. This is particularly important for the evaluation of network services and resources, as there is a direct relationship between the library's technology infrastructure and service and resource implementation architecture and the data that libraries can collect and report about those services and resources. Thus, it is essential for librarians to consider a number of evaluation needs prior to service and resource implementation.

Librarians need to consider several key questions to initiate an evaluation process. Minimally, these include the following:

- Who will use and/or review the data regarding library network services and resources?
- What do decision makers, staff, others want to know regarding library network services and resources?
- For what purposes will decision makers, staff, and others use the data?

- What are the goals, objectives, desired outcomes, level of service quality, and other key aims of the network services and resources that the library intends to provide?
- Where and in what formats will the library report its data?

These questions should guide librarians as they develop evaluation strategies and efforts regarding their network services and resources.

## Planning the Evaluation Process

Figure 1-1 demonstrates the overall evaluation planning process. It is important to note that the evaluation process resides within the context of a number of situational and organizational factors that will impact the evaluation efforts libraries undertake in several key ways.[1] The following are examples of situational and organizational factors that can influence library evaluation activities:

- **Externally imposed reporting requirements**. For example, public and other libraries that receive Library Services and Technology Act (LSTA) funds are required to report service and program outcomes[2] to their state library agencies, who then report such outcomes to the Institute of Museum and Library Services (IMLS). Other examples might include accreditation reporting requirements for academic libraries who reside on campuses that undergo periodic accreditation reviews through such entities as the Middle States Association of Colleges and Schools (see http://www.msache.org/msache/content/pdf_files/characteristicsbook.pdf for the accreditation standards and requirements), or the Southern Association of Colleges and Schools (see, for example, http://www.sacscoc.org/accrrevproj.asp for a review of various accreditation documents).
- **Library placement in the community and/or larger organization**. Factors such as the library's status can affect its reporting needs and requirements. For example, is the library an autonomous unit that reports directly to the city manager or university provost? Or is the library part of the education or other department, thus reporting to the department head rather than the executive? Library placement can influence the reporting demands made from the library.
- **Library stakeholder evaluation data preferences**. Library, community, and organizational decision makers may have a variety of data preferences that will influence a library's evaluation undertakings. For example, some may want to have data that demonstrate the value derived by users of library services and resources given investment

**Figure 1-1**
**The evaluation process.**

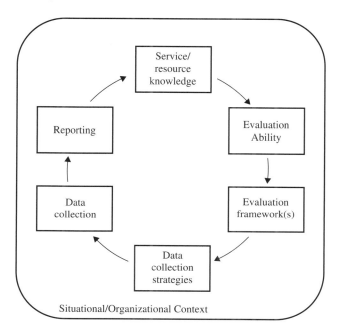

costs (return on investment). Perhaps others may want to know if users consider the service/resource to be of high quality. Others may want to know the reliability of the service (availability over time), while still others may want to know cost factors associated with the use of the service or resource. Others yet may want to know the impacts and benefits users derive from library service and resource use. More likely, librarians need to produce data that meet all of the presented data need examples above. Each of these data preferences requires a particular form of evaluation effort by the library (see Chapter 2 for more detail).

• **Culture of assessment and preparedness**. As Lakos (1999) indicated, a library's ability to engage in evaluation activities is dependent on the extent to which library management and staff believe in the value of evaluation efforts. The ability to engage in evaluation efforts, however, is also dependent on the evaluation skills, tools available, and resources available to those engaging in the evaluation activities.

The foregoing examples are illustrative and serve to demonstrate situational and organizational factors that can affect a library's ability to plan for and engage in evaluation efforts. Specific libraries may have other key contexts, or variations on these examples, that influence their evaluation endeavors.

The first step in the evaluation process is determining the *service/resource knowledge*, or what library managers, staff, or others want to know regarding the network service or resource. For example, is there a need to know

- How much and how often a service or resource is used?
- What users think about the quality of the service or resource provided?
- The impacts, benefits, or changes in knowledge, skills, or behavior that users derive as a result of the service or resource?
- The costs of service/resource provision (financial, human resource, other) versus the perceived benefits?
- Other information?

The situational and organizational context, evaluation participant familiarity with assessment techniques, reporting requirements (both internal and external, mandated and operational), service and resource goals and objectives, and a number of other factors can influence what library managers and others need to know regarding their network services and resources.

Readers should note that there are a large number of e-metrics and performance indicators that library managers, staff, and others can use to assess their network services and resources (see Chapter 4). It is important to determine, however, what *selected* e-metrics and performance indicators will be *most useful* to managers, staff, and others in terms of understanding the uses, impacts, benefits, and quality of the library's network services and resources. Thus, perhaps the most significant effort in which evaluation participants can engage is the data needs determination described earlier—What data are needed for which kinds of reporting, management, and other purposes? It is not the case that libraries should engage in e-metrics data collection for the sake of data collection. Well-done evaluation activities require resources, effort, and commitment. It is better to collect less data that are useful, and to do so in a well-resourced and planned way, than to collect large amounts of data in an under-resourced manner that diminishes the value of the data.

Upon determining the data needs, library managers and others need to engage in a library evaluation capability needs assessment. The evaluation of network services and resources can require a variety of new librarian skills, additional staff, certain technology architecture and configurations, software, and various other requirements in order for the library to engage successfully in data collection efforts. In essence, the library needs to conduct a *gap analysis* that takes into consideration the data needs, data collection requirements, and library preparedness to collect the data (Fig. 1-2). Library managers, staff, and others will then need to develop strategies and solutions to fill the gaps in the ability of the library to collect the desired data.

Once there is a determination of the data that the library needs, based on its evaluation efforts and the ability of the library to collect the data, there is a need to select the evaluation framework that will yield the types of data that the library requires (Fig. 1-3). Chapter 2 discusses various evaluation frameworks and the types of data that they might yield regarding network services and resources. Briefly, however, the *how much*, *how often*, and *by whom* questions tend to rely on outputs assessment techniques; service and resource efficiency and effectiveness questions tend to rely on performance indicator assessment techniques; user satisfaction, user perception of service, and resource quality questions rely on service quality assessment techniques; and questions related to changes in user behavior, skills, and knowledge tend to rely on outcomes assessment techniques. Additionally, there are evaluation frameworks–such as the balanced scorecard–that borrow from outputs, service quality, and outcomes assessment techniques and attempt to provide a balanced view of library services and resources (Matthews, 2004; Self, 2003; Kaplan & Norton, 1996).

The evaluation framework–or combination of frameworks–will influence the development and implementation of data collection strategies in which the library engages. For example, library managers, staff, and others may want to know

- [Outputs] How much and how often a licensed database resource is used? To find out, there is a need to establish data collection and reporting activities regarding the database's usage logs–usually supplied by the database vendor or by the contracting entity, which may be the library, the consortia headquarters to which the library belongs, or the state library agency.

- [Outputs] How many questions a digital reference service receives and answers in a given period? To find out, there is the need to establish a reporting system (perhaps built into the digital reference software the library uses) that logs and tracks reference questions and answers.

- [Performance Indicator] How much each database item downloaded costs, the cost per digital reference transaction, or the percentage of time a service or resource is available to users? To find out, there is a need to develop both service and resource cost figures and service and resource log usage files. Finally, there is a need to develop methods and a process for combining these data to yield appropriate measures of performance.

**Figure 1-2**
**Library evaluation capability assessment tool.**

| Data Needs (what the library desires to know) | Data Collection Requirements (what data need to be collected) | Library Needs (what it will take for library to collect data) | | | | | | |
|---|---|---|---|---|---|---|---|---|
| Remote visitors to library's website (virtual visits) | External sessions to library's website | Web server log files | Have | Need | | | | |
| | | Web log analysis software | Have | Need | | | | |
| | | Staff/person to run analysis | Have | Need | | | | |
| | | | | | | | | |
| | | | | | | | | |
| | | | | | | | | |
| | | | | | | | | |
| | | | | | | | | |
| | | | | | | | | |

**Figure 1-3**
**Selected evaluation frameworks.**

| Outputs/Performance Indicator Assessment | Measures of service and resource use, usage, availability, efficiency, and effectiveness. |
|---|---|
| Service Quality Assessment | Measures of how well a service and resource is performed through user-based assessments and/or predetermined quality standards. |
| Outcomes Assessment | Measures of changes in service/resource user skills, knowledge, and/or behavior; impacts and benefits derived by users of services and resources. |
| Balanced Scorecard | Measures that combine outputs, service quality, and outcomes assessment to develop an overall sense of library performance. |

- [Outcomes] How well a user is able to use a computer to search the Web as a result of training programs offered by the library. To find out, there is a need to develop pre-instruction computer and searching skills tests and post-instruction computer and searching skills tests so as to assess the difference that the training session made in a user's ability to use the technology.
- [Service Quality] How satisfied users are with a library's e-book selection and availability (or perhaps other online resources). To find out, there is a need to develop various data collection efforts (e.g., surveys, focus groups, interviews) that determine user satisfaction and ratings (perceived quality) regarding the library's e-book services and resources.

It is essential, therefore, that those involved in the evaluation process develop evaluation strategies, methods, and approaches that will provide the types of data that they want regarding the library's network services and resources.

One key component of the data collection strategies is to develop what essentially is a data map (Fig. 1-4), that is, a tool that details at least the following elements: 1) Desired data; 2) Source of the data, which includes whether this is branch or system-level data; 3) Type of data and method of collection; 4) Individual and/or group responsible for collecting and reporting the data; 5) Resource needs for collection and reporting; 6) Estimated time required to collect data; 7) Data reporting frequency; and 8) To whom the data are reported for further use. These details, minimally, will enable those involved in the evaluation efforts to keep track of the data collection efforts involved in the evaluation process.

The data map is also useful for assisting libraries to create an evaluation management process. It is not always the case that library managers,

**Figure 1-4**
**E-metric data map.**

| E-metric/Desired Data | Library collection full-content units examined (would include full-text articles downloaded/accessed from a library's database subscriptions). |
|---|---|
| Data Source/Level | Database vendor; System level. |
| Data Type/ Collection Method | Database log file; Collection/access to log data is dependent on the database vendor. |
| Staff Member/ Group | Jane Smith, Serials Librarian |
| Data Collection Resource Needs | Staff member needs to access the database data on a regular basis (e.g., monthly); Manipulate the data (likely across different types of vendor data systems) [Note: this may require another staff member or may be the same individual assigned responsibility for this e-metric/data]; Report number; May need statistical analysis software, or at least spreadsheet software such as Microsoft Excel. |
| Estimated Time Required | 10 hours per month |
| Data Reporting Frequency | Monthly |
| Data Reported To | Abby Jones, Associate Director |

staff, or others know the source of the data that they want, where the data need to be collected (in branches or at a system level), the methods through which collection and reporting might occur, or the effort required to engage assessing a particular service and resource. Indeed, data mapping can be helpful in determining and/or reassessing the value of a particular form of data, given what it might require to acquire and use such data. It can also be helpful in determining what gaps might exist for the library to be able to collect such data, or the need to alter service provider contract language to enable the collection of such data, etc. Said differently, the data map provides library network service and resource evaluators with an at-a-glance picture of the level of effort data collection will require for a particular e-metric or data point.

Once the data collection strategies are developed and in place, those assigned the responsibility for actually collecting the data can engage in their required data collection efforts. While some e-metrics (discussed in Chapter 4) require one-time annual collection efforts, others require ongoing and continual data collection efforts—sometimes monthly, but other times at service provision-dependent intervals (i.e., each time an instructional class is offered). Thus, it is essential to determine the frequency with which the desired data are to be collected and through what means (e.g., survey, log files, etc.). Chapter 3 discusses these and other methodological issues.

Included in the data collection process is data analysis. The analysis process can require data entry (for survey form data, for example), the transfer of datasets (for online survey data or online vendor data, for example), analysis software, and analysis expertise. The analysis process can be as simple as adding the total number of persons who attended library-provided technology instructional sessions during the month of April, or as complex as adding the total number of full-text articles downloaded across different database vendors (see Chapter 9). Once computed, the various data generated from the data collection activities need to be reported to the appropriate person and/or team within the library, who will use the results to generate various library reports for decision-making and reporting purposes regarding the assessed services or resources (see Chapter 4 regarding using the data for decision making purposes).

The foregoing discussion has provided readers with a look at an overall evaluation process regarding network resources and services. The described process is intended to facilitate the data needs–determination activities in which library managers, staff, and others might engage for evaluation planning and implementation efforts. The next section provides readers with two different data needs-assessment frameworks that may be useful. There are certainly other approaches that libraries may find more helpful, given the situational and organizational factors with which libraries must contend.

## Evaluation Planning: Two Approaches

There are a number of approaches, methods, and tools that library managers, staff, and others can use to determine their network service and resource data needs. This section presents two different ways that library evaluators may find helpful as they consider their network services and resources data needs and evaluation strategies. For illustrative purposes, both approaches presented here predominantly use existing selected e-metrics and performance indicators from current International Standards Organization (ISO) and National Information Standards Organization (NISO) library statistics and performance indicator standards efforts. See Chapter 4 for more detail regarding these efforts and specific e-metrics and performance indicators.

## The Network Service and Resource Component Approach

As first described by Bertot and McClure (1998), this approach offers a two-dimensional framework for determining network service and resource data needs, as well as appropriate e-metrics and performance indicators (Fig. 1-5). This framework suggests that there are numerous components to network-based services and resources:

- **Technical infrastructure:** The hardware, software, equipment, communication lines, and technical aspects of the network (e.g., workstations, leased lines, routers, servers);
- **Information content:** The information resources available on the network (e.g., digital collections, local government information);
- **Information services:** The activities in which users can engage and the services that users may use to complete various tasks (e.g., Ebsco-Host, FirstSearch, online applications);
- **Support:** The assistance and support services provided to help users better use the network (e.g., instruction, help desk, technical support); and
- **Management:** The human resources, governance, planning, and fiscal aspects of the network (e.g., network staff, advisory boards, budgeting).

In addition, there are different types of evaluation criteria that library managers, staff, and others can consider against which to measure their network services/resources:

- **Extensiveness:** How much of a network service or resource the library provides (e.g., number of virtual visits per week, number of database sessions);
- **Efficiency:** The use of resources in providing or accessing network services and resources (e.g., cost per session in providing access to remote users of an online database, average number of times users are unable to successfully connect to the library's servers, etc.);
- **Effectiveness:** How well the network service or resource met the objectives of the provider or the user (e.g., success rate of identifying and accessing the information needed by the user);
- **Service quality:** How well a service or activity is done (e.g., percentage of transactions in which users acquire the information they need, percentage of "highly satisfied" service or resource users);

Figure 1-5
Selected e-metrics and performance indicators.

| Types of Measures | Network Components | | | | |
|---|---|---|---|---|---|
| | Technical Infrastructure | Information Content | Information Services | Support | Management |
| **Extensiveness** | ■ (W/I) Public access workstations<br>▲ (W/I) Number of workstation hours available per capita<br>▲ (W/I) Population per public access workstation | ■ (SV) Virtual visits<br>▲ (SV) Percentage of virtual visits to total visits<br>▲ (SV) Percentage of population reached by electronic services | ■ *(EM) Full text titles available by subscription*<br>■ *(EM) E-book titles available*<br>▲ *(EM) Percentage serial titles offered in electronic form*<br>▲ *(EM) Percentage book titles available in electronic form* | ■ (I) Formal user IT instruction<br>■ (I) Point-of-use IT instruction<br>▲ (I) Number of user attendances at electronic service training lessons per capita<br>▲ (I) Number of attendances at formal IT and related training lessons per staff member | ▲ (SV) Percentage of library staff providing and developing electronic services |
| **Efficiency** | ■ (U) Public access workstation users<br>▲ (U) Workstation use rate | | ■ (U) Commercial services sessions<br>■ (U) OPAC sessions<br>■ (U) Commercial services searches (queries)<br>■ (U) Library collections searches (queries)<br>■ U) OPAC searches | | ■ (F/E) Electronic materials expenditures<br>■ (F/E) Electronic network expenditures<br>▲ (F/E) Cost per database session |

(Continued)

Figure 1-5 (Continued)
Selected e-metrics and performance indicators.

| Types of Measures | Network Components | | | |
| | Technical Infrastructure | Information Content | Information Services | Support | Management |
|---|---|---|---|---|---|
| Efficiency (*Continued*) | | | ▲ *(U) Percentage electronic materials use of total library material use* <br> ▲ *(U) Total library materials use* | | ▲ (F/E) Cost per document downloaded <br> ▲ (F/E) Percentage of expenditure on information provision spent on the electronic collection |
| Effectiveness | | | ■ (U) Library collection full-content units examined <br> ■ (U) Commercial services full-content units examined <br> ■ (U) Library collection descriptive records examined <br> ■ (U) Commercial services descriptive records examined <br> ■ (U) OPAC descriptive records examined | | |

| | |
|---|---|
| | ■ (SV) Electronic document delivery<br>▲ (U) Number of documents downloaded per session<br>▲ (U) Percentage of remote OPAC sessions<br>▲ *(SV) Percentage of documents delivered electronically* |
| **Service Quality** | ■ (W/I) Rejected sessions (turnaways)<br>▲ (W/I) Percentage of rejected sessions |
| **Outcomes** | See Chapter 2 for some discussion of outcomes-based evaluation of network services and resources. |
| **Adoption** | ■ (SV) Virtual reference transactions<br>▲ (SV) Percentage of information requests submitted electronically<br>▲ *(SV) Total reference activity*<br>▲ *(SV) Percentage virtual reference to total reference activity* |

W/I = Workstations/Infrastructure U = Usage EM = Electronic Materials F/E = Finances/Expenditures SV = Services I = Instruction

(Continued)

**Figure 1-5 (Continued)**
**Selected e-metrics and performance indicators.**

---

■ E-metric (source: National Information Standards Organization. (2003). *Z39.7-2002 draft standard–Information services and use: Metrics and measures for libraries and information providers.* Available at http://www.niso.org/emetrics. Last accessed December 15, 2003.)
▶ Performance indicator (source: International Standards Organization. (2003). *Technical Report 20983: Information and documentation– performance indicators for electronic library services.* International Standards Organization.)

Those e-metrics/performance indicators presented in *italics* are from Bertot, McClure, & Ryan (2001); Shim, et al. (2001); and ICOLC (2001).

---

- **Outcome:** How a service or resource made a difference in some other activity or situation, or a change in knowledge, skills, or behavior (e.g., the degree to which network users enhanced their ability to gain employment or pursue business);
- **Usefulness:** The degree to which the services are useful or appropriate for individual users (e.g., percentage of services of interest to different types of user audiences); and
- **Adoption:** The extent to which institutions or users integrate and adopt network services and resources into organizational or individual activities (e.g., answering reference questions, generating inter-library loan requests).

These types of criteria provide a matrix approach for thinking about the type of e-metrics and performance indicators that would be necessary to meet library data needs, and evaluation and data collection strategies. It is important to note, however, that existing e-metrics and performance indicators do not yet provide certain types of data–for example, service and resource outcomes data. Nor do they provide user-based service quality data (see Chapter 2 for more on service quality and outcomes-based assessment).

Library managers, staff, and others can use the Network Resource and Component Approach in at least three ways: 1) To map existing e-metrics and performance indicators that library standards adopted, defined, and tested in other library institutions and that meet the data needs of their specific library; 2) To develop measures to meet additional identified data needs of their specific library; and 3) To identify gaps for which e-metrics and performance indicators do not exist. The latter is a particularly important activity, as there are gaps in the matrix for which there are no existing e-metrics or performance indicators. Moreover, it may be the case that an outputs-based approach such as e-metrics and performance indicators will not yield the *best* data for service quality and outcomes data needs (more on this in Chapter 2).

In using the matrix, however, it is possible to look at the technical infrastructure aspect of a library's network and consider e-metrics and performance indicators for that aspect, along with the evaluation criteria of extensiveness, efficiency, etc. For example, library managers and others may want data that reflect the following areas of interest, although this list is not exhaustive:

- **Technical Infrastructure and Extensiveness:** Number of public access workstations; number of workstation hours available per capita; population per public access workstation;
- **Technical Infrastructure and Efficiency:** Number of public access workstation users; workstation use rate;
- **Information Content and Extensiveness:** Virtual visits; percentage of virtual visits to total visits; percentage of population reached by electronic services;
- **Information Services and Extensiveness:** Full-text titles available by subscription; e-book titles available; percentage of serial titles offered in electronic form;
- **Information Services and Efficiency:** Commercial services sessions; OPAC sessions; commercial service searches; electronic materials use as a percentage of total library material use;
- **Information Services and Effectiveness:** Library collection full-content units examined; commercial services full-content units examined; electronic document delivery; number of documents downloaded per session; percentage of remote OPAC sessions;
- **Information Services and Adoption:** Virtual reference transactions; percentage of information requests submitted electronically; virtual reference as a percentage of total reference activity;
- **Support and Extensiveness:** Formal user IT instruction; point-of-use IT instruction; number of user attendances at electronic service training lessons per capita; and
- **Management and Efficiency:** Electronic materials expenditures; cost per database session; cost per document downloaded.

Library service and resource evaluators can use the foregoing criteria as (1) a means through which to determine the types of data that they desire about their network services and resources; (2) a way to use existing and field-tested e-metrics and performance indicators; (3) a tool to develop measures that do not already exist and/or meet the specific needs of the library; and (4) a tool to determine whether other, more appropriate, evaluation frameworks may provide the data necessary (e.g., service quality tools such as LibQUAL+, or outcomes assessment tools such as those found at http://www.lstatoolkit.com) for certain types of network service and resource data (see Chapter 2).

### The Balanced Scorecard Approach

Kaplan & Norton (1996) developed the balanced scorecard as a means to measure the overall performance of an organization along four dimensions: financial, customer, internal, and innovation/learning. The notion of the balanced scorecard is to review organizational effectiveness, efficiency, use, and other factors through multiple measures that allow managers to determine overall performance. Thus, the balanced scorecard approach does not favor any one particular evaluation perspective or philosophy (e.g., outputs, service quality, outcomes).

More recently, library organizations have been experimenting with the balanced scorecard as an evaluation tool (Matthews, 2004; Self, 2003). Approaches that libraries take can vary, and do not necessarily use the initial financial, customer, internal, and innovation/learning dimensions recommended by Kaplan & Norton. Of more importance than the original scorecard dimensions is that libraries create their own scorecard dimensions and measures that they will use to determine service and resource goal and objective attainment, quality standards, performance indicators, or other indicators of success, use, efficiency, effectiveness, etc. Such an approach will provide an evaluation master plan tailored to meet the specific data needs of a particular library, rather than a prescribed approach that does not factor in the situational and organizational context of one's own library.

Figure 1-6 presents a balanced scorecard-based approach to measuring network services and resources through e-metrics and performance indicators. The scorecard example uses four dimensions:

1. **Resources, Accessibility, and Infrastructure**, which includes items such as technology infrastructure (i.e., public access workstations); resources to which the library subscribes (e.g., e-journals, e-books); and capacity (i.e., simultaneous use licenses and rejected session rates).

2. **Use of Services and Resources**, which includes items such as instruction (e.g., users who attend library instruction sessions, courses offered); database and/or online resource sessions, searches, items and content examined, and documents and items downloaded.

3. **Cost Efficiency**, which includes items such as materials and network expenditures (e.g., subscription costs, telecommunications line costs); and expenditures per service or resource use (e.g., cost per document and item downloaded, cost per session).

Figure 1-6
**Balanced scorecard approach to e-metrics and performance indicators.**

## Resources, Accessibility, & Infrastructure

| E-metric | Performance Indicators |
|---|---|
| (W/I) Public access workstations | (W/I) Number of workstation hours available per capita |
| (W/I) Public access workstation users | (W/I) Population per public access workstation |
| (W/I) Rejected sessions | (W/I) Percentage of rejected sessions |
| (EM) *Full text titles available by subscription* | (EM) *Percentage serial titles offered in electronic form* |
| (EM) *E-book titles available* | (EM) *Percentage book titles available in electronic form* |

## Use of Services & Resources

| E-metric | Performance Indicators |
|---|---|
| (I) Formal user IT instruction | (I) Number of user attendances at electronic service training lessons per capita |
| (I) Point-of-use IT instruction | (SV) Percentage of virtual visits to total visits |
| (SV) Electronic document delivery | (SV) Percentage of information requests submitted electronically |
| (SV) Virtual visits | (SV) Percentage of population reached by electronic services |
| (SV) Virtual reference transactions | (SV) *Total reference activity* |
| (U) Commercial services sessions | (SV) *Percentage virtual reference to total reference activity* |
| (U) OPAC sessions | (SV) *Percentage of documents delivered electronically* |
| (U) Commercial services searches | (U) Percentage of remote OPAC sessions |
| (U) Library collections searches | (U) Number of documents downloaded per session |
| (U) OPAC searches | (U) *Percentage of remote commercial services sessions* |
| (U) Library collection full-content units examined | (U) *Percentage of electronic materials use of total library material use* |
| (U) Commercial services full-content units examined | (U) *Total library material use* |
| (U) Library collection descriptive records examined | (W/I) Workstation use rate |
| (U) Commercial services descriptive records examined | |
| (U) OPAC descriptive records examined | |

(Continued)

**Figure 1-6 (Continued)**
**Balanced scorecard approach to e-metrics and performance indicators.**

| Cost Efficiency | |
|---|---|
| **E-metric** | **Performance Indicators** |
| (F/E) Electronic materials expenditures<br>(F/E) Electronic network expenditures | (F/E) Cost per database session<br>(F/E) Cost per document downloaded |

| Potentials & Development | |
|---|---|
| **E-metric** | **Performance Indicators** |
| *(I) Formal staff IT instruction* | (F/E) Percentage of expenditure on information provision spent on the electronic collection<br>(I) Number of attendances at formal IT and related training lessons per staff member<br>(SV) Percentage of library staff providing and developing electronic services |

W/I=Workstations/Infrastructure  U=Usage  EM=Electronic Materials  F/E=Finances/Expenditures  SV=Services  I=Instruction

E-metric source: National Information Standards Organization. (2003). *Z39.7-2002 draft standard – Information services and use: Metrics and measures for libraries and information providers*. Available at http://www.niso.org/emetrics, accessed December 15, 2003.
Performance indicator source: International Standards Organization. (2003). *Technical Report 20983: information and documentation - performance Indicators for electronic library services*. International Standards Organization.

Those e-metrics/performance indicators presented in *italics* are from Bertot, McClure, & Ryan (2001); Shim, et al. (2001); and ICOLC (2001).

4. **Potentials and Development**, which includes items such as resources (e.g., human, financial, equipment, other) required to develop, maintain, and provide network services and resources (e.g., cost to digitize resources and develop digital collections, maintaining and updating staff skills training programs).

This approach enables library managers, staff, and others to develop measures in a number of key areas that they will then use to guide the evaluation and data collection process. The approach requires two key decisions: 1) The dimensions that the library will use to assess itself; and 2) The actual measures the library will use to determine the success, issues, etc., associated with its network services and resources.

## Putting the Evaluation Planning Pieces Together

Preparing your library to evaluate its services and resources involves both *planning to evaluate* and operational/implementation activities. Thus, library managers, staff, and others need to engage in both *thinking* and *doing* strategies. Too much thinking with little or no doing leads to a lack of data to meet important library decision making and reporting needs, whereas too much doing with little or no thinking can lead to an abundance of data without purpose, data of poor quality, and a considerable expenditure of resources (e.g., human, financial) for little or no benefit. The challenge, therefore, is to strike the right balance between thinking (evaluation strategizing and data needs determination) and doing (engaging in targeted data collection efforts with a well-constructed and managed data collection, analysis, and reporting process).

To do this, library managers, staff, and others need to complete the following steps.

- **Conduct a data needs assessment**. Discussed more thoroughly in previous sections of this chapter, this is a critical first step in developing a library's network service and resource evaluation plan. It is imperative that key staff and decision makers determine what data they need to fulfill library decision making, management, and reporting needs.

- **Create an evaluation process**. Once the library determines its data needs, it is important to develop an overall network service and resource evaluation plan.[3] This includes
  - Defining clear goals and objectives of the evaluation process;
  - Selecting an evaluation approach that facilitates the selection of measures, methods, and other key items related to acquiring the data the library wants;

- Understanding and selecting various evaluation frameworks (e.g., outputs, service quality, outcomes, balanced scorecard, other) that are *most likely* to provide the data that the library needs;

- Determining what the library will need in terms of resources, staff, staff training, equipment, etc., in order to engage in the evaluation activities;

- Preparing various areas of the library for data collection activities, to include explaining to the staff what the purpose of the evaluation is, as well as the duration, process, and other key activities and needs; and

- Creating a clear data reporting structure and process so that those involved with the actual data collection know what to do with the collected data.

- **Manage the process**. There needs to be an overall command and management structure in place that governs the evaluation process. The evaluation of network services and resources can occur in many locations (e.g., branches, systems, particular service areas), involve a number of people and resources, and require data collection from a wide range of sources (e.g., vendors, users, and county/city/campus IT shops). Thus, the evaluation process is complex and requires management. Work by the authors and others (Bertot, McClure, & Ryan, 2001; Matthews, 2004; Hernon & Whitman, 2001) indicates that evaluation efforts in libraries work best when responsibility for a library's overall evaluation activities is assigned to one particular individual or group of individuals (perhaps as part of a quality management team, or some other configuration).

- **Devote, reassign, or reconfigure resources to evaluation**. In conducting the data needs assessment and creating an evaluation process, it may become apparent that the library is not fully prepared to engage in evaluation activities that will yield key data. Indeed, it may be the case that it is necessary to train and/or reassign staff, hire staff with specific skills, purchase equipment, reconfigure certain systems implementations (e.g., OPACS, websites, firewalls, etc.) to meet various evaluation and data needs.

- **Use the data**. The results of the evaluation activities need to feed back into the library's decision making, planning, and strategy development efforts. As other chapters in this book mention, these data can be used for collections development decisions, resource allocation, staffing needs, and any number of decisions. It is important to integrate the evaluation results with strategic and operational library undertakings, so as to better meet the information needs of the library's community of users through network services and resources.

- **Report the data**. It is unfortunate that many libraries report their various data only through standard, and often mandated, reports. This practice often leaves a number of key individuals–particularly library staff–with a lack of understanding about the results, uses, and significance of their evaluation efforts. Staff buy-in regarding evaluation is critical, and one way to enlist staff cooperation and participation is to demonstrate how the data are used for various decision making, management, and service and resource provision purposes. Also, given the level of effort that libraries can expend on evaluation, it is important to maximize the use of the results through a number of reporting outlets: reports, brochures, and/or presentations to external library stakeholder groups, community-based organizations, users, and others that may benefit the library on various occasions.

By following this process, with modifications to better meet the specific needs of a particular library, library managers and staff can develop a productive, useful, and meaningful evaluation process to assess a library's network services and resources.

## Notes

1. A library's evaluation of its network services and resources may or may not occur as a separate evaluation process from other services, resources, and activities that a library offers. The focus of this book is on the evaluation of network services and resources, and thus presents issues that librarians and others should consider while evaluating those types of resources. Depending on how a library manages its evaluation activities, network service and resource evaluation may or may not occur separately from larger evaluation efforts.
2. Outcomes assessment is a particular type of evaluation framework discussed in more detail in Chapter 2.
3. As noted earlier, the focus of this book is on the evaluation of network services and resources, and thus presents issues that librarians and others should consider while evaluating those types of resources. Depending on how a library manages its evaluation activities, network service and resource evaluation may or may not occur separately from larger evaluation efforts.

## References

Bertot, J.C. (2001). Measuring service quality in the networked environment: Approaches and considerations. *Library Trends*, 49 (4): 758–775.

Bertot, J.C., McClure, C.R., & Ryan, J. (2001). *Statistics and performance measures for public library networked services.* Chicago, IL: American Library Association.

Hernon, P., & Whitman, J.R. (2001). *Delivering satisfaction and service quality: A customer-based approach for libraries.* Chicago, IL: American Library Association.

Kaplan, R. & Norton, D. (1996). *Translating strategy into action: The balanced scorecard.* Boston, MA: Harvard Business School Press.

Lakos, A. (1999). The missing ingredient: Culture of assessment in libraries. *Performance Measurement and Metrics,* 1(1), 3–7. Retrieved 20 March 2003 from http://www.aslib.com/pmm/1999/aug/opinion.pdf.

Matthews, J.R. (2004). *Measuring for results: The dimensions of public library effectiveness.* Westport, CT: Libraries Unlimited.

Self, J. (2003). From values to metrics: Implementation of the balanced scorecard at a university library. *Performance Measurement and Metrics,* 4(2), 57–63.

Shim, J.W., McClure, C.R., Fraser, B.T., Bertot, J.C., Dagli, A.,& Leahy, E.H. (2001). *Measures and statistics for research library networked services: Procedures and issues (ARL e-metrics phase II report).* Washington, DC: Association of Research Libraries. Retrieved 15 February 2003 from http://www.arl.org/stats/newmeas/emetrics/index.html.

# CHAPTER 2

# Selecting Evaluation Approaches for a Networked Environment

John Carlo Bertot and J.T. Snead

## Introduction

The selection process for determining the *best* evaluation approaches for assessing both traditional and network services and resources within library settings can be difficult for library managers and staff. In the past, and today, library managers and staff use various evaluation approaches that inform the planning and decision making processes regarding library services and resources. Many of these approaches, however, were developed originally for use within a traditional library setting. Some of these are still effective, but technology creates demands for evaluation approaches for the network environment. Broad areas of evaluation within a context of network services and resources include the following:

- Access, use, and availability of network services (e.g., digital reference, interlibrary loan, online training sessions, etc.) and network resources (e.g., databases, e-books, e-journals, online training modules, etc.);

- Development of both electronic non-Internet and Internet-accessible services and resources;
- Management of all network services and resources;
- Assessment of the quality of network services and resources;
- Allocation of resources and other aspects of developing and providing network services and resources; and
- Determination of the effectiveness and efficiency of providing both traditional and network services and resources.

The foregoing list illustrates some of the network applications that require evaluation. Determining which areas within a networked environment to target for evaluation is part of a larger evaluation and planning process such as that described in Chapter 1.

Additionally, the prevailing *anywhere/anytime* atmosphere created by technology fosters situations in which many libraries offer some of their services and resources both online and within the physical library setting. For example, libraries may provide reference services to both the walk-in desk patrons and to patrons accessing online services and resources from remote stations *within* the library setting, as well as from remote stations located at a distance. Libraries must also balance budget cuts, storage restrictions, and (at times) the difficult process of obtaining current hard copies of some resources—such as journal editions—against patron demands for immediate *online* access to articles and the practice by a growing number of publishers of providing *only* electronic versions of journals.

Other examples of library services and resources that increasingly require online availability include:

- Databases of collections of hard copy items such as books, documents, and media materials such as CDs and microfiche, etc.;
- Databases of indexes and abstracts;
- Digital collections of materials such as those found in PALMM (Publication of Archival Library and Museum Materials)[1], including *Florida Environments Online, Florida Heritage Collection, Literature for Children, Linking Florida's Natural Heritage,* etc.;
- Vendor-provided digital collections and databases;
- Services such as material lending and interlibrary loan; and
- Programs delivered and available via the Web (e.g., online training sessions, etc.).

With the growing use of technology in the development of library network services and resources, patrons increasingly use libraries in sophisticated ways via networks from home, work, coffee houses, hotels, remote work stations within libraries, etc. Library managers must ask the question: How can we determine the extent to which library network services and resources meet the information needs and information-seeking behavior of the library community?

Library managers find themselves in a position in which they must apply limited, and sometimes decreasing, resources (funds, personnel, etc.) effectively and efficiently to provide costly network services and resources. Library managers have to make decisions regarding which types of services and resources they can provide, weighed against what library patrons expect and often demand. To implement, manage, and maintain library services and resources effectively and efficiently, library managers must learn to assess both the traditional and the network settings and to account for multiple patron perspectives and needs.

This chapter presents an overview of some of the types of evaluation approaches developed for and used in a library network service and resource context. The chapter also presents some questions addressed by each approach, as well as some examples of applications of each approach in the evaluation of library network services and resources.

## Which Evaluation Approaches, and When?

Library managers need a range of types of evaluation approaches from which to select (based on specific library evaluation data needs), and each of the evaluation approaches should effectively assess a broad range of library services and programs. These evaluation approaches can often be adapted to fit a manager's need for a specific evaluation effort and adjusted for particular situational factors and contexts within a library setting (e.g., library placement within a community, externally required reporting, stakeholder data evaluation preferences, etc.). See Chapter 1 for a discussion of library situational factors and contexts.

Fortunately, continuing research within the library field has led to evolving evaluation approaches with developed assessment techniques and methods for the networked environment. Evaluation approaches such as *best practice, benchmarking, service quality,* and the *balanced scorecard* are available from research initially developed within the business field. In addition, *outcomes assessment* is receiving substantial attention from researchers and library practitioners.

A relative newcomer to library evaluation, outcomes assessment has been practiced within the fields of medicine, education, and sociology for some time. Recently, government organizations have been engaging in, or requiring the use of, outcomes assessment as a means of producing accountability for government funded projects and programs. Outcomes assessment has also become a favored approach within library evaluation circles, driven largely by the adoption of outcomes requirements of accrediting bodies for higher education institutions (academic libraries), outcomes requirements of Library Services and Technology Act (LSTA) funds (public libraries, state library agencies, and other libraries that receive such funds), and outcomes requirements of National Leadership Grants provided by the Institute of Museum and Library Services (Library and Information Science/Studies schools, museums, and libraries of all types that receive such grants).

These evaluation approaches offer library managers many options for conducting evaluation efforts regarding library network services and resources. The key to these options, however, is matching available evaluation approaches to specific library network services and resources data needs.

There are many factors to consider in choosing evaluation approaches, such as the following:

- Data needs of the library (type of information needed);
- Purpose of the evaluation;
- Knowledge and skills of library staff related to evaluation, data collection, data analysis, and data reporting;
- Difficulty associated with understanding and implementing evaluation approaches;
- Organizational factors related to the library;
- Situational factors related to the library (such as available resources);
- Community factors, such as diversity within the population and the special interests and needs of stakeholder groups, governing boards, etc.; and
- Political contexts and their effects on the library (funding, legislation, etc.).

Library managers and staff face the challenge of determining which evaluation approaches are the *best* or *most appropriate* to address factors such as those in the foregoing list. Library managers need to understand fully the factors related to conducting successful evaluations if their libraries are to conduct the most useful types of network service and resource evaluations (see Chapter 1 for more information on factors and evaluation planning). Libraries also must have insight into the use and application of specific, developed, planned, and managed evaluation approaches.

Library managers and staff also need to understand the usefulness, impact, and overall benefit of different approaches to library evaluation in order to answer questions related to specific evaluation needs. Without this understanding, libraries cannot meet the needs of the library or the diverse community that the library serves. Library managers and staff need to make informed choices about the:

- Different types of available evaluation approaches;
- Data produced by each type of evaluation approach;
- Best application of the different evaluation approaches;
- Adaptability of evaluation approaches; and
- Specific situations within the library, the library community, and the external government sphere that may affect the evaluation.

Understanding and utilizing the best evaluation approach to meet specific needs produces the most useful data and results. These data can inform the library decision making process as to the best use of library services and resources to meet the information needs of the community that the library serves.

## Evaluation Approaches

Library managers and staff can choose to evaluate their network services and resources in a number of ways. The issue is less one of the availability of assessment techniques and more one of selecting the *best approach(es)* that will yield the *most useful* data regarding the network services and resources under evaluation. The key issue that library managers and staff face is determining what their evaluation data needs are and then implementing an evaluation strategy that will yield the evaluation data that they need. More often than not, libraries will need to engage in multiple evaluation approaches to meet their services and resources evaluation needs, because no one evaluation approach is likely to provide all the necessary data.

### Evaluation Approaches Frameworks

Researchers, library managers, and library practitioners have developed and/or adapted a number of evaluation approaches for data collection efforts used in the management of library services and resources. These individuals typically are familiar with approaches such as *output assessment, performance measurement, service quality assessment,* and *outcomes assessment.* In practice, however, each of these evaluation approaches typically is utilized, implemented, and the results assessed independently of the others. Output assessment occurs as one practice, whereas service quality occurs as another, and outcomes assessment as yet another.

In addition, the presentation of the results of these evaluative efforts tends to focus on a single evaluation approach or method. Although this has the benefit of enabling libraries to present the evaluation results in a comprehensive way, it has the unfortunate consequence of essentially endorsing one assessment approach over others. Evaluation in a complex library service and resource environment requires a number of evaluation approaches to truly describe, understand, and facilitate the decision making activities of the library manager.

As information-based organizations, libraries already engage in a number of decision making activities that govern the selection, design, management, and evaluation of resources and services provided to communities served. In general, these decisions involve three fundamental aspects of library services and the use of library resources (Bertot & Snead, 2004):

- *Inputs* are the resources libraries invest (e.g., funds, personnel, computer work stations, etc.);
- *Activities* are the library services and resources generated by the use of inputs (e.g., virtual reference services, online training modules, etc.);
- *Outputs* are the count data of the number of services or resources generated from inputs (e.g., the number of online reference questions answered, the number of training sessions, etc.).

These three aspects are already being used to inform library managers in the decision making process regarding usage of library services and resources (Fig. 2-1).

Inputs, activities, and outputs provide vital baseline information regarding budgeting, services, and resources for evaluation approaches (Bertot & Snead, 2004). Moreover, evaluation methods, information sources, and—to a degree—indicators (see the sections on *Output Assessment and Performance Measurement* and *Outcomes Assessment* later in the chapter) guide the evaluation approaches. Inputs, activities, outputs, methods, sources, and/or indicators contribute to an overall evaluation approach framework that forms the core of library network services and resources evaluation efforts. The particular focus and direction of a library's evaluation strategy determines the type of evaluation approach: long-term changes in skills, knowledge, and behavior among patrons (*outcomes assessment*) or the quality of virtual reference services (*quality assessment*).

Research suggests that library managers, staff, and researchers have developed and/or adapted a number of evaluation approaches for use in the management of library network services and resources (Bertot, 2003;

**Figure 2-1**
**Library services and evaluation frameworks.**

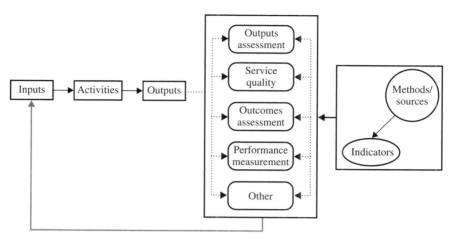

Bertot & McClure, 2003a, b; Matthews, 2004). Initial research suggests that among the most widely used evaluation methods and approaches available, there are three primary evaluation strategies that encompass many of the individual evaluation methods and approaches: *output/performance measures* (combined for purposes of discussion in this chapter), *outcomes assessment,* and *quality assessment* (Bertot & Snead, 2004). Additionally, the past few years have seen the development and testing of a fourth approach for library assessment–the *balanced scorecard.*

Differences in focus and direction for each evaluation approach will be addressed in the following pages, but it should be noted that these are certainly not all of the available evaluation approaches used in a library network setting. The evaluation approaches identified for this chapter and by prior research are the predominant approaches used most often and/or combined by common evaluation focus (*outputs/performance measures*). Other approaches, such as *benchmarking* and *best practices,* have received a lot of attention among library researchers and practitioners. Some, such as *LibQUAL+* (electronic evaluation of a comparison of the quality of network delivered services and resources across peer organizations), are being tested, developed, and honed for use in evaluating network services and resources (see http://www.libqual.org for additional detail).

## Conceptual Framework

Evaluation approaches are affected by situational factors and situational contexts within a library environment (see Chapter 1). The context of particular library evaluation efforts creates an overall environment that influences nearly all aspects of assessment, including data needs, reporting requirements, and other key components. Figure 2-2 provides a conceptual framework that demonstrates the evaluation environment and the relationship between:

- Stakeholders (those who have various interests in library network services and resources);
- Stakeholder evaluation perspectives (the types of data that the stakeholders would prefer to have reported regarding library network services and resources. Some stakeholders prefer outcomes data, whereas others prefer return on investment, outputs, or some combination of various types of data.); and
- Evaluation approaches (used in the evaluation of library network services and resources to meet stakeholder data needs).

**Figure 2-2**
**Library evaluation conceptual framework.**

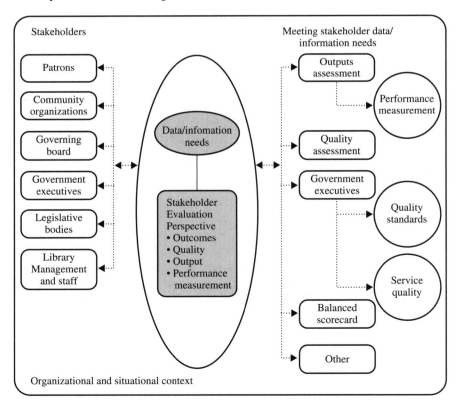

These relationships also exist within specific organizational and situational contexts. A brief overview is presented in Table 2-1.

Relational effects among library stakeholders, stakeholder perspectives, evaluation approaches, and organizational and situational contexts create an overall evaluation perspective. Figure 2-2 depicts this perspective and provides a conceptual view that describes and facilitates an understanding of the use of selected evaluation approaches: *outputs assessment/performance measures, outcomes assessment, service quality assessment,* and the *balanced scorecard.*

## Types of Evaluation Approaches

Each type of evaluation approach—output assessment/performance measurement, outcomes assessment, service quality assessment, and the balanced scorecard—represents multiple versions of similar evaluation approaches. It is possible to adapt and develop these evaluation approaches for the assessment of different areas within a library setting and for specific goals within an overall evaluation effort.

These four approaches represent both user-centered perspectives and library-centered perspectives. Evaluations of library-centered approaches tend to focus on the presentation of resources and services, with an emphasis on efficiency and effectiveness. Evaluations of user-centered approaches tend to focus on the quality of the presentation of resources and services and the inclusion of the needs of diverse library communities in accessing resources and services. User-centered approaches may include the library community in general within the approach, or may target specific stakeholder groups. Table 2-2 provides brief descriptions and some key literature examples of the four types of evaluation approaches presented in this chapter.

### Output Assessment and Performance Measurement

Libraries have traditionally collected outputs as counts from circulation records, reference services, facility usage, and others. These count units have been the staple for evaluation of use of services and resources for decades, and are incorporated into numerous national annual data collection efforts such as those by the Association of Research Libraries (ARL), the Federal-State Cooperative System (FSCS), and the Public Library Data Service (PLDS). These types of measures, however, do not account for the use of library network services and resources, and thus undercount the services and resources that libraries provide and the use of such resources.

Table 2-1
**Examples and relational effects among library stakeholders, their perspectives, evaluation approaches, and situational factors.**

| | Examples | Relational Effects |
|---|---|---|
| **Stakeholders** | 1. City/county executives,<br>2. Community leaders,<br>3. Funding sources, etc. | May want to know a number of things regarding the investments made in the public library, such as:<br>■ In what ways do patrons benefit from reading library online or print material?<br>■ For every dollar we invest in the library, what does the community get in return? Do we need to continue to fund print collections in the same amount, or can we divert more resources to online material?<br>■ What do users of library services think about the quality of the services that they receive from the library? |
| **Stakeholder Evaluation Perspective** | 1. Return on investment,<br>2. Impacts/benefits,<br>3. Quality,<br>4. Value, etc. | Drives the *stakeholder* data/information needs and questions that library managers must answer to make resource allocation decisions. The Stakeholder Evaluation Perspective influences the *evaluation approaches* library managers will use in order to meet stakeholder data demands. |
| **Evaluation Approaches** | 1. Outputs assessment,<br>2. Outcomes assessment,<br>3. Quality assessment,<br>4. Balanced scorecard,<br>5. Other | Assessment frameworks that library managers may use in order to answer *stakeholder* questions and make resource allocation decisions. These tend to occur in isolation and may not be integrated in effort, resource devotion, and data/reporting activities. |
| **Organizational & Situational Context** | 1. Online database usage by branch,<br>2. Digital reference sessions, etc. | Operating environment where *evaluation* activity occurs. It can create a number of constraints on the *evaluation* activities in which libraries can engage. These can include limited staff resources and expertise, limited evaluation resources, time frame, and limiting technology and other infrastructure that does not permit the collection of critical data. |

Table 2-2
Presentation of key evaluation approaches.

| Approach | Description | Key Literature Examples |
|---|---|---|
| **Outputs/ Performance Measures** | Involves: <br>■ Identification of library activities patrons use (e.g., number of database sessions, number of database items examined, number of training sessions conducted, etc.) <br>■ Breadth and scope of such services (e.g., training attendance per capita, cost per database session, etc.), and <br>■ Measurement of the efficiency or effectiveness of the activities (e.g., usability of service, accessibility to services, etc.). | 1. Output Measures for Public Libraries: A Manual of Standardized Procedures (Van House, Lynch, McClure, Zweizig, & Rodger, 1987). <br>2. Planning for Results (Himmel & Wilson, 1998). <br>3. Statistics and Performance Measures for Public Library Networked Services (Bertot, McClure, & Ryan, 2000). |
| **Outcomes Assessment** | Seeks to determine: <br>■ Impact of the library's services/resources on the library service and resource users; or <br>■ Benefits as changes in skill/knowledge that library users derive from library services/resources. | 1. Outcomes Assessment in the Networked Environment: Research Questions, Issues, Considerations, and Moving Forward (Bertot & McClure, 2003a). <br>2. Counting on Results: New Tools for Outcomes-Based Evaluation of Public Libraries, Workbook: Outcome Measurement of Library Programs (Lance, et al., 2002). <br>3. An Action Plan for Outcomes Assessment in Your Library (Hernon & Dugan, 2002). <br>4. ARL E-metrics Project: Toward a Framework of Library and Institutional Outcomes (Fraser & McClure, 2002). |

(Continued)

**Table 2-2 (Continued)**
**Presentation of key evaluation approaches.**

| Approach | Description | Key Literature Examples |
|---|---|---|
| **Quality Assessment** | Involves:<br>■ Determining the degree to which users find the library services and resources to be satisfactory and/or meet expectations; and<br>■ May also include the extent to which library services/resources meet library-determined quality standards. | 1. Delivering Satisfaction and Service Quality: A Customer-Based Approach for Libraries (Hernon & Whitman, 2001).<br>2. Quality Management for Information and Library Managers (Brophy & Kouling, 1996).<br>3. Statistics, Measures and Quality Standards for Assessing Digital Reference Library Services: Guidelines and Procedures (McClure, Lankes, Gross, & Choltco-Devlin, 2002). |
| **Balanced Scorecard** | Involves:<br>■ Use of outputs, outcomes, and quality assessment evaluation approaches to provide an overall assessment of library services along financial, customer, internal, and innovation/learning dimensions; and<br>■ Although not widely employed in libraries, this approach has the potential to offer a comprehensive and integrated evaluative approach. | 1. The Balanced Scorecard: Translating Strategy into Action (Kaplan & Norton, 1996).<br>2. From Values to Metrics: Implementation of the Balanced Scorecard at a University Library in Performance Measurement and Metrics (Self, 2003).<br>3. Performance-based Management: Eight Steps to Develop and Use Information Technology Performance Measures Effectively (General Services Administration Office of Governmentwide Policy, 1996). |

The anytime/anywhere atmosphere within modern libraries creates opportunities for patrons to access many of a library's network services and resources at any time. This access from remote locations, both within the library setting and from a distance, can represent a large percentage of the volume of use of services and resources. If a library does not add additional network evaluation methods to its information collection tools to account for use of network services and resources, it is substantially undercounting overall library use.

Online databases, Web pages, digitized collections of materials, and a growing number of other services and resources available through electronic means are increasingly a mainstay in the overall portfolio of library services and resources to the communities that libraries serve. It is imperative that a library have the means to collect this information for the following uses:

* Resource allocation;
* Management of resources;
* Evaluation and planning of networked services;
* Budget allocation and accountability to the library community, library boards, etc.;
* Benchmarking and best-practice efforts;
* Peer comparisons; and
* Competition for limited community resources.

Chapters 3 and 4 provide guidance on the specific e-metrics to collect, methods of collection, and assessment methodologies. Readers should refer to these chapters for assistance regarding such outputs-oriented e-metrics.

Output assessment is just one of the evaluation tools available to libraries for evaluating network services and resources. And, as one approach, outputs assessment essentially provides counts of resources and services availability, resources and services amounts, and resources and services uses.

Performance measurement is an evaluation method that also has a long history of use in library evaluation. In general, performance indicators are combinations of individual library statistics (e.g., population served, circulation) that provide measures of library service and resource penetration, efficiency, and effectiveness (e.g., circulation per capita/population served). Performance indicators in the networked environment use combinations of both traditional metrics and e-metrics. The following are some examples of network services and resources performance indicator applications:

- Indication of how well network services and resources are presented and received;
- Measurement of the effectiveness and efficiency of online services and resources;
- Determination of levels of user satisfaction;
- Identification of needs of users; and
- Recognition of problems for users within the network services and resources.

Thus, performance indicators are *measurable indicators* of the effectiveness and efficiency of library network services and resources.

Bertot, McClure, & Ryan (2001), as well as Brophy et al. (2000), suggest composites of outputs to create performance indicators. Creating composites is a means of (1) compounding collected statistical information of different outputs for a library service or resource area, and (2) creating ratios for analysis (with a warning not to compare apples and oranges, within reason, for credibility purposes). Some examples of composite performance indicators are:

- The percentage of virtual reference transactions to total reference questions (the number of virtual reference transactions compared to the total number of reference transactions, both traditional and virtual);
- User information technology instruction as a percentage of total reference activity (the number of users instructed in information technology as a percentage of total reference activity); and
- Total library visits (physical attendance at the library and the number of virtual visits, collected electronically, combined into one total.

*Technical Report 20983* of the International Organization of Standardization (ISO) 11620 Library Performance Indicators incorporates these and other network service and resource performance indicators. These are also detailed in Chapter 4 of this book.

### Quality Assessment

In general, quality assessment is an evaluation of how well a library provides services and resources. There are two perspectives involved in determining quality: (1) the library community's perceptions of excellence in the provision of the services and resources (user-centered perspective), and (2) the evaluation of the quality of the services and resources in providing information (library-centered perspective). The broad goal of quality assessment is to identify and resolve gaps, either between the community's perception of excellence and its perception of actual services and resources provided, or between the *potential* quality of presented library network services and resources and the *actual* effectiveness and efficiency of presentation by the library of those services and resources.

Evaluation may be within and of a single institution; across libraries as a field, or by types of libraries (academic, public, special, etc.); or some combination using evaluative approaches to compare and contrast levels of quality. Within the area of evaluation of library network services and resources, measuring quality in quantifiable terms occurs using a number of evaluation approaches and methods. SERVQUAL and LibQUAL+ are examples of Web-based instruments designed as tools to assess library services and resources.

SERVQUAL was originally developed by a research marketing team—Berry, Parasuraman, and Zeithaml (1990)—for use within the service industry. Qualitative studies identified five dimensions of service quality that are important to customers:

- **Tangibles** such as equipment, the appearance of facilities, communication capabilities, and personnel;
- **Reliability** in performing and delivering promised services accurately and dependably;
- **Responsiveness** to helping and meeting customers' needs;
- **Assurance** to customers of employees' abilities to convey trust and confidence in a knowledgeable and courteous manner; and
- **Empathy** of attention and caring provided to customers.

SERVQUAL can also be used to identify gaps between perceptions of excellence and customers' perceptions of actual provision of services and resources (Nitecki, 1997). Cook & Heath (1999) identified specific strategies for the use of SERVQUAL in an academic setting, using three dimensions to determine quality: tangibles, reliability, and affect of library service.

Both the original developers and Cook & Heath found this product to be most effective when applied within an institution, as opposed to ranking across institutions.

LibQUAL+ was developed from the SERVQUAL program. It is an attempt to develop a tool for use across institutions (ranking), as well as for local planning. LibQUAL+ addresses questions such as:

- How do patrons rank information delivery?
- What are patrons' levels of satisfaction with the quality of services?

- Are patrons satisfied with facilities, including equipment and communication levels?
- How aware are patrons of the full range of services and resources available?

Both LibQUAL+ and SERVQUAL seek to produce outcome measures. Outcome measures can be used by libraries in measuring and comparing the quality of services such as reference, interlibrary loan, and reserves. Both LibQUAL+ and SERVQUAL are currently being tested in a number of university library settings on an international scale, with plans to expand into other library types. To date, however, the efforts of LibQUAL+ focus on the overall quality of library services and resources. There are plans to develop an "E-QUAL" version of LibQUAL+ that would focus on library network services and resources. See http://www.libqual.org for developments in that area.

Total Quality Management (TQM) is another approach developed within the business field. TQM was developed in the early 1950s to measure quality throughout an organization based on customer needs and perceptions. Key components of TQM are employee training and involvement, problem-solving teams, statistical methods for measures, and thinking in terms of long-term goals. The TQM approach is based on 14 steps developed to implement TQM within an organization. Masters (2003) identifies three ways that libraries can benefit directly from implementing TQM:

1. Interdepartmental barriers are broken, creating cross-department cooperation and participation by employees;
2. Beneficiaries of library services and resources are internal (employees) and external (patrons); and
3. A state of continuous improvement within the organization is created.

Libraries can use TQM to rethink and rewrite vision and mission statements and to understand and address misrepresented issues (e.g., network issues considered by staff to be critical and not thought of as critical by patrons).

SERVQUAL, LibQUAL+, and TQM are three approaches that have received a lot of attention within the area of library evaluation of quality assessment. Other areas of focus for developing quality within networked systems and network-based information sources include:

- Building quality non-WWW and WWW services and resources;
- Evaluation of Web-based services and resources;

- Assessment of Internet resources;
- E-references and e-citations;
- E-publishing and information quality;
- User interface design issues;
- Web development;
- Database quality criteria;
- Web ethics and netiquette;
- Development of information standards (such as NISO Z39.7 Library Statistics and ISO 2789 Standard on Library Statistics); and
- Measuring the quality and impact of WWW-available services and resources.

Quality assessment has many applications within the network environment. Of primary importance, and linked to almost all approaches within this area, is the idea that quality can be measured and information gaps can be identified to improve the quality level of library network services and resources.

**Outcomes Assessment**

The intent of outcomes assessment is to determine the potential long-term impact(s) or effects (outcomes) of library services, resources, or programs in terms of benefits to participants. Benefits are changes in knowledge, skill level, behavior, attitudes, or any change that may be seen as a benefit for the participant as a direct result of interaction with services, resources, or programs. Outcomes assessment is an approach created to evaluate services and resources by directly influencing the impact of library services and resources. It is the process of identifying, understanding, measuring, and assessing changes that occur within individuals, where the changes are directly related to specific programs and where the changes *indicate* meeting specific, predetermined long-term outcomes (Bertot & McClure, 2003; Hernon & Dugan, 2002; Institute of Museum and Library Services, 2000; United Way, 1996).

Outcomes are derived from goals that may be developed from mission and vision statements, an institution's standards, or from goals that may preexist as part of a library's planning process. However derived, these goals represent long-term planning efforts that directly tie the direction and scope of an organization's future to outcomes-based programming and to the individuals who participate in those programs. Outcomes assessment addresses the following issues:

- Questions concerning accountability for the use of services and resources;

- Budgeting needs for planning and implementing services and resources;
- Program and resource allocation costs;
- Patron and organization needs;
- Effectiveness of programming in meeting patron and organization needs; and
- Effectiveness of programming in meeting long-term goals.

The methodology of outcomes-based evaluation in assessment is developed to identify the long-term effects of programming and to develop an understanding of relationships between those effects and the goals of the organization. This assessment is accomplished by quantifying the results of programs and assessing these results in terms of outcomes.

Outcomes assessment is also intended as an ongoing process. It is a means of evaluating outcomes produced by programming over an extended period of time (Bertot & McClure, 2003). Initial outcomes assessment activities evaluate only the initial success and/or immediate impact of the program. The analysis includes:

- The input-activity-output process;
- Outcome indicators;
- Methods used to gather data;
- Interpretation of that data; and
- The immediate impact the program has on participants.

The initial assessment evaluates the program as to immediate (short-term) identifiable changes in the learning process of participants. Changes that are directly related to the program and all of the program's aspects are assessed. The process relates these changes to organizational goals. Library managers and staff would need to engage in ongoing outcomes assessment to determine the long-term changes in user knowledge, skills, or behavior due to library services and resources.

Developing outcomes assessment as an approach in a networked environment can involve a reevaluation of an organization's mission or vision statements, departmental specific goals (reference, circulation, systems, and technical services), etc. Changes within the environment in which libraries present network services and resources suggest necessary changes within the process of determining how future service and resource goals will be accomplished.

Outcomes are meant to show that the organization is moving toward these future goals in a positive mode, through the introduction of programming designed to measure benefits for participants of the programs. Outcomes are meant to measure the effects or impacts upon individuals as a result of programming, and through this process to link those impacts directly to long-term goals.

Outcomes assessment within a library setting is relatively new, and additional research is needed to understand the impact of this approach on evaluating a library's network services and resources. Library managers and staff who would like to have additional assistance regarding outcomes assessment may wish to consult http://www.lstatoolkit.com. This is a Web-based interactive instructional outcomes assessment planning and evaluation website created by the Florida Division of Libraries and the Information Management Use and Policy Institute at Florida State University, with a National Leadership Grant from the Institute of Museum and Library Services (IMLS). The website provides instruction on developing outcomes assessment plans, including methods of assessment, for libraries that receive Library Services and Technology Act (LSTA) grants. The content of the site does, however, have application beyond LSTA grant recipients.

### Balanced Scorecard

The balanced scorecard was developed by Kaplan & Norton (1996) as a means of improving performance within an organization over time. The balanced scorecard originally was applied within a business environment, but has since seen application within a library environment as well. As an approach, the balanced scorecard attempts to improve performance within an organization in two ways: (1) by evaluation of current performance levels within an organization to create a baseline effect, and (2) by enhancement of the future performance of the organization. The balanced scorecard is a top-down process in which future performance is determined by the mission, or vision, of the organization. The overall goal of this approach is the development of new practices or processes that will produce, or meet, future desired performance standards.

The balanced scorecard is meant to provide a framework for the transformation of vision and strategy statements into terms of operational performance. The balanced scorecard is a cycle in which:

- **Vision and strategy** are translated by management into goals, objectives, and desirable measures, where measures are the targeted areas of improvement. The purpose of this is to develop goals, objectives, and measures instigated and created through consensus of management, for implementation throughout the organization.

- **Communication** occurs when the goals, objectives, and measures are communicated throughout the organization, at every level, in every department, and to every employee. The purpose of this is to establish understanding of strategic goals and to mobilize each employee, at every level, to take action to meet goals.
- **Planning and target setting** occur at the implementation stage to meet objectives, measures, targets, and initiatives. Targets are typically long-term objectives such as improving customer service satisfaction by 50 percent, for example. Measures, however, are ongoing and provide continuous feedback so the cycle can be monitored as the process unfolds.
- **Strategic feedback and learning** take place at the final stage, where feedback is given to management for future strategic planning, as part of a learning process, and for use in perpetuating the cycle.

Measurement falls within the planning and target setting phase in four areas, or dimensions, of the organization: internal business process, financial, customer, and learning and growth. Performance is measured using multiple methods (e.g.,outputs, performance measures, outcomes, service quality) without favoring one over another.

Recently, some libraries have begun experimenting with the balanced scorecard as an evaluation approach (Mathews, 2004; Self, 2003). As one of the few U.S. libraries trying this approach, the University of Virginia (UVA) library has used the balanced scorecard within the library since 2001. UVA library management focuses on a few measurement methods related directly to the library's mission statement and within four perspectives: user, finance, internal processes, and learning and the future. Four to eight metrics have been developed for each perspective, and each metric has two specific potential targets to gauge success. These targets are successfully reaching either 95 percent (success) or 90 percent (partial success) retention of commended employees for the retention goal: *retention rate of commended employees* (Self, 2003).

The balanced scorecard offers libraries an evaluation approach for assessing performance in key areas of a library's operation. Some advantages of the balanced scorecard include:

- Inclusion of all members of an organization in meeting performance goals;
- Direct and continuous feedback to management on the progress toward the targets (where the initial process begins);
- Focus on key areas within the library;
- Control of the evaluation process;

- Incentive to complete scheduled evaluations (all employees are involved from management down, so all are aware of targets, etc.);
- Development of balanced, open evaluation of areas within the library;
- Identification of areas within a library needing evaluation but not receiving evaluation previously through prior evaluation attempts; and
- Creation of a management tool to focus resources where they are needed most and to maintain a balance throughout the organization.

Perhaps most important is the ability of each library to identify specific needs within the organization and to develop evaluation approaches best suited to meet those needs. The library develops dimensions for identifying areas for evaluation, and the measures the library uses in evaluation determine the success of the provision of services and resources. Areas within the library include the network environment.

Chapter 1 presents a modified balanced scorecard approach for evaluating library network services and resources through e-metrics and performance indicators. The approach offers a means through which to assess library network services and resources in the aggregate, along a number of dimensions.

## Comparison of Approaches

Selecting the appropriate evaluation approach is essential for a successful evaluation effort. Determining the type of data needed and specific evaluation approaches available to capture those data begins with an evaluation strategy development process as outlined in Chapter 1. One key aspect of that evaluation strategy development process is to review the various evaluation frameworks presented in this chapter and match the frameworks to the types of assessment data needs your library has.

- Do you need to know what network services and resources patrons use, how often, and in what ways? Do you need to know how efficiently and effectively your library provides these network services and resources? If so, your library needs to engage in Outputs and Performance Measurement efforts.
- How do patrons rate the network services and resources your library provides? Are patrons satisfied? Is the library not meeting, meeting, or exceeding patron service expectations? Is the library not meeting, meeting, or exceeding library developed quality standards? To answer these questions, your library needs to engage in Quality Assessment efforts.

- What are the short-term and long-term impacts of library network services and resources on patron skills, knowledge, and behavior? How do library network services and resources impact or provide benefits to users of the services and resources? To answer these questions, your library needs to engage in Outcomes Assessment efforts.

- How can resources be utilized for maximum benefits throughout an organization (measuring overall performance of an organization)? To answer this question, your library may wish to consider Balanced Scorecard-based efforts.

Deriving answers to the foregoing questions—either individually or collectively—essentially dictates which evaluation approach libraries should use in order to evaluate their network services and resources. The issue is less one of having evaluation and assessment approaches and techniques available to library managers and staff, and more one of selecting the *best* evaluation approaches and techniques to meet the assessment needs of the library. The following books and manuals can provide details on selecting evaluation approaches within a library networked setting.

- *Statistics and Performance Measures for Public Library Networked Services* (Bertot, McClure, & Ryan, 2001);
- *Evaluating Networked Information Services* (McClure & Bertot, 2001);
- *Data Collection Manual for Academic and Research Library Network Statistics and Performance Measures* (Shim, et al., 2001);
- *Measuring for Results: The Dimensions of Public Library Effectiveness* (Mathews, 2004).

In addition to the current text, these books can assist library managers in selecting evaluation approaches. They address issues specific to a networked environment, planning an evaluation process, and applying the results of the data collection efforts to the decision making process.

The overall purpose of conducting evaluation and collecting information is to assist library managers in the decision making process. As shown in Fig. 2-3, library managers need to match the appropriate evaluation approaches with library network services and resources to meet information needs.

The following list includes some of the types of questions library managers need to address in determining the appropriate evaluation approaches.

1. What types of data do evaluation approaches provide library managers?

**Figure 2-3**
**Matching evaluation approaches to library network services and resources.**

2. What do such data enable library managers to say about their library services?

3. What are the strengths, weaknesses, and uses of the evaluation approaches?

4. Which evaluation approaches are best suited to meeting specific data needs?

5. How successful are evaluation approaches at meeting identified specific data needs?

6. How adaptable are evaluation approaches to specific evaluation needs?

7. Is your library able and/or ready to engage in the evaluation approaches that best meet the identified data needs?

For library managers to understand meaningfully the uses of a library's network services and resources, to improve those services and resources, and to plan for future network services and resources, selecting the most appropriate evaluation approach or set of approaches is critical. The foregoing questions, and others more specific to a particular library, will assist library managers in determining which evaluation approaches will deliver the most impact for the  evaluation effort resources available.

## Conclusion

Using evaluation approaches can require a significant amount of effort and allocated resources (funds, personnel, etc.) to provide library managers with information about network services and resources that is timely, appropriate, informative, and applicable. Data provided by evaluation approaches must inform the decision making process; otherwise, the collection efforts are not effective, nor are they efficient in the use of allocated personnel and resources. Selecting the most appropriate evaluation approach(es) is part of a larger process that includes:

- Identification of the data needs of patrons, library staff and management, library boards, library vendors, etc. (see Chapter 1);
- Development and prioritization of evaluation questions to address information needs (see Chapter 1);
- Creation of an overall evaluation methodology (see Chapter 3);
- Selection of the most effective and efficient evaluation approaches (outputs/performance measures, outcomes, service quality, etc.) to answer evaluation questions , as discussed in this chapter);
- Collection, dissemination, and application of collected data (see Chapter 4); and
- Assessment of the evaluative process as to impact, effectiveness, and efficiency in meeting the data needs (see Chapter 4).

In short, library managers need to have a clear understanding of what they need to know for the decision making process and which evaluation approaches *best fit* the information collection process. Additionally, library managers need to understand that:

- No one evaluative approach will fit all data needs (multiple approaches may be necessary to solve specific data needs);
- Evaluation approaches need to be *doable* (factors such as funding and personnel must be adequate to complete the evaluations); and
- Evaluation approaches should be sustainable.

The collection of data is part of an overall planning effort and includes the selection of evaluation approaches. Data collection using evaluation approaches to meet specific needs requires commitment, effort, and the allocation of sufficient resources. The results of that commitment, effort, and use of resources, however, will inform the decision making process of library managers. The results will provide library managers with the ability to understand some of the impacts and benefits of library network services and resources.

## Notes

1. For additional information about PALMM and other materials in the PALMM collection, go to http://susdl.fela.edu/collection.html.

## References

Bertot, J.C. (2003). Libraries and networked information services: Issues and considerations in measurement. *Proceedings of the 5th Northumbria International Conference on Performance Measurement in Libraries and Information Services.* University of Northumbria at Newcastle, Durham, England: 15–25.

Bertot, J.C., & McClure, C.R. (2003a). Outcomes assessment in the networked environment: Research questions, issues, considerations, and moving forward. *Library Trends,* 51(4): 590–613.

Bertot, J.C. & McClure, C.R. (2003b). *Assessing LSTA project outcomes: Methods and practice.* Retrieved 14 January 2004 from http://www.ii.fsu.edu/index.cfm.

Bertot, J.C., & McClure, C.R. (2003). Outcomes assessment in the networked environment: Research questions, issues, considerations, and moving forward. *Library Trends,* 51(4): 590–613.

Bertot, J.C., McClure, C.R., & Ryan, J. (2001). *Statistics and performance measures for public library networked services.* Chicago, IL: American Library Association.

Bertot, J.C. & Snead, J.T. (2004). Social measurement in libraries. In K. Kempf-Leonard, (Ed.). *Encyclopedia of Social Measurement.* San Diego, CA: Academic Press.

Brophy, P., Clarke, Z., Brinkley, M., Mundt, S., & Poll, R. (2000). EQUINOX library performance measurement and quality management system performance indicators for electronic library services. Available at http://equinox.dcu.ie/reports/pilist.html. Last accessed November 18, 2003.

Brophy, P. & Kouling, K. (1996). *Quality management for information and library managers.* Aldershot, UK: Gower Publishing Co.

Fraser, B.T. & McClure, C.R. (2002). Toward a framework of library and institutional outcomes. *Association of Research Libraries (ARL) e-metrics project.* Retrieved 14 January 2004 from http://www.arl.org/stats/newmeas/emetrics/contract00-01.html.

General Services Administration Office of Governmentwide Policy. (1996). *Performance-based management: Eight steps to develop and use information technology performance measures effectively.* Retrieved 14 January 2004 from http://www.defenselink.mil/nii/org/cio/ciocert/sum-step.html.

Hernon, P. & Dugan, R.E. (2002). *An Action plan for outcomes assessment in your library.* Chicago, IL: American Library Association.

Hernon, P., and Whitman, J.R. (2001). *Delivering satisfaction and service quality: A customer-based approach for libraries.* Chicago, IL: American Library Association.

Himmel, E.E., and Wilson, W.J. (1998). *Planning for results: A public library transformation process.* Chicago, IL: American Library Association.

Institute of Museum and Library Services. (2000). *Perspectives on outcome based evaluation for libraries and museums.* Washington, D.C.: Institute of Museum and Library Services.

International Standards Organization. (2003). *ISO/CD 11620 information and documentation–library performance indicators technical report 20983.* Stockholm, Sweden: Swedish General Standards Institute.

Kaplan, R. & Norton, D. (1996). *Translating strategy into action: The Balanced scorecard.* Boston, MA: Harvard Business School Press.

Lance, K.C., et al. (2002). *Counting on results: New tools for outcomes-based evaluation of public libraries.* Aurora, CO: Biographical Center for Research. Retrieved 15 January 2004 from http://www.lrs.org/html/about/CountingOnResults.htm.

Masters, D.G. (2003). Total quality management in libraries. *ERIC Digest.* Retrieved 12 March 2004 from http://michaellorenzen.com/epic/tqm.html.

Matthews, J.R. (2004). *Measuring for results: The dimensions of public library effectiveness.* Westport, CT: Libraries Unlimited.

McClure, C.R., Lankes, R.D., Gross, M., & Choltco-Devlin, B. (2002). *Statistics, measures and quality standards for assessing digital reference library services: Guidelines and procedures.* Syracuse, NY: Information Institute of Syracuse.

Nitecki, D.A. (1997). SERVQUAL: Measuring service quality in academic libraries. *Association of Research Libraries.* Retrieved 12 March 2004 from http://www.arl.org/newsltr/191/servqual.html.

Self, J. (2003). From values to metrics: Implementation of the balanced scorecard at a university library. *Performance Measurement and Metrics,* 4(2), 57–63.

Shim, W., McClure, C.R., Fraser, B.T., & Bertot, J.C. (2001). *Data collection manual for academic and research library network statistics and performance measures.* Washington, D.C.: Association of Research Libraries.

United Way of America. (1996). *Measuring program outcomes: A Practical approach.* Alexandria, VA: United Way of America.

Van House, N.; Lynch, M.J.; McClure, C.R.; Zweizig, D.L., & Rodger, E.J. (1987). *Output measures for public libraries: A manual of standardized procedures.* Chicago: American Library Association.

Zeithaml, V.A., Parasuraman, A., & Berry, L.L. (1990). *Delivering quality service: Balancing customer perceptions and expectations.* New York, NY: The Free Press.

# CHAPTER 3

# Methods and Tools for Assessing Network Services and Resources

**John Carlo Bertot**

## Introduction

This chapter describes a number of methods, approaches, and tools that libraries can use to assess their network services and resources, as well as some issues associated with using these various methodologies. The chapter presents these methods in the context of a larger evaluation approach as described in Chapter 1, evaluation frameworks as described in Chapter 2, and the e-metrics and performance indicators provided in Chapter 4. This chapter does not detail social science research methods and practices, but rather, it does offer various practical approaches and considerations with the discussed methodologies. Readers who want a basic primer on research methods should consult Babbie (2003), Creswell (2002), or Powell (1997).

The methods in this chapter are not presented as definitive. Rather, they are examples of methods used by the author and others during a variety of public and academic library, state library agency, and regional consortia projects that involved different network service and resource evaluations–portal websites, statewide database licenses, instructional programs, and outcomes assessment, for example (see Bertot, 2003, 2002; Bertot & Davis, 2001; Bertot & McClure, 2002a, 2002b, 1999; McClure, Ryan, & Bertot, 2002). Librarians will also need to consider making modifications to the questionnaires and other examples to better meet the situational factors in which their libraries operate. In addition, one method, approach, or one-time measurement may not yield the desired assessment results–it may be the case that the desired data may require more than one approach at various time intervals (e.g., review log files monthly, or survey users before and after a service or resource use). While the tools provided in this chapter may be helpful to get librarians started in building their evaluation methods, librarians should review, make modifications, and consider strategies for data collection that will yield the *best results for their particular evaluation projects and libraries.*

Finally, approaches for assessing network services and resources involve a combination of new methodologies and variations on existing methods. They also require some creativity and a spirit of experimentation, because the services and resources that libraries provide are in a continual state of change, adaptation, and development. As a result, new services and resources are available on a regular basis and thus may require new approaches and tools through which to assess them.

## Building a Methodology

There are a number of factors that library managers, staff, and others should consider as they build an evaluation methodology. At minimum, these include the following:

- **Resources necessary and/or available for the evaluation effort**. There is a need to consider the resources available and/or necessary for the evaluation effort in general (see Chapter 1), and the method(s) under consideration, in particular. These include staff, funding, equipment, and other resources associated with conducting an evaluation effort.
- **Timeframe**. By when do library managers and others need the results? A shorter timeframe will dictate a less complex methodology that has the ability to provide useful data in a short period of time.
- **Expertise**. What expertise do library staff and others need in order to conduct project evaluation activities–such as create surveys, conduct focus groups, analyze systems log files (e.g., Web log files, circulation system files), and analyze survey and focus group data. Staff expertise may determine the method(s) chosen, rather than a more preferred approach. [Note: Library managers and others may consider hiring

experts, or perhaps soliciting assistance from research faculty or others, as a means of gaining access to research experience and knowledge].

- **What you want to know about the network services and resources**. There are a number of ways to assess network services and resources: use and usage counts (e.g., number of e-books downloaded, number of full-text articles accessed, number of users that attended library technology training sessions); user satisfaction (e.g., the satisfaction with the services/resources that users identify, such as ratings of "excellent" for library technology training sessions); and outcomes (e.g., changes in technology skills as a result of attending a library technology training session). It may be the case that library managers want to have data regarding all of the above, or just one particular type of data. Some *need to know* data may be driven by external reporting requirements or internal management needs. Knowing the context or need for the data helps in the overall evaluation effort (as discussed in Chapter 1).

- **What you want to be able to say about the network services and resources**. Depending on the nature of your library's data needs, there may be a need for both quantitative and qualitative data. For example:

  - If you want to report data such as "45% of training session attendees indicated that they could now search the consumer information databases more effectively," or "Database sessions increased by 30% after the training program began," then you will need to use approaches that yield quantitative data (in the first example, likely a user survey; in the second example, the use of database log files).

  - If you want to report user-based anecdotal data such as "Thanks to the training session, I can now look up all sorts of information regarding investing, products, and other important information. I am now so much more informed and am able to make better life decisions on my own," then you will need a user focus group, interviews, or a survey that uses open-ended questions with selected training session participants.

  - If you want to present both types of data, then you need to think about focus groups or interviews *and* a survey, or a survey that has both numeric and open-ended questions.

These factors form the core considerations that library managers and others need to consider as they develop a research methodology for assessing their network services and resources.

## What is Measurement?

There are entire books devoted to social science measurement (see Babbie, 2003; Creswell, 2002). This chapter takes a basic and pragmatic approach to the measurement process (Fig. 3-1). Briefly, those involved in measuring social phenomena (e.g., user satisfaction, changes in knowledge) try to be as accurate (reliable) and close to the phenomena (e.g., actual satisfaction, real changes in knowledge) as possible (valid). To do this, researchers and others use *indicators.* Said simply, to measure the use, quality, outcomes, etc., of the library's network services and resources, library managers, staff, and others need to decide what they will actually examine in order to determine, for example, user satisfaction with or perceived quality of the library's digital reference program, changes in user skills due to the training sessions, or uses of the online databases.

Thus, in order to measure the extent to which a library's training sessions dealing with online searching strategies have changed a user's searching skills or knowledge about searching strategies in general (an outcomes-based evaluation strategy), one would need to determine a user's online searching skills both *before* and *after* the training session through *indicators* of the user's skills and knowledge. As discussed in more depth later in this chapter, these pre- and post-training data could be obtained through a simple skills/knowledge questionnaire, brief interviews, or even a "treasure hunt" in which training session attendees are given a few items to find online. However you choose to ascertain change in skills or knowledge, you will measure and analyze indicators of skills or knowledge change. The development, measurement, and analysis of indicators are best viewed as part of a larger methodology planning process.

**Figure 3-1**
**Measurement of network services and resources through indicators.**

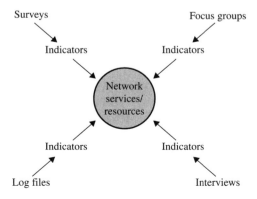

## Planning a Methodology or Measurement Approach

An ad hoc approach to measurement inevitably results in wasted resources, missed opportunities, and poor or useless data. A more beneficial approach is to consider a variety of factors (e.g., desired data, available resources, timeframe, reporting requirements, other) prior to any type of data collection activity. One way to facilitate the measurement and data collection process is to develop an overall methodology plan (Fig. 3-2). Engaging in such a process can assist library managers, staff, and others in determining the network service or resource they are assessing; the goals and objectives for the assessment and data collection; what they will actually measure (indicators); how they will measure the indicators (e.g., survey, focus group, log files, other); and the source of the data (e.g., users, vendors, library staff). This methodology planning process not only can help to avoid a number of data collection pitfalls, but also can assist library managers and staff in determining the feasibility of the overall evaluation approach. To a large extent, the methodology plan is the operational plan of the evaluation plan described in Chapter 1; thus, the two plans work together in critical ways.

At minimum, the components of the methodology plan include the following:

- **Network service or resource being assessed**. Planners should identify up front the network service or resource for which the methodology plan is being developed, e.g., a particular vendor set of databases, a particular product, technology instructional sessions, digital reference services, etc. It is important to identify the resource or service in its implementation context—for example, if you are examining a particular database or online journal within a larger vendor package.

- **Objectives of the data collection and identification of desired data**. Identify the specific objectives for collecting data on this e-metric or e-metric grouping. Why is the library collecting these data? For what management, external reporting, or other reasons is it important to collect the data? What do library managers and staff desire to know about this network service or resource?

- **Inputs**. These are the resources invested in providing the network service or resource, such as funds, staff, technology and equipment, or facilities. Inputs may not be as straightforward to identify in cases in which state library agencies or other entities provide at least part of the resources necessary for the network service (e.g., statewide licensing of databases), but the library should strive to identify the inputs to the extent possible.

Figure 3-2
Methodology plan.

Network Service/
Resource: _____

Desired Data/
Objectives: _____

| Inputs | Activities | Assessment Type | Measurement | | |
| --- | --- | --- | --- | --- | --- |
| | | | Indicators | Sources/Methods | |
| | | | | | |

- **Activities**. These are the actions generated by the inputs, such as actually licensing selected databases, creating an instructional technology lab, purchasing software or equipment, or any other actions generated by the inputs.
- **Assessment Type**. This is the assessment framework(s) that the library intends to use for collecting data (see Chapter 2), for example:
  - **Outputs**, which are basically counts of how many units of a service or resource are used and/or provided, and how often;
  - **Service quality**, which can range from user satisfaction with a service or resource to an assessment of the service or resource by field experts. This form of assessment essentially gauges how well a library provides a service or resource, as determined by some user population(s); and
  - **Outcomes**, which are the changes in knowledge, skill, or behavior exhibited in users due to their use of the library's network service or resource.
- **Indicators**. These are what the library will actually measure to determine *how many* (outcomes), *how well* (service quality), and *changes in users* (outcomes). Thus, indicators are the questions you ask users on surveys, in interviews, or focus groups regarding a service or resource; they are the specific log file data (e.g., database sessions, searches, content units examined) that you examine; or they are other forms of assessment that the library uses to measure a service's use, success, etc.
- **Sources and Methods**. Sources are the entities from which libraries will collect data regarding the service or resource. This entails a number of issues and considerations, including
  - **Ownership of data:** Does the library actually own the data of interest (e.g., Web log files, circulation files), or are the data in the hands of others (e.g., vendors, Internet Service Providers (ISPs), academic computing, county IT department, other)? Once ownership is established, libraries will need to establish a process and/or system to gain access to data that are not under the control of the library.
  - **Location of collection:** Will the data collection occur on a system level or on a branch level? In general, the point of service or resource delivery (e.g., instructional room, reference desk, website) determines the location of data collection.
  - **Provider of data:** Who or what actually provides the data to the library? The data of interest can come from service or resource users, log files (e.g., Web server, database, circulation, digital reference software), or library staff (e.g., reference transactions, instruction attendance counts, counts of public access workstation users).

Methods are the ways in which libraries will actually collect the data. This also involves key issues, including

- **Data collection approach**, which identifies the way(s) in which the library will actually collect the desired data—for example, through a survey of users (which can take the form of a print/mail survey, e-mail survey, Web-based survey, Web-based pop-up surveys, or any combination); machine-generated log file analysis (e.g., Web server, database vendor); librarian-maintained log file analysis (e.g., reference desk transactions); focus groups or interviews with library staff and/or service or resource users, other;

- **Sampling**, which identifies who or what, specifically, the library will involve in the data collection approaches. There are entire text-books and numerous chapters on sampling techniques (see Babbie, 2003; Creswell, 2002), but there are three basic approaches to sampling: (1) **Random** (all service/resource users have an equal chance of being asked to complete a survey, for example); (2) **Purposeful** (selection of patrons—such as decision makers, those most informed, etc.—is nonrandom and intentional; and (3) **Convenience** (select whomever is available to participate at that time, using exit surveys, handing out surveys at the circulation desk, etc.). Libraries need to consider how they will actually select participants. This is increasingly difficult for remotely offered network services and resources (e.g., licensed database resources and Web-based resources), and is highly dependent on how the library offers the service or resource to its users. Another issue to consider is whether to sample at all. Some data collection is actually a census; that is, all data are collected. This is the case with database and Web server log files, circulation transaction logs, and reference transactions.

- **Desired data** (as identified earlier), which involves the type(s) of reporting library mangers and staff desire and/or have to provide. For example, numeric data that quantify the uses, impacts, or quality of library services, or data that explain—from a user's perspective—the value of library services, or both. Different methodologies can provide different data types, so library managers and staff will need to engage the methods that *best provide* the types of data needed. It may be the case that *more than one method* (e.g., a combination of usage logs and focus groups) are necessary to present a robust description of the network service or resource under analysis.

- **Type of analysis**, which involves the varying levels of effort and knowledge necessary to conduct data analysis. For example, the calculation of measure of central tendency (mean, median, mode) or counts requires only basic knowledge of statistical analysis and can be conducted with a spreadsheet tool such as Microsoft Excel. More sophisticated analysis requires additional statistical skills, as well as more powerful statistical analysis software (e.g., SPSS). Also, the analysis of qualitative data (e.g., from focus groups, interviews, or open-ended survey questions) requires the ability to synthesize text into meaningful and useful findings.

- **Library staff skills and time**, which means that library managers and staff need to determine the extent to which library staff have a) the skills, experience, and abilities to collect the desired data through the identified methods; b) the necessary skills to analyze and present the data; and c) the necessary release from other duties to engage in data collection and analysis. Some data and approaches may require temporary reassignment of staff to assist in the process, training, or other forms of preparation.

In considering the foregoing issues and putting the key components together, as demonstrated in Fig. 3-2, library managers and staff can develop a comprehensive methodology plan that facilitates the collection of data regarding network services and resources. When used in combination with the overall evaluation plan as described in Chapter 1, the methodology plan provides an operational and implementation guide for the actual collection of data for evaluation purposes.

## Methods in Brief

There are a number of methodologies through which libraries can collect data about their network services and resources. This section identifies selected methods, considerations for using such methods, and issues associated with these methods. Where possible, the section provides sample questions and designs–though these are generic and may not fit exactly what your library needs to assess a particular service or resource. Thus, library managers and staff will need to consider what changes to make to the various examples in order to *best meet* the library's service and resource evaluation needs.

One basic way to categorize network service and resource methods is by the source of collection–either the user of the service or resource, or the service or resource usage data (Fig. 3-3). Library managers and staff need to ask and answer three basic questions regarding their data collection efforts:

1. From what or whom can we *collect* data?
2. From what or whom do we *want* data?

**Figure 3-3**
**Selected data collection approaches by source of data.**

| User Data Collection | Resource/Service Data Collection |
|---|---|
| Surveys<br>Focus groups<br>Interviews | Web site usage logs<br>Database usage logs<br>OPAC usage logs<br>Circulation logs<br>Reference transaction logs<br>Instructional session logs<br>Counts of workstation users |

3. What do we want to be able to *say* about the library's network services and resources?

As discussed earlier, the answers to these questions are essential to creating a methodology design. As discussed later, it is not the case that libraries may engage in *either* user-based *or* resource usage methods. Indeed, the two often work well together, providing different perspectives and data regarding a resource or service such as IT instructional sessions, public-access workstations, library websites, and licensed resources.

## User-Based Data Collection Approaches

This section discusses three forms of user-based data collection methods: surveys, focus groups, and interviews. To facilitate the discussion, focus groups and interviews are discussed together, as there are a number of similarities in approach and considerations. This section does not describe all methodological issues associated with survey, focus group, or interview research. Readers interested in specific methodological information should consult such texts as Fowler (2001), Punch (2003), and Krueger & Casey (2000).

### Surveys

There are numerous types of surveys that librarians can use in order to collect data from users regarding library network services and resources:

- **Mail** surveys, which libraries could distribute to registered borrowers, students, or faculty;
- **Handouts**, which libraries distribute to users at various locations in the library or after participation in or use of a library resource (e.g., training session);
- **E-mail** surveys, which libraries distribute to users through e-mail accounts;

- **Web-based** surveys, which libraries make available through the library (or other) website for users to complete; and
- **Web-based pop-up** surveys, which appear as users access various areas of the library (or other) website.

Libraries can also use combinations of these surveys for data collection purposes—for example, distribute a mail survey to registered borrowers, as well as a Web-based survey form.

Survey forms and the questions asked on such forms can exhibit a wide range of formats, layouts, and question wording and presentation. To a large extent, the actual design of a survey questionnaire is a creative process that has few limits. Regardless of survey appearance and other methodological issues, there are two important factors that library managers and staff need to consider regarding survey design: 1) Survey participants must be able to move through the survey form itself with ease, understand the questions asked, and not be too burdened in terms of the level of effort required to answer the questions asked; and 2) Survey question responses must actually provide useful, informative, and meaningful data regarding the service or resource.

To satisfy these two criteria of a successful survey, the library needs to engage in a survey design process that includes pre-tests of both the survey questions and forms (be they electronic or print). These pre-tests should involve users with backgrounds similar to those who will ultimately complete the survey (e.g., patrons, faculty, students, etc.). The results of the pre-test process should be incorporated into the final survey form. It may be necessary to engage in a multiple-test process, depending on the number of comments received regarding the survey design and questions, and on the complexity of the survey.

The two broad types of questions on surveys include *closed*, or *forced-choice*, questions and *open-ended* questions. Closed/forced choice questions provide survey participants with the answers to the questions asked, and participants may choose among a series of answers (e.g., age groupings, gender, household income categories). Included in such questions would be agreement and/or satisfaction questions that provide a scale (e.g., 1–7, with 1 being *not at all* s*atisfied* and 7 being *extremely satisfied*) (Fig. 3-4). Open-ended questions allow participants to supply their own answers to the questions. These can take many forms, but typically consist of fill-ins (such as actual age, annual household income) or short answers (Fig. 3-5). Library managers and staff will ultimately need to decide which questions to ask, the ways in which to ask the questions, and the presentation of the questions. As discussed earlier, these decisions should be made in consideration of the goals and objectives of the evaluation, the specific data needs, and the types of data that library managers want to use and report.

**Figure 3-4**
**Closed (forced choice) survey question examples.**

| | |
|---|---|
| Please tell us your age (fill in the oval):<br><br>　　　　○ Under 20<br>　　　　○ 20–25<br>　　　　○ 26–30<br>　　　　○ 31–35<br>　　　　○ 36–40<br>　　　　○ 41–45<br>　　　　○ Over 45<br><br>*Note:* Libraries should select age categories that matter to the service or resource under assessment. | |

| Please indicate your agreement with the following statements (circle your choice): | Strongly<br>Disagree | | | | Strongly<br>Agree |
|---|---|---|---|---|---|
| I am able to search the Web and find information I want with ease. | 1 | 2 | 3 | 4 | 5 |
| The library's online databases meet my research needs. | 1 | 2 | 3 | 4 | 5 |

**Figure 3-5**
**Open-ended survey question examples.**

| |
|---|
| In the space below, please tell us up to three ways that our training program improved your ability to use the consumer information databases:<br><br>　　　1.<br>　　　2.<br>　　　3. |
| In the space below, please tell us up to three ways that our training program can better meet your needs:<br><br>　　　1.<br>　　　2.<br>　　　3. |

### Key Survey Components

Although the composition of each specific survey depends on a number of factors, there are four key components to surveys in general:

• **Privacy/confidentiality statement** (Fig. 3-6). Such a statement should let participants know how the library will use the data; whether

**Figure 3-6**
**Sample privacy/confidentiality statement.**

The data we collect on this survey help us to assess our training program. We do not collect names, or other forms of identification, that will allow us to trace your answers back to you. Once we analyze the data, we will destroy all individual completed survey forms.


*Note*: This statement should come at the beginning of the survey, perhaps in the form of a tear sheet (if print) or a consent screen with an "ok" button (if Web-based).

responses are anonymous (no way to trace back to the participant) or confidential (can trace back to the participant, but specific answers will not be disclosed or attributed to the participant); or what will happen to the survey data once the evaluation is finished.

- There may also be a need to ask permission from a parent/guardian for a minor to participate in the survey.

- Given the passage of the USA Patriot Act and its impact on library records, libraries may want to develop an overall records management policy that includes survey form/database records (see Jaeger, Bertot, & McClure, 2004 for issues concerning libraries and the Patriot Act).

- **Introduction and instructions** (Fig. 3-7). These should introduce and explain the survey to the participants and tell participants how to complete the survey (e.g., fill in the blank, circle their choice, etc.). Instructions may need to appear periodically throughout the survey, particularly as question types change.

- **Demographic questions**. These questions can provide important information regarding service and resource users: gender, income, zip code, status (e.g., faculty, student, staff), etc. These types of questions enable various forms of data analysis that may help with service and resource planning. For example, perhaps the results show that women need specific forms of instruction, students require specialized information literacy skills, or other interesting findings.

- **Content questions**. These provide library managers and staff with data regarding the outcomes, service quality, or other aspects of the library's network service(s) and resource(s) under assessment. Answers to these questions will inform the overall evaluation, planning, and other aspects of the network service(s) and resource(s).

**Figure 3-7**
**Sample introduction and instructions.**

> **Introduction:** We are conducting this survey to assess our training program. Your answers will help us to understand how our training helped you, as well as areas for improving our training program. Thank you for your willingness to help by completing this survey.
>
> **Instructions:** This survey form has questions that ask you to fill in ovals, fill in blanks, and write out your answers. Please look at each question and select the appropriate way to complete that question. When you are done with the survey, please pass the completed form to the training session instructor. If you have any questions while completing the survey form, please ask the instructor.

Together, the foregoing items form the core elements of a survey. Appendix 3-A provides some sample survey questions that libraries may find helpful as they develop their network service or resource surveys.

There is not enough space in this book to provide a detailed presentation of how to analyze survey findings. Readers will find a PowerPoint tutorial on analyzing and presenting survey data, including the creation of a survey codebook, at http://www.ii.fsu.edu/neteval. The tutorial also includes assistance with analyzing focus group and interview data.

### *Selected Survey Issues and Considerations*

Regardless of survey type, questions asked, or other survey specifics, there are several issues regarding surveys–particularly web-based and/or electronic survey forms–that librarians should consider. Selected issues are identified in the following list:

- **Identifying users**. Increasingly, users access library network services remotely, and may or may not be *active borrowers* in the traditional sense. Thus, it is increasingly challenging to identify actual users of services through the systematic research method approaches of developing a sample frame (list of users to sample), drawing a sample (selecting participants), contacting those sampled, and knowing who responded (for survey response, representation, and other methodological purposes).

- **Eliciting participation**. Across the board, survey response rates are low. For various reasons, users simply do not participate in survey research as they used to do. Thus, libraries face the challenge of collecting enough data that are *meaningful* and *useful* through survey research.

- **Collecting data more than once**. Depending on the data the library wants, it is likely to be necessary to collect data more than once. More often than not, library managers and staff will want to have longitudinal data—data that show service and resource use trends over time. Thus, library managers and staff will need to consider the frequency of data collection. Finally, certain evaluation frameworks, such as outcomes assessment, measure the change in user skills, knowledge, and behavior. By definition, therefore, libraries will need multiple measures—both *before* and *after* library resource or service use and/or contact.

- **Web-based and pop-up surveys**. Over the years, Internet-based data collection has taken hold. On the one hand, these forms of surveys have great advantages (e.g., postage cost savings, duplication cost savings, and automated data entry). On the other hand, they bring challenges such as technical infrastructure needs, and design and survey administration issues (details on Web surveys are available in such texts as Junion-Metz & Metz, 2001a, b; Ward, 2000). Other issues with Web surveys include

  - **Spam filters and pop-up blockers**. Many of us now use these defensive tools to stop—or at least attempt to stop—the unwanted flow of advertisements or solicitations. The effect of these software programs also extends to survey research—spam filters may rule that an e-mail from the "library" is spam, or pop-up blocking software may halt a pop-up survey form that the library might have been able to use. Thus, even if libraries establish a methodologically sound approach to e-mail and pop-up surveys, the surveys may actually never reach the identified participants. This may skew the survey results in many unknown ways.

  - **Implementation**. Notices of Web surveys generally include only a URL to where the survey is, along with general information regarding the survey. Participants are not necessarily able to preview the survey to determine whether they are able and/or willing to complete the survey based on its contents. Also, pop-up surveys cannot be lengthy. Research on previous studies by the author and others (Bertot & McClure, 1999; 2002a,b) demonstrates that a pop-up survey, in general, has to be as easy to complete as it is for the user to decline participation. Thus, there is a real limitation to such a survey.

    On the other hand, libraries can target pop-up surveys to appear systematically (e.g., every 10th page accessed) on a particular location after a user engages a particular action (e.g., a search of library holdings). This can be quite useful and can help libraries target a specific Web-based service or resource.

- **Developing your own surveys, or outsourcing**. Depending on data needs, available resources, and expertise, library managers may want to hire consultants to conduct, analyze, and report a survey and its findings. There are even types of surveys and expertise that library managers can contract for. For example, the Association of Research Libraries (ARL) now offers its LibQUAL+ survey (a service-quality survey developed for academic libraries) on a fee-for-service basis (see http://www.libqual.org for more details). Library managers and staff would need to engage in a resource cost/benefit process to determine which is more cost effective: outsourcing or library-conducted survey work.

The list just presented identifies various factors and considerations regarding surveys of the use of library network services and resources. The next section discusses using focus groups and interviews to assess library network services and resources.

### Focus Groups and Interviews

This section provides some basic guidance, issues, and examples of focus groups and interviews regarding library network service and resource evaluation efforts. Readers are encouraged to consult Creswell (2002) and Kruger & Casey (2000) regarding additional methodological information concerning qualitative methods such as focus groups and interviews.

Focus groups and interviews with network service and resource users provide library managers and staff with detailed comments, issues, suggestions, and anecdotes regarding the library's service(s) and resource(s). Focus groups and interviews are excellent methods for gathering in-depth feedback from users that is simply not possible through surveys. From an outcomes perspective, for example, focus groups and interviews can provide significant user-based data regarding:

- How a training program gave them new skills and knowledge;
- What in particular about the training program provided patrons with new skills and knowledge; and
- Life changes, such as fostering reading habits with children.

The ability to engage users in a conversation and/or guided data collection process facilitates the exploration of topics and issues in ways that surveys simply cannot. Furthermore, these forms of data collection provide library managers and staff with quotes and anecdotes that can be quite powerful in describing the impact of a service or resource in ways that numbers alone cannot.

Focus groups bring a group or groups of people together to focus on a particular issue or set of issues. Interviews are generally one-on-one and can occur in person, via the telephone, through iChat, or even by e-mail. They can occur in real time (in person, or by telephone or iChat) or asynchronously (e-mail), depending on how the library desires to access service and resource users. Depending on how rigorous the library wishes to be regarding its qualitative data efforts, focus groups and interviews can be either: 1) formal, that is, structured with a set of questions and *probes* (probes to initiate discussion, clarify participant statements, or get participants to consider ideas or issues (see Appendix 3-B); or 2) informal, that is, unstructured and exploratory. Those involved in the evaluation effort will need to decide on the expectations and intent of their qualitative data collection, as it has implications for the conduct of the sessions or interviews, data analysis, data presentation, and data use.

Some issues and considerations regarding focus groups and interviews include:

- **Participant selection**. There are a number of ways to select focus group and interview participants. As discussed previously in the survey section of this chapter, there are random, purposeful, and convenience methods for participant selection.

- **Need to decide on similar or dissimilar participants**. For example, you may decide to have all retirees, all students, or only faculty in a session, or you may decide to mix the participants. Both have advantages—similar types of participants may have more in common, and so may create camaraderie in the group (e.g., retired individuals, Spanish speakers, other). Dissimilar participants may provide more diversity in views regarding the service or resource.

- **Number of participants and duration**. In general, focus groups with more than 8 to 10 people get unwieldy, and it is difficult to elicit participation from all who attend. Participant tolerance, time constraints, and energy levels last for up to two hours. It is difficult to maintain focus beyond that amount of time.

- **Getting participants to come**. Not all invited participants will actually come to the session(s). Thus, it is good practice to overinvite by at least a few people (if your target is 10 participants, consider inviting 15 to the session). Ways to solicit participation include advertising the sessions in various library locations or correspondence; contacting participants individually, if possible; scheduling the sessions at times that are convenient to the participants; holding the sessions at locations that are convenient to the users (e.g., don't make participants travel to the library if it is more convenient for the sessions to occur in dorms, community centers, etc.); and offering incentives, such as small gifts (e.g., tote bags, mouse pads, other) and refreshments.

- **Decide on how many focus groups and interviews are enough**. This is difficult to determine and depends on a number of factors, including the number of program participants and the resources at the library's disposal. A general rule of thumb is that you have had enough when (a) you no longer find new information from the participants; (b) no longer have the anecdotes, stories, or quotes that you need; or (c) your library runs out of resources. Library managers and staff need to make a decision as to when is an appropriate time to halt the focus groups and interviews, given resources, findings, and other factors.

- **Librarian expertise**. There are a number of skills involved in focus groups and interviews, including the ability to plan and organize a session or series of sessions; facilitate a session; take good notes, particularly if recording devices will not be used (a choice that should be left up to the participants); and the ability to analyze, organize, and present session findings (see Appendix 3-C).

- **Privacy and confidentiality**. The same issues regarding confidentiality and privacy described earlier in the *Surveys* section apply with focus groups and interviews. A key difference, however, is that focus groups and interviews are not anonymous—session facilitators and participants know who participated in the session and provided answers to questions, comments, etc. It is the job of the data analyzer(s) and report writer(s) to ensure the anonymity and confidentiality of participant comments, unless otherwise requested.

The foregoing list presents selected, pragmatic issues regarding focus groups and interviews. There are others, as described in various texts (Kruger & Casey, 2000). It may be the case that library managers decide to hire consultants or work with faculty to assist in the focus group and/or interview process, given the level of effort such data collection activities require.

There are a number of considerations regarding the analysis of focus group and interview data that space does not permit discussing. Readers are encouraged to review the data analysis module (PowerPoint presentation format) located at http://www.ii.fsu.edu/neteval. The tutorial also includes assistance with analyzing and presenting survey data. Appendices 3-B and 3-C provide sample focus group protocols and an issues-based writeup based on a study the author conducted regarding the establishment of a Spanish language Web portal service. Appendix 3-B also contains additional sample focus group and interview protocols. The intent of the appendices is to provide guidance regarding focus group and interview question probes, as well as one approach to presenting the findings.

### Service and Resource Use Data Collection

In general, service and resource use data collection activities involve the analysis of various log files. There are four basic types of log files that library managers and staff can analyze regarding various network services and resources:

- **Librarian-maintained log files**. These include reference transaction logs, training attendance logs, public-access workstation sign-up sheets, or others that librarians use to keep tallies for various service and resource uses;

- **Library information system-generated files**. These include OPAC, circulation, or Web server log files. While not always the case, libraries generally run and maintain these types of systems, and thus have access to the log files. In some cases, libraries are limited by proprietary log analysis software in their ability to analyze these files;

- **Licensed resource vendor systems files**. These include licensed databases, e-books, and e-journals. With these log files, libraries do not have access to the raw log files, nor do they necessarily control how they gain access to the data. Each vendor supplies libraries with resource usage data differently (see Chapter 9 for a discussion about using vendor data);

- **Service and resource user logs**. These include service and resource user logs that users complete as they use selected library network resources and services. This approach provides users with feedback regarding the service or resource under assessment as they make use of it.

Each of these types of log files can provide library managers and staff with a wide range of service and resource use data. Examples are website use, including pages accessed, files downloaded, and various other user actions; user search strings and bibliographic records examined; books circulated; journal articles downloaded or accessed and e-book titles circulated; and user-based assessments of the library network services and resources that they accessed and used. There are other data that such files can provide, depending on the types of analysis desired, the technology infrastructure configuration of the library, and the availability of the data.

Library managers and staff should consult their system managers regarding library system log files and the ability to run analysis on these files. Though not always the case, some integrated systems have proprietary log files that can be analyzed only by using the vendor's analysis software program or scripts. Web server log files are standardized text files that libraries can analyze by using a variety of software (e.g., WebTrends, at http://www.netiq.com/webtrends/default.asp; WebTracker, at http://www.tacticit.com/en-US/; or Analog (which is available for free) at http://www.analog.cx/). Additional information and assistance in analyzing Web server log files is available in Stern (2002) and Rubin (2002). Licensed resource vendor log files are the property of the respective vendors, and libraries are provided indirect access to the log file data through vendor-developed interfaces. Also, in most cases, vendors will provide various use data to libraries in a variety of formats (see the Shim chapter on using vendor data).

### Issues Regarding Log Files

Log files can provide library managers and staff with service and resource use data: how much use, how often, from what location, and what actions users took while engaging the service or resource (e.g., viewed files, downloaded an article, etc.). There are limitations and issues associated with log files, however, that librarians should consider:

- **Service and resource configuration matters**. If the library uses a firewall or proxy server for its network services, this affects substantially what a log file collects in terms of data. Indeed, as Fig. 3-8 shows, network services such as vendor provided databases, library websites, etc., can be woven together in a complex configuration that requires a number of distinctions about what is counted where and by what log, and what the numbers actually mean. For example, a vendor who receives a session request from a library that uses a firewall or proxy server receives only the IP address of the firewall or proxy server. Thus, if libraries want any breakdowns such as sessions initiated by IP address, the library will need to run Web log analysis from the firewall or proxy server's Web log files. Database vendors will *not* be able to provide that type of data to the library.

- **Multiple log files of the same service or resource**. With the advent of federated and cross-resource search and retrieval systems (e.g., WebFeat, at http://www.webfeat.org/; Ex Libris' MetaLib/SFX, at http://www.exlibris-usa.com/), libraries now face multiple log files regarding similar actions by different providers. For example, federated or cross- resource searching products also maintain logs of user-initiated sessions, searches, and items retrieved. Vendor logs also provide session, search, and items retrieved data. Thus, librarians have access to multiple log files, with some differences, of the same resource or service use. On the one hand, this provides multiple views of the usage. On the other hand, this can be confusing, and librarians will need to know which log files provide what types of data and how those data meet the library's service and resource evaluation data needs.

**Figure 3-8**
**Complexity of access to network services and resources.***

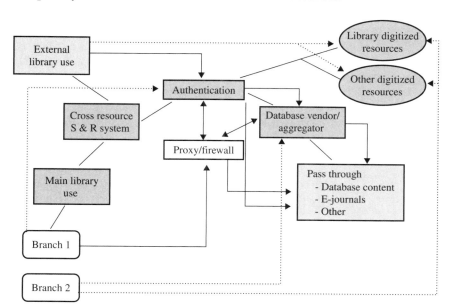

*An earlier version of this diagram appeared in Bertot (2003).

- **Making sense of the numbers**. The numbers reported by the federated or cross-resource and vendor systems will likely differ. Although they examine the same service or resource use broadly, they have different vantage points and views on sessions, searching, and retrieving information. On top of that, libraries have websites through which these services and resources are accessed, and which generate another set of log files. Thus, library managers and staff need to consider which log files contain the necessary data for the library's evaluation purposes.

- **Know the definitions and terminology**. Although vendors and others claim ICOLC, COUNTER, or NISO/ISO compliance (see Chapter 4 for a discussion of these), not all vendors and providers count and report sessions, searches, downloads, etc., in the same way, or with the same definitions. Thus, librarians need to know how a vendor counts and defines such items. Finally, it is important to remember that the library's implementation of a service or resource has an impact on what shows up on the vendor side in terms of user actions.

These issues associated with log files require that library managers and staff know what services and resources maintain log files; what those log files contain; the definitions used by the service providers regarding reported items (e.g., searches, sessions); what the reported data or log analyses mean; and how the various log files interrelate.

## Concluding Comments

This chapter has presented a brief discussion of several key methods for assessing library network services and resources. In particular, the chapter offered suggestions, approaches, and issues for library managers and staff to consider while using selected methods—such as surveys, focus groups, and interviews—and log file analysis for service and resource analysis. The chapter also provided readers with sample surveys, focus group and interview protocols, and focus group write-up strategies. Finally, readers are encouraged to access the web-based content identified throughout this chapter for additional assistance in analyzing survey and focus group data. The chapter did not provide a detailed methodological discussion of each method. Readers should consult specific texts such as Babbie (2003), Creswell (2002), Powell (1997), or Krueger & Casey (2000) for such assistance.

Following are some final thoughts for readers:

- **No one method tells the whole story**. Each method has limitations in what service and resource data it can provide. Log files provide only use and usage data—they do not provide user-based assessments of the service or resource. Surveys can yield various user assessments of a service or resource, and can assist libraries in quantifying such evaluations. Surveys do not, however, provide an expanded understanding (through stories, anecdotes, or life changes) of the service or resource use by library customers. Focus groups and interviews yield a greater understanding through stories, anecdotes, and other user-provided explanations of a service or resource, but they provide no quantification of such experiences. Thus, for libraries to truly understand their network services and resources, it is likely that librarians need to use a combination of methods: log file analysis, surveys, and focus groups and/or interviews. Each method provides a different perspective on the service or resource, and library managers and staff will need to decide which view(s) they want.

- **Get help**. Depending on a library's available resources, staff and management knowledge and skills, time constraints, and other factors, it may simply not be possible or feasible for a library to conduct its own data collection—or even key aspects of the collection, analysis, and reporting of data. Library managers may want to consider hiring consultants, seeking faculty on campus (or faculty at nearby Library and Information Science, Education, or other relevant departments), contacting the state library's consultants, or drawing on other sources to assist in the process. Library managers do have options and alternatives to internal data collection efforts.

In the end, the primary objective of using the methods discussed here (and others) is to assist library managers and staff to better understand the uses, quality, impact, and value of the library's network services and resources. As this chapter has described them, there are a number of options, tools, and approaches available to library managers and staff to assist in this process.

# References

Babbie, E.R. (2003). *Practice of social science research* (10th ed.). Belmont, CA: Wadsworth Publishing.

Bertot, J.C. (2002). Building a statewide digital public library: A case study. *Public Library Quarterly*, 21(2): 5–33.

Bertot, J.C. (2003). Libraries and the networked environment: Future issues and strategies. *Library Trends*, 52(2): 209–227.

Bertot, J.C., & Davis, D.M. (2001). *Building a Maryland digital public library: Issues, findings, and recommendations.* Baltimore, MD: Division of Library Development and Services.

Bertot, J.C., & McClure, C.R. (1999). *The DelAWARE evaluation: User survey findings and recommendations.* Dover, DE: Delaware Division of Libraries.

Bertot, J.C., & McClure, C.R. (2002a). *Assessing SEFLIN's virtual libraries.* Ft. Lauderdale, FL: Southeast Florida Library Information Network, Inc.

Bertot, J.C., & McClure (2002b). *Assessing SEFLIN's Virtual Library Mi Servicio de Biblioteca: User and Reference Librarian Focus Group Report.* Ft. Lauderdale, FL: Southeast Florida Library Information Network, Inc.

Creswell, A. (2002). *Research design: Qualitative, quantitative, and mixed methods approaches* (2nd ed.). Thousand Oaks, CA: Sage Publications.

Fowler, F.J. (2001). *Survey research methods* (3rd ed.). Thousand Oaks, CA: Sage Publications.

Jaeger, P.T., Bertot, J.C., & McClure, C.R. (2004). The effects of the Children's Internet Protection Act (CIPA) in public libraries and its implications for research: A statistical, policy, and legal analysis. *Journal of the American Society for Information Science*, forthcoming.

Junion-Metz, G., & Metz, D.L. (2001a). *Instant web forms and surveys for academic libraries.* New York, NY: Neal-Schuman Publishers, Inc.

Junion-Metz, G., & Metz, D.L. (2001b). *Instant web forms and surveys for public libraries.* New York, NY: Neal-Schuman Publishers, Inc.

Krueger, R.A. & Casey, M.A. (2000). *Focus groups: A practical guide for applied research* (3rd ed.). Thousand Oaks, CA: Sage Publications.

McClure, C.R., Ryan, J., & Bertot, J.C. (2002). *Public library Internet services and the digital divide: The role and impacts from selected external funding sources.* Tallahassee, FL: Chief Officers of State Library Agencies.

Powell, R.R. (1997). *Basic research methods for librarians* (3rd ed.). Norwood, NJ: Ablex Publishing.

Punch, K.F. (2003). *Survey research: The basics*. Thousand Oaks, CA: Sage Publications.

Rubin, J. (2002). Introduction to log analysis techniques: Methods for evaluating networked services. In *Evaluating Networked Information Services* (McClure, C.R., & Bertot, J.C., eds.). Medford, NJ: Information Today.

Stern, J. (2002). *Web metrics: Proven methods for measuring website success*. New York, NY: John Wiley & Sons.

Ward, D. (2000). *Getting the most out of web surveys*. Chicago, IL: American Library Association.

# Sample Surveys and Questions

## SAMPLE LIBRARY PATRON TECHNOLOGY/DATABASE ASSESSMENT SURVEY (Pre-test)

The purpose of this survey is to help us (1) know a little bit about you, (2) determine your comfort level with computers and the Internet, and (3) understand a bit about your use of the library's online databases. Please provide the requested information and hand back the survey to the instructor before the training session begins. Thanks!

The data we collect on this survey is for the express purpose of assessing our services/resources. We do not collect names, or other forms of identification, that will allow us to trace your answers back to you. Once we analyze the data, we will destroy all individual survey forms.

Please fill in the circle completely to indicate your response:

### Part I: Patron Information

(1) **Age:** (select one)
  ○ Under 12   ○ 18–21   ○ 26–35   ○ 46–55   ○ over 65
  ○ 13–17        ○ 22–25   ○ 36–45   ○ 56–65

(2) **Gender:** (select one)
  ○ Male        ○ Female

(3) **Race:** (select one)
  ○ White, non-Hispanic        ○ Native American
  ○ Hispanic                   ○ Asian/Pacific Islander
  ○ African-American           ○ Other

**(4) Occupational status:** (select one)

     ○ Currently employed    ○ Student    ○ Other

     ○ Currently unemployed    ○ Retired

**(5) Highest level of education:** (select one)

     ○ Not completed high school

     ○ High school or equivalent

     ○ Some college

     ○ Community college (e.g., completed AA, AS)

     ○ College (e.g., completed BA, BS)

     ○ Graduate school (e.g., completed MA, MS, Ph.D.)

     ○ Professional degree (e.g., completed JD, MD)

**(6) Florida county of residence:** (select one)

     ○ Broward

     ○ Palm Beach

     ○ Martin

     ○ Miami/Dade

     ○ Other Florida county: (Please specify) _____

     ○ Not a Florida resident

**Part II: Self-Assessment of Technology.** Circle the number that indicates the degree to which you agree or disagree with each of the statements below.

|  | Strongly Agree | | | | Strongly Disagree |
|---|---|---|---|---|---|
| 7. I feel very comfortable around computers–they don't intimidate me at all | 1 | 2 | 3 | 4 | 5 |
| 8. I am able to troubleshoot basic computer problems (e.g., documents not printing, frozen screen) with ease | 1 | 2 | 3 | 4 | 5 |
| 9. I am familiar with using spreadsheet software such as Microsoft Excel | 1 | 2 | 3 | 4 | 5 |
| 10. I am familiar with using word processing software such as Microsoft Word | 1 | 2 | 3 | 4 | 5 |
| 11. I use email regularly–at least four times a week | 1 | 2 | 3 | 4 | 5 |
| 12. I surf the Web regularly–at least four times a week | 1 | 2 | 3 | 4 | 5 |

|  | Strongly Agree | | | Strongly Disagree | |
|---|---|---|---|---|---|
| 13. I am able to search the Web and find information I want with ease | 1 | 2 | 3 | 4 | 5 |
| 14. I am familiar with HTML and developing Web pages | 1 | 2 | 3 | 4 | 5 |
| 15. I am able to search the library's databases with ease | 1 | 2 | 3 | 4 | 5 |
| 16. I am able to view, print, download, or otherwise access the information I want in the library's databases with ease | 1 | 2 | 3 | 4 | 5 |
| 17. I use the library's databases regularly—at least four times a week | 1 | 2 | 3 | 4 | 5 |

**Part III: Treasure Hunt.** Please take the next 10 minutes to access the [fill in name] database and look for the following sources.

| Resource Description | How To Look | Treasure | Could Not Find |
|---|---|---|---|
| Article entitled "[fill in]" | By Title | Author Name:<br><br>Date Published: | |
| Article by [fill in author name] published in August 2002 | Author name | Title:<br><br>Name of publication: | |

## THANK YOU FOR COMPLETING THE SURVEY.
### PLEASE RETURN THE COMPLETED SURVEY FORM
### TO THE INSTRUCTOR

## SAMPLE LIBRARY PATRON TECHNOLOGY/DATABASE ASSESSMENT SURVEY (Post-test)

The purpose of this survey is to help us assess the extent to which our training program helped you understand how to use selected computing technology and our databases. Please provide the requested information and hand back the survey to the instructor once you are done. Your answers will help us to improve our training programs, so please do take the time to complete the survey. Thanks!

The data we collect on this survey is for the express purpose of assessing our services and resources. We do not collect names, or other forms of identification, that will allow us to trace your answers back to you. Once we analyze the data, we will destroy all individual survey forms.

**Part I: Technology Skills Assessment.** Circle the number that indicates the degree to which you agree or disagree with each of the statements below.

**After this training session, I am now . . .** (please indicate your agreement with the completed sentences by circling your choice)

|  | Strongly Agree | | | | Strongly Disagree |
|---|---|---|---|---|---|
| 1. Comfortable around computers | 1 | 2 | 3 | 4 | 5 |
| 2. Able to troubleshoot basic computer problems (e.g., documents not printing, frozen screen) with ease | 1 | 2 | 3 | 4 | 5 |
| 3. Familiar with using spreadsheet software such as Microsoft Excel | 1 | 2 | 3 | 4 | 5 |
| 4. Familiar with using word processing software such as Microsoft Word | 1 | 2 | 3 | 4 | 5 |
| 5. Comfortable using email | 1 | 2 | 3 | 4 | 5 |
| 6. Able to search the Web and find information I want with ease | 1 | 2 | 3 | 4 | 5 |
| 7. Familiar with HTML and developing Web pages | 1 | 2 | 3 | 4 | 5 |
| 8. Able to search the library's databases with ease | 1 | 2 | 3 | 4 | 5 |
| 9. Able to view, print, download, or otherwise access the information I want in the library's databases with ease | 1 | 2 | 3 | 4 | 5 |

**Part II: Specific comments.** Please tell us what you think about our training session.

10. What was the most significant thing you learned in this training session?

_____

_____

11. How will this help you with work, your education, retirement, or other endeavors?

_____

_____

**Part III: Treasure Hunt.** Please take the next 10 minutes to access the [fill in name] database and look for the following sources: **Note: these items should be similar to items searched for in the pre-test, but they should not be the same items. See additional note below for further explanation.**

| Resource Description | How To Look | Treasure | Could Not Find |
|---|---|---|---|
| Article entitled "[fill in]" | By Title | Author Name:<br><br>Date Published: | |
| Article by [fill in author name] published in August 2002 | Author name | Title:<br><br>Name of publication: | |

**Note: The items searched at the end of the program should be similar ("author/date published" or "title/name of publication" as in example above), but different items from those presented in the pre-training session survey.

• Participants should "find" or "locate" the items searched for during the pre-test to instill a sense of successful searching. This is a positive reinforcement of the training program as it is offered.

• Some participants will have "found" the items during the pre-test; success finding them again at the end will not show any change in knowledge.

• Items searched for with the post-test should be more challenging and should reflect the level of training the participants just received.

- Using the same item at the beginning of the training and at the end of the training will not reflect the level of training given to the participants or show any significant change in knowledge.

## THANK YOU FOR COMPLETING THE SURVEY.

PLEASE RETURN THE COMPLETED SURVEY FORM
TO THE INSTRUCTOR

# Spanish Portal Librarian Focus Group Questions[1]

http://www.miserviciodebiblioteca.org

## "Mi Servicio de Biblioteca" Librarian Focus Group Questions

### Project Concept Issues:

1. "Mi Servicio de Biblioteca" is planned as an Internet portal that will provide Spanish-speaking users with electronic access to the catalogs of libraries throughout Southeast Florida, various reference resources, and various community information resources and services.
   - (a) What are your overall thoughts about this concept?
   - (b) What do you like about it?
   - (c) Do you have any concerns about this concept? (If yes, what would they be?)
   - (d) What, if anything, is missing from this concept?

### Information Resources Issues:

2. Based on your experience serving Hispanic populations, what information needs could be met through a service like Mi Servicio de Biblioteca?

3. Do you have suggestions for types of online services or specific information to include in the community information area of this portal?

4. Do you have suggestions for Spanish-language websites to be incorporated into the reference resources that will be a part of the site?

### Library Issues:

5. Would such a Web portal assist you in providing better service to your Spanish-speaking customers?

6. What issues would you or your staff face in supporting a Spanish-language library service like Mi Servicio de Biblioteca?

### Marketing Issues:

7. What would be the best ways to promote this service to Spanish-speaking library users?

8. What name would you recommend for this service (the name should also be the URL)?

## "Mi Servicio de Biblioteca" Patron Focus Group Questions

### Library and Website Usage Issues:

1. What have been your experiences with computer technology and the library?

    (a) Do the library services in general meet your needs? Why or why not?

    (b) Have you used any library websites? For what reasons?

    (c) Do library websites meet your information needs? Why or why not?

### Project Concept Issues:

2. "Mi Servicio de Biblioteca" is planned as an Internet portal that will provide Spanish-speaking users with electronic access to the catalogs of libraries throughout Southeast Florida, various information resources, and various community information services.

    (a) What are your overall thoughts about this concept?

(b) What do you like about it?

(c) What, if anything is missing from this concept?

(d) Do you have suggestions for types of online services or information resources to be incorporated into the community information area of this portal?

(e) What Spanish-language websites do you find the most helpful and informative?

(f) *Would* you utilize such a service?

(g) *How* would you utilize such a service?

## Marketing Issues:

3. What name do you suggest for this online service (the name should be the URL)?

4. How could this service be best promoted?

# Additional Sample Focus Group/Interview Questions

## Service/Resource User (Training Program)

1. Please describe your ability to use the following before you began the training session:

    (a) Computers?

    (b) The Internet?

    (c) The library's databases?

2. If you used computers, the Internet, or the library's databases prior to the training session, how did you typically use them?

    (a) Computers?

        i.   Write letters
        ii.  Track personal finances
        iii. Games
        iv.  Other

    (b) The Internet?

        i.   E-mail
        ii.  Web surfing
        iii. Read online newspapers
        iv.  Take online classes/courses
        v.   Pay bills
        vi.  Job searching/application

       vii.   Other

  (c) The library's databases?

       i.   Which ones or which subjects?

       ii.   What types of information do you typically look for?

3. How did your use of computers, the Internet, or the library's databases change after the training session?

  (a) For example:

       i.   "As a result of this session, I am now able to use a computer to. . . ."

       ii.   "As a result of this session, I am now able to use the Internet to. . . ."

       iii.   "As a result of this session, I am now able to use the library's databases to. . . ."

4. If you still have some difficulties in using computers, the Internet, or the library's databases, could you please describe what they are and how the library might help in resolving those difficulties?

  (a) Computer use. . . .

  (b) Internet use. . . .

  (c) Database use. . . .

5. If you had one key recommendation for improving the library's training program, what would it be?

6. Please provide us with any additional comments that you might have regarding the project's success and/or issues.

## Outcomes-Based Librarian Focus Group and Interview Questions

1. Please describe the network service or resource.

  (a) What were its initial goals and objectives?

  (b) Who or what communities did the project target?

  (c) Time frame?

2. What specific outcomes did you anticipate from the service or resource?

  (d) Please complete the sentence, "As a result of this service or resource, customers or patrons would be able to. . . ."

3. What specific outcomes were you able to identify from the service or resource?

  (e) How were these different, if applicable, from what you anticipated from the service or resource at the outset?

4. What issues did the library encounter in implementing and maintaining the service or resource?

    (f) Staffing needs

    (g) Infrastructure (e.g., bandwidth, computers, space)

    (h) Community interest

    (i) Other

5. If you had to do it again, what would you do differently (if anything) to implement the service or resource?

6. Please provide us with any additional comments that you might have regarding the service or resource's success and/or issues.

## Notes

1. This series of focus groups was conducted by the author for the Southeast Library Information Network (SEFLIN) as SEFLIN was establishing its MiServiciodeBiblioteca website (http://www.miserviciodebiblioteca.org) in January 2002.

# Sample Issues-Based Focus Group Write-Up

## *Information Use Management and Policy Institute*

### Assessing SEFLIN's Virtual Library Mi Servicio de Biblioteca: User and Reference Librarian Focus Group Report

A Report Submitted To:

Southeast Florida Library Information Network, Inc.
100 S. Andrews Avenue
Fort Lauderdale, FL 33301

By:

**John Carlo Bertot** <bertot@lis.fsu.edu>
Associate Professor and
Associate Director
(850) 644-8118 phone
(850) 644-4522 fax

Information Use Management and Policy Institute
School of Information Studies
Florida State University
101 Shores Building
Tallahassee, FL 32306

March 2002

School of Information Studies
Florida State University
Information Institute
http://www.ii.fsu.edu

## INTRODUCTION

The Southeast Florida Library Information Network (SEFLIN) began planning a variety of virtual library services in 2000. At the same time, SEFLIN implemented a Technology Training Program (TTP) for its member library staff. Through a phased approach, SEFLIN intends to introduce a number of network-based services and resources to both its members and the southeast Florida area. Phase I of the virtual library project had the following goals:

• To provide a single public gateway to access the collective resources of SEFLIN member libraries and other selected resources;

• To provide a comprehensive collection of information about SEFLIN member libraries;

• To provide SEFLIN members with products and services that enhance library and information services; and

• To provide an organized and comprehensive resource for accessing information about Southeast Florida non-profit and government organizations.

These goals serve as the foundation for the virtual library efforts of SEFLIN. Additional goals will be developed as the project progresses, as well as specific applications that are produced and made available to users.

An LSTA grant from the State Library of Florida provided initial funding for the SEFLIN virtual library service, now called MyLibraryService.org. One component of the project was to conduct an overall evaluation of SEFLIN virtual library activities in general and the MyLibraryService.org site in particular. LSTA grant money also provided funding for the TTP voucher and password programs. SEFLIN requested that the consultants conduct such an assessment to:

• Review and assess SEFLIN virtual library services with a focus on possible areas of assessment and evaluation;

• Develop an approach for ongoing assessment strategies for networked services offered through SEFLIN;

• Provide guidance on the types of data and statistics to collect for assessment purposes;

• Provide analysis and reporting strategies;

- Gain a sense of member librarian and administrator issues with SEF-LIN networked services in general and MyLibraryService.org in particular; and
- Assess the overall effectiveness of the TTP as a means to provide technology education for library staff.

This evaluation project continues and has expanded to include an evaluation of the latest virtual library service underway by SEFLIN, the Mi Servicio de Biblioteca Spanish Web-based service.

The goals of the Mi Servicio de Biblioteca virtual library service are to provide:

- A multiservice, library-oriented portal on the World Wide Web, presented in Spanish;
- A single-search public gateway to Southeast Florida's library catalogs and other databases with Spanish-language content;
- Enhanced access to the Spanish-language materials in the collections of libraries in the region;
- User initiated interlibrary loan capabilities;
- An interactive directory, in Spanish, promoting Southeast Florida libraries and highlighting library resources and services for the Spanish-speaking population;
- Resources for library staff in the region that will enhance services to Spanish-speaking patrons; and
- Library staff recruitment services that target Spanish-speaking librarians and promote the Southeast Florida job market for librarians.

These goals serve as the basis for the evaluation activities regarding the Mi Servicio de Biblioteca service.

This report is one of a series of reports that will inform SEFLIN between March 2002 and September 2002 regarding its virtual library services, including the MyLibraryService.org, the TTP, and Mi Servicio de Biblioteca services. In particular, this report:

- Reviews a broad cross section of literature regarding the U.S. Hispanic population, including identifying information needs of and library services to the Hispanic population;
- Provides a descriptive demographic of the Hispanic population based on the 2000 U.S. Census; and
- Summarizes reference librarian and user focus groups regarding the Mi Servicio de Biblioteca service conduced in December 2001.

The report begins with the summary of the reference librarian and user focus groups.

# Mi Servicio de Biblioteca Focus Group Summaries

In December 2001, the consultants conducted two focus groups to assist SEFLIN in defining the information needs of the Southeast Florida Hispanic community—with a particular emphasis on creating a Spanish-based virtual library service to meet those needs. To assist in the process, the consultants conducted a morning focus group session with a wide range of Hispanic reference librarians from throughout the Miami-Dade Public Library (MDPL) system. The afternoon session included library users from the Miami area (see Appendix 3-A for a copy of the focus group questions for each group). It is important to note that the user focus group was conducted in Spanish (see the *User Session* section of this report for more detail). Accordingly, a member of SEFLIN staff facilitated the session and a member of the MDPL system translated notes from the session for the consultants.

## Reference Librarian Session

Attendance at the reference librarian session was high, with a total of about 20 participants. Those in attendance reflected a wide range of reference services in the MDPL system, including children's, business, foreign language, social sciences, and Hispanic, to name a few. This section summarizes the key issues and findings raised by the reference librarian focus group session.

### One Hispanic Nation, Many Villages

As participants discussed an organizational framework for the site, all indicated clearly that one size does not fit all. As one participant stated, "We talk about an 'Hispanic population,' but we really have a great diversity in that population. For example, we are Cuban, Puerto Rican, Mexican, Guatemalan, or something else." The key issue that the participants raised is this: while there may be some general information needs that cut across the Hispanic community as a whole (generic), information needs differ substantially within the various populations (community-specific). For example, common information needs that participants identified are:

• Immigration information that includes legal residency requirements and citizenship (generic);

- "Living here" survival-type information that assists immigrants and others in learning about their new environment (generic);
- Health (generic);
- Education, such as GED requirements, English as a Second Language classes, and what is happening in local schools that children attend (generic);
- Jobs, such as work requirements and availability by type of work and skills requirements (generic);
- Spanish-based search engines and capabilities (generic);
- Keeping up with current events "back home" through newspapers, radio shows, and other formats (community-specific);
- Local consulate information (community-specific);
- Discussion/networking forums (community-specific); and
- Calendar of events that pertain to ethnic celebrations and other activities (community specific).

According to the participants, therefore, a useful Spanish virtual library will meet the generic as well as the specific information needs of the various Hispanic groups that reside within Southeast Florida.

### Organizing the Site

The focus group participants identified three distinct aspects for the Mi Servicio de Biblioteca site:

1. A portal site that links to existing Spanish resources such as Spanish CNN, Yahoo!, REFORMA, Informe, and others.
2. An online community that fosters social communications that facilitate communication exchange and interaction among the Hispanic community with education, social, and communications services (e.g., Web mail).
3. A source of unique resources and services developed specifically for the Southeast Florida Hispanic community.

Within each of these service areas, there is a need to provide services that meet a variety of needs of the user communities, including librarians, members of differing Hispanic background (as detailed above), and different user groups within those Hispanic communities (e.g., seniors, parents, and youth).

Carrying this organizational framework further, the participants envisioned a site that provided information resources and services to the Hispanic community at large (e.g., links to existing resources, e-mail

**Figure 3-C-1**
**Possible organization of the Mi Servicio de Biblioteca virtual library.**

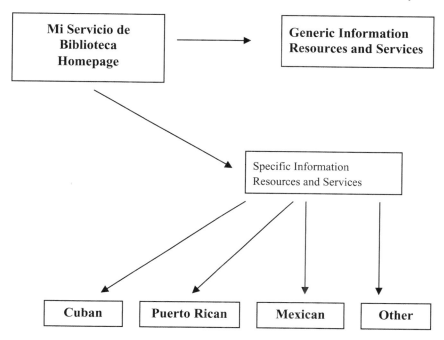

services, immigration, etc.) and to specific communities (e.g., Web pages that serve the Cuban population with links and content for Cuban newspapers and newsletters, radio stations, etc.) (Fig. 3-C-1).

There are a number of web-based usage statistics that the consultants recommend SEFLIN consider for collection, analysis, and reporting. The statistics, provided in Table 1, reflect three areas of understanding/ evaluation:

- **Overall**. These statistics provide an overall assessment of the use and uses of various Website areas, services, and documents. In addition, these statistics indicate where users enter and exit the site. Further sub-categories include 1) core statistics–those the consultants recommend that SEFLIN should collect and report externally, and 2) optional statistics–those statistics that the consultants recommend that SEFLIN consider collecting and reporting externally.

- **Administrative**. These statistics provide more technical assessments of the use, uses, and traffic on the Website that would be of primary interest to SEFLIN staff–particularly the technical staff. The consultants recommend that these statistics be collected and reported internally.

- **Design**. These statistics inform the design, display, and navigation of Website content and services.

As mentioned, a further consideration that participants raised is that there are other communities within the Hispanic population in general, and within ethnic communities in particular. For example:

- Parents will want to know about what is happening in their childrens' schools;
- Children and youth in the K–12 age range have school assignments that require research and resources, plus having specific social and entertainment interests;
- Seniors require a variety of government and community services (e.g., health, social services) and have a number of social needs;
- Immigrants require a number of general and specific information services and resources related to living, acclimating, and making the transition to a new area; and
- Latin American corporations require a wide range of location information in making their decisions to build a presence in the Southeast Florida area. Examples of the information needs of corporations include the educational environment (for children, as well as to meet organizational business demands), the business climate for particular services and products, and business compliance regulations and legal issues.

The extent to which these are either generic information needs that cut across the Hispanic community or community-specific needs requires additional study.

In this mix, there is a need to also consider the library professional as a user community. The consultants were impressed by how well the library staff identified the information needs of the communities that they serve. One cannot forget that librarians are users as well and, as such, need to have their information needs met to facilitate the services that they provide their patrons.

Although the participants did not indicate that they would need separate resources for themselves, they did indicate that they may require a different form of access to the content on the site. Accordingly, it may be necessary to consider different Web pages (perhaps password protected) that provide a more professional form of access to the site's content. For example, a business reference librarian may want comprehensive and quick access to a variety of business resources that would be scattered throughout the site for general users. This may be the case, in particular, for online databases or other forms of online content.

### What is Spanish?

Participants identified three issues strongly when the discussion centered on providing a Spanish-focused virtual library.

1. The content and services need to be in Spanish. As is sometimes the case, Spanish sites are about issues that pertain to Hispanic populations–but they are not necessarily in Spanish. Participants insisted that the content and services be in Spanish.

2. Spanish is not Spanish. The participants indicated that Spanish exists in a number of forms and dialects, thus having a number of different vocabulary words for the same item (e.g., car, bus, etc.). As such, participants indicated that the site should adopt the *real* or *prime* Spanish as defined by the Real Academa. This is particularly important because some colloquialisms in one form of Spanish are offensive in other forms.

3. Translation should not be machine-generated. Participants indicated unanimously that machine translators do not translate appropriately and are problematic. Therefore, the content and services on the site require human intervention and translation so as to ensure proper translation and adherence to appropriate usage, syntax, and composition.

These issues point to the need for SEFLIN to work closely with the library community so as to ensure appropriate Spanish on the site.

### Tie In to Library Services

The librarians indicated a number of initiatives that library systems or particular branches have under way. These initiatives include story time in Spanish, computer literacy courses in Spanish, Internet skills lessons in Spanish, and other special-content courses in Spanish. The participants indicated the need to integrate and coordinate the Mi Servicio de Biblioteca site with those existing efforts–and perhaps develop new services and/or partnerships as the site evolves.

Examples of partnerships and coordinating activities include:

• Integrating the Mi Servicio de Biblioteca site into computer and Internet training courses;

• Integrating the Mi Servicio de Biblioteca site into online information resources training sessions; and

• Working with library staff to develop online tutorials and help services for patrons.

Although others are possible, the foregoing activities provide a starting point.

The librarians raised the issue of coordination and integration in another context as well: getting people into the library. The envisioned site may well serve people who would not ordinarily consider the library as a source of information related to their needs, as traditionally underserved populations tend to try meeting their information needs through trusted individuals and community-based organizations, such as community centers and churches. There is a need, therefore, to consider ways to bring members of the community into the libraries for instruction, assistance, and access—or to consider outreach programs that take the technology, training, and other services out to the community organizations that members of the community frequent.

The access issue is one that SEFLIN and its member libraries need to consider in particular. As presented in the *Technology Access* section of the report, the Hispanic population in general lags behind in both computer and Internet access in the home, compared to the White and Asian-American populations. Although the specific data concerning Southeast Florida Hispanic computer and Internet access in the home are unavailable, they are likely to reflect the national trend. Thus, substantial portions of the Hispanic community in Southeast Florida—the target audience of the Mi Servicio de Biblioteca site—are likely to be without access to essential technology for use of a virtual library. Accordingly, it is essential to develop a coordinated approach that joins Mi Servicio de Biblioteca site/service development and in-library services to inform and instruct users about the site and its contents.

## User Session

The user focus group had six participants, and an additional two library participants who could not attend the morning session. The library participants primarily observed the session and assisted in clarifying issues that users raised during the session. The user focus group was conducted in Spanish, with a member of SEFLIN staff facilitating the session and a member of the MDPL system translating notes from the session for the consultants. The consultants relied on the language skills of the facilitator and note taker to accurately communicate the outcomes of the user session.

During the introductory phase of the session, all participants indicated that they used a variety of the services and resources that the MDPL system offered. None of the users was a recent immigrant, and they represented a broad range of professions: local government employee, homemaker, and professor. Consequently, the findings from the user session are best viewed as indicators of user information needs that will require additional assessment and determination.

To a large extent, the user session mirrored that of the reference librarian focus group. To the consultants, this is an indication of the reference librarians' understanding of the information needs of their patrons–patrons who visit the library facilities to interact with the library's services and resources. It is unclear, at this point, what nonlibrary users would want from a virtual library service.

In particular, the user participants identified the following services and resources that should be part of the Mi Servicio de Biblioteca site:

- Library Services
  - Access to the Miami-Dade Public Library System's catalog in Spanish
  - Access to one's own patron record
  - Access to e-books
  - Ability to initiate holds
  - Ability to read newspapers from native country
  - Access to newspapers and magazines through the Internet/database subscriptions
- Government and Immigration Services
  - Immigration and citizenship information as well as other legal information
  - Information on Medicare/Medicaid
  - Translation of County web pages/services into Spanish
- Health Information
  - General health care and services information
  - Cancer information
  - Link to the Liga Contra el Cancer web site
  - Link to Miami Children's Hospital (http://www.mch.com)
  - Information about support groups dealing with drug and alcohol problems
- Educational Information and Services
  - GED requirements
  - Information on classes to learn English
  - Information on classes to learn to use the computer and computer programs
  - Availability of educational games
  - Link to the public school system
- Employment Information and Services

- Listing of job opportunities
- Ability to write resumes
- Ability to exchange job services and post resumes
- Cultural and Community Information
  - Cultural activities for children and adults
  - Information on U.S. holidays
  - Information on holidays in different countries
  - Calendar of events
- Other Services
  - Access to the Internet for persons who do not have a computer/connection at home
  - Access to e-mail services
  - Include Yahoo! en Español, CNN en Español
  - Information about volunteer groups

Participants indicated that all services should be (1) communicated in "pure" Spanish, and (2) translated by people, rather than by machine-generated translators.

# CHAPTER 4

# E-metrics and Performance Indicators: Availability and Use

**John Carlo Bertot**

## Introduction

This chapter presents and discusses several e-metrics and performance indicators developed through a number of research projects, library groups, and publishers in a variety of contexts and library types. Ultimately, the chapter focuses primarily on those e-metrics and indicators that standards bodies–International Standards Organization (ISO) and National Information Standards Organization (NISO)–have adopted, or are in the process of adopting, in their relevant standards. It is worth noting that there are a number of e-metrics and performance indicators for library network services and resources. This chapter does not present all e-metrics and indicators–rather, it presents a selected number to provide library managers, staff, and others with a smaller number of key e-metrics and indicators that measure services and resources in which libraries invest substantial resources, such as databases, instruction, and technology infrastructure. Finally, the chapter concludes with a section designed to help library managers, staff, and others use the e-metrics for a variety of decision making and resource allocation issues. For those interested in pursuing other e-metrics and indicators, Appendix 4-A provides readers with a reasonably comprehensive listing of e-metrics from a number of key initiatives and standards.

It is possible to point to several research projects that are responsible for many of the field-tested e-metrics and performance indicators that exist as of this writing. These research efforts include the following:

- Bertot, John Carlo, McClure, Charles R., & Ryan, Joe. (2001). *Statistics and performance measures for public library network statistics.* Chicago, IL: American Library Association.
- Bertot, John Carlo, McClure, Charles R., & Davis, Denise M. (2002). *Developing a national data collection model for public library network statistics and performance measures: Final report.* Washington, DC: Institute of Museum and Library Services. Available at http://www.ii.fsu.edu/Projects/IMLS/final.report.natl.model.pdf. Last accessed November 17, 2003.
- Brophy, Peter, Clarke, Zoë, Brinkley, Monica, Mundt, Sebastian, & Poll, Roswita (2000). *EQUINOX library performance measurement and quality management system performance indicators for electronic library services.* Available at http://equinox.dcu.ie/reports/pilist.html. Last accessed November 18, 2003.
- Project COUNTER, at http://www.projectcounter.org.
- Shim, Wonsik, McClure, Charles R., Fraser, Bruce T., & Bertot, John Carlo. (2001). *Data collection manual for academic and research library network statistics and performance measures.* Washington, DC: Association of Research Libraries.

Readers who wish to have more in-depth insight into the methodologies for developing and field-testing the various e-metrics and performance indicators should consult these resources directly. Appendix 4-B presents the historical evolution of the e-metrics developed by the inaugural studies identified above.

## The Playing Field

The landscape regarding e-metrics and performance indicators that measure library network services and resources involves several organizations and is often complex. This section provides a brief synopsis of selected key stakeholders and efforts. In particular, this section focuses on the three major library statistics and performance indicator standards, as well as work by library consortia and publishers. These efforts include:

- ISO 2789 Library Statistics and ISO 11620–Library Performance Indicators;
- NISO Z39.7–Library Statistics;
- International Coalition of Library Consortia (ICOLC); and
- Project COUNTER.

Each of these initiatives has different goals and objectives, and carries differing levels of influence in libraries, with publishers, and in the research community. Thus, it is useful to provide some background on the "official" standards process, as well as on other efforts.

## The Role of Standards Regarding E-metrics and Performance Indicators

As they relate to e-metrics and network service and resource performance indicators, standards serve at least four purposes:

1. A forum to review current practices and measures within libraries of all types on a national and/or international scale;
2. A means through which to develop agreed-upon data elements and definitions that enable and facilitate data collection across libraries, regions, and nations;
3. A resource that provides guidance to library managers and staff regarding what data to collect and some possible methods through which to collect the data; and
4. An official source of data elements, indicators, definitions, and methods of collection for librarians and others (e.g., publishers, vendors) to reference regarding the types of data libraries collect and use in decision making and management practices.

Ultimately, data elements and indicators within a standard go through a lengthy discussion and definitional process, are reviewed widely through a public comment and review period, and are voted upon and adopted (or rejected) according to the standards body's rules and regulations. Standards bodies do not, however, actually develop e-metrics and performance indicators. Rather, they review practices in the field and engage in a multistage review and decision making process that determines the viability and value of an element or elements as part of a standard.

In the case of e-metrics and performance indicators, the library community–with input from vendors, publishers, researchers, and others–developed a set of statistics (ISO/NISO) and indicators (ISO) that provide a wide range of measures that enable libraries to measure how much, how often, and with what quality the library provides certain network services and resources. The standards efforts emphasized resources and services (e.g., databases, e-books, Web-based digital collections) in which libraries are investing considerable resources.

## The Role of the International Coalition of Library Consortia (ICOLC)

Simply put, one can credit ICOLC with beginning the entire movement regarding the measurement of online database usage. Briefly, ICOLC (http://www.library.yale.edu/consortia/) is an informal group (as of September 2000, it had approximately 150 members) of library consortia, or libraries that are members of consortia, that meets to discuss issues that are relevant to consortia. Founded in 1997, a particular focus of ICOLC has been issues related to network services and resources, particularly the reporting of online journal and database usage. In November 1998, ICOLC issued its first set of guidelines regarding what members of consortia wanted online vendors to report in terms of licensed resource usage. These guidelines were updated in December 2001 (see http://www.library.yale.edu/consortia/2001webstats.htm for the guidelines). The 2001 guidelines also included sample reporting formats for vendors to follow when reporting usage data to libraries. Appendix 4-B includes ICOLC data elements and definitions and shows them side-by-side with other standards and initiative definitions.

Nearly all developmental work (Bertot, McClure, & Ryan, 2001; Shim, et al., 2001; Brophy, et al., 2000) relied on ICOLC's embryonic work in the area of vendor e-metrics and reporting. The ISO and NISO standards also reflect ICOLC's efforts, though there have been a number of updates to the e-metrics and definitions, primarily due to changes in vendor and library technologies regarding the provision of online database and journal services. It is also important to note that vendors were involved with ICOLC, or if not, were made aware of ICOLC's activities. It is not uncommon to see vendor promotional material indicating that the vendor is "ICOLC compliant." Thus, it is clear that ICOLC's efforts had substantial impact on the library and vendor communities.

## The Role of COUNTER

COUNTER (Counting Online Usage of NeTworked Electronic Resources, http://www.projectcounter.org) was established in March 2002 as an effort by publishers to develop usage data reporting standards. COUNTER worked with several publishers (primarily of scientific and scholarly journals), database aggregators (e.g., Ebsco), and selected academic libraries and academic library associations (e.g., Association of Research Libraries–ARL) to achieve this goal.

COUNTER took essentially a three-stage approach in its efforts to create standard usage data reports across publishers and vendors:

1. **Review, creation, and adoption of data elements.** To the extent possible, COUNTER relied on the e-metrics and data elements defined by the ISO and NISO standards initiatives. Where elements were lacking, COUNTER participants created, defined, and adopted additional elements.

2. **Usage report formatting and element standards.** As ICOLC and various research efforts had determined, libraries and library consortia wanted a) standardized elements and definitions, and b) a uniform reporting structure so that library managers could look across vendor- and publisher-supplied data in a meaningful and statistically reliable manner. COUNTER's efforts are a significant step forward in this regard, as those involved are indeed agreeing to such standard reporting and data element structures.

3. **Ensure data reliability and validity**. A key hurdle to overcome regarding publisher and vendor data continues to be the reporting and comparison of reliable and valid data *across* vendors and publishers—even for the same institution. Even with vendors claiming ICOLC compliance or ISO 2879/NISO Z39.7 compliance, libraries could not easily, if at all, compare data across vendors and publishers. A number of factors, such as library technology configurations (e.g., firewalls, timeouts) and vendor technology infrastructure and service delivery, create a situation in which a database session, for example, is not the same across vendors. Thus, reported numbers from one vendor are not comparable to reported numbers from another vendor. COUNTER is in the process of establishing a reporting process that will ensure comparable vendor data within a library/consortia arrangement.

To achieve its three key goals in the foregoing list, COUNTER is relying on a compliance, auditing, and certification process. COUNTER has established a *Code of Practice* (see http://www.projectcounter.org/code_practice.html) that details the responsibility of vendors who wish to attain a COUNTER-compliant certification. The certification process requires various auditing and data-quality checking processes that are ongoing, so that vendors and/or publishers adhere to the Code over time. A key component of this certification process is a data auditing feature– vendors and/or publishers will need to use a COUNTER-certified data auditing agency to ensure that the vendor's and publisher's data in fact adheres to the Code.

# Standards, ICOLC, COUNTER: What Does it All Mean?

All of these various initiatives can seem to be in competition and con-tradiction, and can lead to confusion on the part of librarians, vendors, and publishers. With some analysis, however, these efforts do work together, and they can be helpful and even complementary. One way in which to reduce the confusion is to analyze these efforts in regard to the issue of compliance. In essence, each of these initiatives attempts to engender some form of compliance, such as e-metric names and defini-tions and methods of collection and reporting. Compliance can assume a number of forms when network services and resources are considered:

- **Definitional**. This is perhaps the most basic form of compliance, and the one over which groups, organizations, corporations, and individu-als have expended a substantial amount of effort. The main purpose of definitional compliance is to identify network service and resource data elements (e-metrics) and performance indicators, and the defini-tions that accompany such elements. This is the primary focus of the ISO, NISO, and ICOLC efforts.

- **Reporting**. Based on agreed-upon definitions, libraries and other enti-ties (e.g., vendors) are asked to report the data regarding selected data elements in a uniform way through often-centralized data reporting systems (discussed earlier). In general, the collection and reporting of data are executed through a decentralized process left in the hands of participating libraries, with the understanding that all parties will adhere to the definitions as closely as possible. This approach has pro-vided various degrees of flexibility for libraries, because no two librar-ies operate in exactly the same manner—particularly when it comes to electronic services. Again, this is a focus of the ISO, NISO, and ICOLC efforts, as they enable comparison between libraries through regional, national, and international reporting systems for library data. The COUNTER project should facilitate the standardized reporting of key vendor and publisher data, as well.

- **Methodological**. Most library data collection and reporting efforts rely on accepted research methodologies, such as focus groups, inter-views, and surveys, that are used with appropriate approaches such as sampling. Libraries, however, are left to create those surveys and/or focus group protocols to best fit the situational and organizational fac-tors of the library, albeit with the accepted definition of elements as described above. Through this form of compliance, libraries combine the standards definitions with various methods and data collection tools.

• **Data**. Through project COUNTER's efforts in general, and the Code of Practice mentioned above in particular, there is a movement to create a conformity of vendor data across vendors. The intent is to allow libraries to receive online resource usage data in a standardized format that allows comparability of data across vendors and publishers. This should enable the comparison of vendor and publisher data across vendors and publishers within a library system.

Clearly, the standards body, ICOLC, and COUNTER efforts and initiatives work together along the above dimensions of compliance. Each may have a particular focus, set of goals and objectives, and set of participants, but the efforts intersect and integrate in a number of key ways that facilitate a library's ability to describe the usage of its network services and resources. Chapter 10 presents a vendor perspective on the significance of these efforts and initiatives.

The next section provides details on selected e-metrics that libraries may want to consider to assist them in assessing their network services and resources.

## Selected E-metrics to Measure Library Network Services and Resources

As Appendix 4-A shows, there are a number of e-metrics that libraries can use to assess their network services and resources. Appendix 4-A also contains the full definitions of these e-metrics. Appendix 4-C contains network service and resource performance indicators and definitions as contained in the *ISO 11620 Library Performance Indicators Technical Report 20983*. Chapter 1 describes an evaluation planning process in which libraries should engage to determine which e-metrics *best* meet the data needs of library managers, staff, and others. This section offers some definitional and methodological detail regarding several key e-metrics of core library network services and resources (Fig. 4-1). Complete details for a range of e-metrics and performance indicators are available in Bertot, McClure, & Ryan (2001), Shim, et al. (2001), Brophy, et al. (2000), ISO 2789, ISO 11620, and NISO Z39.7. The definitions rely on both ISO 2789 (Annex A) and NISO Z39.7.

We recommend that readers who wish additional guidance regarding the collection and use of e-metrics consult the Information Use Management and Policy Institute's E-Metric Instructional System (EMIS). This Web-based interactive instructional system (http://www.ii.fsu.edu/emis), funded in part through a National Leadership Grant from the Institute of Museum and Library Services (IMLS), provides its librarians (and others) with guidance regarding the definition, collection, reporting, and evaluation management of selected e-metrics.

**Figure 4-1**
**Selected e-metrics and collection issues.**

| E-Metric | Location of Collection | Collection Process |
|---|---|---|
| **Workstations/Infrastructure (W/I)** | | |
| **Public-Access Workstations** | Branch level | Determine at one point in time annually during fiscal year period |
| **Public-Access Workstation Users** | Branch level | One-week sample, estimate annual count |
| **Rejected Sessions (turnaways)** | System level/vendor | Likely monthly, aggregated to get an annual count |
| **Usage (U)** | | |
| **Commercial Services Sessions** | System level/vendor | Likely monthly, aggregated to get an annual count |
| **OPAC Sessions** | System level/vendor | Likely monthly, aggregated to get an annual count |
| **Commercial Services Searches (queries)** | System level/vendor | Likely monthly, aggregated to get an annual count |
| **Library Collection Searches (queries)** | System level | Likely monthly, aggregated to get an annual count |
| **OPAC Searches** | System level/vendor | Likely monthly, aggregated to get an annual count |
| **Library Collection Full-Content Units Examined** | System level | Likely monthly, aggregated to get an annual count |
| **Commercial Services Full-Content Units Examined** | System level/vendor | Likely monthly, aggregated to get an annual count |
| **Library Collection Descriptive Records Examined** | System level | Likely monthly, aggregated to get an annual count |
| **Commercial Services Descriptive Records examined** | System level/vendor | Likely monthly, aggregated to get an annual count |

**Figure 4-1 (Continued)**
**Selected e-metrics and collection issues.**

| E-Metric | Location of Collection | Collection Process |
|---|---|---|
| **Usage (U)** | | |
| **OPAC Descriptive Records Examined** | System level/vendor | Likely monthly, aggregated to get an annual count |
| **Services (SV)** | | |
| **Virtual Reference Transactions** | Branch or system level | One-week sample |
| **Virtual Visits** | System level | Likely monthly, aggregated to get an annual count |
| **Instruction (I)** | | |
| **Formal User Information Technology Instruction** | Branch level | Count instruction sessions throughout month, aggregate to get annual count |
| **Point-of-Use Information Technology Instruction** | Branch level | One-week sample, estimate annual count |

# Some General Considerations in Preparing Your Library to Collect E-metrics

Chapter 1 presents readers with a number of issues to consider when planning to evaluate library network services and resources. Readers should review Chapter 1 for evaluation planning assistance, though the following are some key points presented in that chapter:

1. **Assemble a team**. Choose an overall e-metrics coordinator for your library, if there is not one at the present time. It may be useful to enroll staff to help coordinate local data collection activities, collect the data, and prepare associated reporting and commentary. It is best that a single individual have ultimate management responsibility for the data collection process, though collection actually will occur throughout the library.

2. **Determine which statistics your library will collect**. Not all of the e-metrics apply to your library, or your library may simply not be able to collect some statistics for a variety of reasons. It is important to determine which e-metrics your library will collect and report as part

of a management process. This section describes *several* e-metrics; focus on the ones that your library will collect. Not all library systems have branches, but the system or branch designation is used for those libraries that *do* have branches. If your library does not have branches, then consider all branch-level data collection to mean *system-level* collection.[1]

3. **Determine how your library will collect the data.** The e-metrics require different intervals for collection—some use sampling approaches, and others are "always on." The library needs to determine the collection period.

4. **Develop local data collection procedures.** Identify the local, step-by-step, procedures necessary to collect the chosen network statistics. Who is going to do what, and when, and why? Refer to Fig. 1-4 (Data Map) to assist in this process.

5. **View the process with a constructively critical eye.** Keep the big picture in mind—for what purpose are you collecting these data, what do you want to know so that the data are collected efficiently and used effectively, etc.?

## Collecting E-metrics: Issues and Considerations

This section presents readers with a variety of issues that library managers, staff, and others should consider as they collect data for selected e-metrics. Readers should consider the following as general guidelines that may require adjustment to best meet the particular needs, situation, and operating environment of a library.

### Workstations and Infrastructure (W/I)

### Public-Access Workstations (Branch-Level Statistic)

#### *Definition*

This is the annual count of the total number of library-owned public-access graphical workstations that connect to the Internet for a dedicated purpose (to access an OPAC or specific database) or for multiple purposes. This statistic is counted and collected for each participating branch, if applicable.

#### *Procedure*

Count and report the number of graphical workstations with Internet access (no matter the speed or type of connection) that are made available to the public as of a certain date (e.g., beginning or end of the fiscal year) for each participating branch, if applicable. Include the bookmobile, should your library have one that is Internet-ready.

Computers in computer labs used for public instruction–if graphical and connected to the Internet–should be counted. Public-access graphical workstations that connect to the Internet and that are used by both staff and the public should be counted, if the workstation is used by the public for at least half of the hours during an average week that the library is open to the public. Reference desk computers used by staff to assist the public should *not* be counted.

### Public-Access Workstation Users (Branch-Level Statistic)

#### *Definition*

This is the annual count of the number of users of all of the library's graphical public-access workstations connected to the Internet, computed from a one-week sample.

#### *Procedure*

1. Select a one-week period during the test period. One week equals the number of hours the library is open over a consecutive seven-day period. Note: Data may be collected for more than one week and averaged, *but* report this change in procedure when reporting the data.

2. Prepare a written, step-by-step plan for collecting this e-metric. Identify the dates of the week(s) chosen to collect these data. The number of users may be counted by observation (continuous or every X minutes), manually using registration signup sheets, via computer software, or through the "circulation" of workstations through your library's circulation system. Indicate whether you observed (and for how long), used signup sheets, or used software to collect the data for this e-metric.

3. Count the number of users of all of the library's graphical public-access workstations connected to the Internet during the chosen sample week. Count each user that uses the graphical public-access workstations connected to the Internet, regardless of the amount of time spent on the computer. A user who uses the library's workstations three times a week would count as three users in the count. Internet use includes all types of usage, including web, e-mail, telnet, chat, etc. Users of multipurpose workstations present a challenge, as it is not always possible to determine whether the workstation is being used to access the Internet. Do not include staff use of these workstations.

4. Obtain a total figure of users for the week (or an average weekly use figure if you counted users over a two-week period) and report that

number for each participating branch, if applicable. If you collect the user data over a two-week period, for example, and during the first week 70 users were counted and 80 users were counted the second week, the average number of users would be 75 (obtained and reported by adding the first week's users to the second week's [70 + 80 = 150] and dividing by the number of weeks surveyed [150 ÷ 2 = 75]). Multiply by 52 to get an annual count.

### Rejected Sessions (Turnaways) (System-Level/Vendor Statistic)

*Definition*

A rejected session (turnaway) is defined as an unsuccessful log-in to an electronic service by exceeding the simultaneous user limit. Note: Failure of log-in because of wrong passwords is excluded.

*Procedure*

1. Request from commercial database vendor(s):
   (a) Count the number of started sessions to each database for the field test month; and
   (b) Calculate the total sessions to host by adding the number of sessions from each database.
2. Obtain from OPAC network administrator or vendor:
   (a) Count the number of started sessions to the OPAC for the field test month; and
   (b) Calculate the total sessions to host *by adding the number of sessions from each day.*
3. Obtain from OPAC administrator, network administrator, and/or vendor:
   (a) Count the number of rejected sessions to each database or OPAC

## Usage (U)

### Commercial Services Sessions (System-Level/Vendor Statistic)

*Definition*

A session is defined as a successful request of a commercial service (e.g., online database). It is one cycle of user activities that typically starts when a user connects to a database and ends by terminating activity in the database that is either explicit (by leaving the database through log-out or exit) or implicit (timeout due to user inactivity). *Note* 1: For multiple databases compiling several individual databases, further information should be provided as to the separate databases hosted. *Note 2*: In some cases, e.g., database use inside the library, several users one after the other might make use of the same workstation, and sessions could not be separated. In most systems, a session is cut off after a specified time of nonuse, thus avoiding part of the problem. The average timeout setting would be 30 minutes. If another timeout period is used, this should be reported. Browser or proxy caching will be likely to reduce the number of requests registered in log files.

### OPAC Sessions (System-Level/Vendor Statistic)

*Definition*

A session is defined as a successful request of the library's online catalog. It is one cycle of user activities that typically starts when a user connects to the OPAC and ends by terminating activity in the OPAC that is either explicit (by leaving the database through log-out or exit) or implicit (timeout due to user inactivity). In some cases, e.g., OPAC use inside the library, several users one after the other might make use of the same workstation, and sessions could not be separated. In most systems, a session is cut off after a specified time of nonuse, thus avoiding part of the problem. The average timeout setting would be 30 minutes. If another timeout period is used, this should be reported. Browser or proxy caching will be likely to reduce the number of requests registered in log files.

### Commercial Services Searches (Queries) (System-Level/Vendor Statistic)

*Definition*

A search is defined as intending to represent a unique intellectual inquiry. Typically, a search is recorded every time a search request is submitted to the server. These searches are limited to commercial services. Mistyped search strings do not represent unique intellectual inquiries. Include menu selection searches; exclude spider/crawler searches.

### Library Collection Searches (Queries) (System-Level/Vendor Statistic)

*Definition*

A search is defined as intending to represent a unique intellectual inquiry. Typically, a search is recorded every time a search request is submitted to the server. These searches are limited to library electronic collection services. Include menu selection searches; exclude spider/ crawler searches. This excludes OPAC searches.

## OPAC Searches (Queries) (System-Level/Vendor Statistic)

### Definition

A search is defined as intending to represent a unique intellectual inquiry. Typically, a search is recorded every time a search request is submitted to the server. These searches are limited to the library online catalog service. Include menu selection searches; exclude spider/crawler searches.

### Procedure for Searches

Request from a licensed database vendor(s), or obtain from OPAC network administrator or vendor:

(a) Count the number of searches performed in each online library collection, commercial service, or OPCA for the field test month; and

(b) Calculate total searches in all hosts by adding the total number of searches in each database.

## Library Collection Full-Content Units Examined (System-Level/Vendor Statistic)

### Definition

This is the number of full-content units from the library electronic collection examined, downloaded, or otherwise supplied to a user. Exclude OPAC or commercial services (i.e., online databases).

## Commercial Services Full-Content Units Examined (System-Level/Vendor Statistic)

### Definition

This is the number of subscription service full-content units examined, downloaded, or otherwise supplied to the user, to the extent that these are recordable and controlled by the server rather than the browser. *Note* 1: Journal articles—by journal title with ISSN and title listed. *Note* 2: E-books—by book title with ISBN and title listed. *Note* 3: Reference materials—by content unit appropriate to the resource (e.g., dictionary definitions, encyclopedia articles, biographies, etc.). *Note* 4: Nontextual resources—by file type as appropriate to resources (e.g., image, audio, video, etc.).

### Procedure

Request from the network administrator and licensed database vendor(s). Count the number of views in each database for:

- Full text articles
- Full text pages
- PDF articles
- PDF pages
- Abstracts
- Citations
- Text only,
- Text and graphics.

Then calculate the total views to host by adding the total views in each database. Consider using the Fig. 4-2. Chapter 9 (Shim) has additional worksheets and offers guidance on using vendor-provided data.

### Library Collection Descriptive Records Examined (System-Level/Vendor Statistic)

*Definition*

This is the number of descriptive records concerning the library's electronic collection delivered to a user. It is determined by the record type appropriate to the resource, e.g., abstract, archive, and index. Exclude OPAC or commercial services (i.e., online databases).

### Commercial Services Descriptive Records Examined (System-Level/Vendor Statistic)

*Definition*

This is the number of descriptive records concerning the library's commercial services delivered to a user. It is determined by the record type appropriate to the resource, e.g., abstract, archive, index. Exclude OPAC or library collection descriptive records (i.e., library website services and collections).

### OPAC Descriptive Records Examined

*Definition*

This is the number of descriptive records from the library's online catalog delivered to a user. Exclude commercial services or library collection descriptive records (i.e., library website services and collections).

*Procedure*

1. Request from network administrator and licensed database vendor(s).

**Figure 4-2**
**Worksheet for the number of items (#) examined using subscription services.**

| Type of View | Database 1 | Database 2 | Database 3 |
|---|---|---|---|
| # Full-text articles | | | |
| # Full-text pages | | | |
| # Abstracts | | | |
| # Citations | | | |
| # Text only | | | |
| # Text/Graphics | | | |
| # PDF articles | | | |
| # PDF pages | | | |
| Total Views to Host | | | |

2. This item may also appear as part of the **Full-Content Units Examined** count. Consult the network administrator or licensed database vendor(s) for confirmation to avoid duplicate counting.

## Services (SV)

### Virtual Visits (System-Level Statistic)

*Definition*

This is a user's request of the library website from outside the library premises, regardless of the number of pages or items viewed. It excludes website visits from within the library. *Note*: This statistic is the equivalent of a session for a library's website. As such, there is a need to exclude various actions (e.g., hits, downloads) by users during any given visit.

In the case of a user visit to a library website, a user who looks at 16 pages and 54 graphic images registers one visit on the Web server. Due to various Web server issues and differing software, this measure is an *estimate* of the visits to the web site. One definition (from the *MS Site Server* manual) of a virtual visit is:

> A series of consecutive requests from a user to an Internet site. If your log file data includes referrer data, then new visits begin with referring links external to your Internet site. Regardless of whether

or not you have referrer data, if a user does not make a request after a specified time period, the previous series of requests is considered to be a completed visit.

Another log analysis software provider, *WebTrends*, defines a visit using the phrase *user session*: "A session of activity (all hits) for one user of a web site. A unique user is determined by IP address or domain name. By default, a user session is terminated when a user falls inactive for more than 30 minutes." An alternative approach is to assign each visitor unique authentication tags that are attached to each transaction.

Count of visits to the library via the Internet, with a breakdown by:

- # *Internal virtual visits*: Visits while library users are in the library using public-access Internet workstations (excludes library staff and staff workstations);
- # *External virtual visits*: Visits while library users access the library remotely (excluding the visits made by library users within the library, using the public-access Internet workstations); and
- *Total # virtual visits*: A total count of both internal and external virtual visits.

Only report the number (#) of external virtual visits, however.

### Procedure

1. Identify all sources of electronic visits to the library. This may involve activity that takes place on more than one computer server. The library may own some of the computer servers, another local government agency may own some others, or an Internet Service Provider (ISP).

2. Separate the various sources of virtual visits into staff internal, public internal, and public external. Two common approaches are using IP address or some form of authentication tagged to each transaction. Exclude staff internal sourcesfrom the counts for this measure, where possible.

3. Develop strategies for collecting the necessary data from each of these sources of virtual visits. Different software may be needed to measure each electronic source of virtual visits. In some cases, the library may calculate the virtual visits using one or more log analysis software packages. In other cases, the external owner of the computer server or service (the Internet Service Provider) must provide the data. Discussions may need to be held with these service providers to obtain the

needed data. In still other cases, computer-monitoring software may be appropriate.

4. In the case of a library Web page housed on a library server: Identify, configure and install appropriate log analysis software. Determine the log analysis software definition that corresponds to the virtual visit definition. *Note:* All log analysis software may not track virtual visits the same way, so the count obtained will necessarily be an estimate. Arrange with the server technical staff for regular (e.g., monthly) reporting of internal staff visits (for your own internal use, if interested); internal library user visits at the various public-access Internet workstations, external library user virtual visits and total virtual visits (internal public visits plus external visits, excluding staff use). Run the log analysis software.

5. In the case of library Web pages housed on an Internet Service Provider's (ISP) server, identify which log analysis software the ISP uses. With the assistance of the ISP, determine the definition of *visit* used by the log analysis software that corresponds to the virtual visit definition. Arrange with the ISP for regular (monthly) reporting of internal staff visits (for your own internal use if interested); internal library user visits at the various public-access Internet workstations, external library user virtual visits, and total virtual visits (internal public visits plus external visits, excluding staff use). Another option is to create a Web log file transfer arrangement (perhaps monthly) with the library's ISP, through which the library receives the log files and can conduct its own log file analysis.

**Virtual Reference Transactions (Branch- or System-Level Statistic)**

### Definition

This is the annual count of the number of virtual reference transactions conducted via e-mail, website, or other network-based medium designed to support virtual reference. *Note:* Questions either received or responded to are included.

### Procedure

1. Select a one-week period. *Note:* Data may be collected for more than one week and averaged if desired. Multiply by 52 to get an annual count. It may be the case that your library uses specialized digital reference software that provides usage logs. If so, generate an annual count of virtual reference transactions through the software used by your library.

2. Prepare a written, step-by-step plan for collecting this e-metric. If your library offers virtual reference services and it is centralized through a single location, simply report the number of virtual reference transactions at the end of the week. If virtual reference is a distributed feature throughout the library system and its branches (if applicable), then you will need to aggregate the number of virtual reference transactions per branch.

3. Count the number of electronic reference requests received during the week. Be sure to report only transactions that occur virtually—both in receipt and answer. Report an electronic reference transaction as you would a face-to-face reference transaction. Thus, for example, one e-mail request may contain several reference questions taking varying amounts of time to complete. Say one e-mail request contained one ready-reference question and one reference question that took 10 or 15 minutes to answer. Count the number of questions, not the number of requests. So, in this example you would report 2 as the number of electronic reference transactions.

4. Report the number of virtual reference transactions for the sample week—either for the system, if this is a centralized service, or for each branch that offers the service. Should you conduct the count over more than the one-week period, you will need to obtain an average weekly number of virtual reference transactions. To get it, add the total number of virtual reference transactions each week and divide by the number of weeks this statistic was surveyed. For example, during the first week 7 electronic reference requests were counted, and 9 were counted the second week. An average of 8 electronic reference requests is obtained and reported by adding week one's transactions to week two's [7 + 9 = 16] and dividing by the number of weeks surveyed [16 ÷ 2 = 8]. Multiply by 52 to get an annual count. Again, if your library uses specialized digital reference software, generate an annual count through the software's usage logs.

## Instruction (I)

### Formal User Information Technology Instruction (Branch-Level Statistic)

#### *Definition*

This involves a count of the number of users instructed and the hours of instruction offered in the use of information technology or resources, obtainable using information technology in structured sessions. Instruction is either delivered in the library using a computer lab or other instructional setting, or delivered electronically through online-based instruction.

*Procedure*

1. Include only instruction in the use of information technology or resources obtainable using information technology. Examples of user instruction include use of the Web, Internet searching, use of public-access Internet workstations or personal computers, subject-based resources available on the Internet, and social implications of information technology (e.g., filtering and the public library).

2. Count all users attending and record the session length of formal, structured lectures, public meetings, or courses in the use of information technology or resources obtainable using information technology the library offers, the library contracts for, or that uses library facilities. A signup sheet may be the most appropriate technique. Consider using the tally sheet shown in Fig. 4-3). In the count, include the number and duration of online training sessions (e.g., online tutorials or contracted training services such as those offered by ElementK (http://www.elementk.com/). Obtaining online training session counts will likely require the assistance of the account or system administrator.

3. A user need not be a registered library user. A single individual may attend multiple training sessions of the same or different types, each of which is counted. So if a single individual attended multiple training sessions (even if he or she repeated a particular course), you would count each of those attendances and time intervals.

**Point-of-Use Information Technology Instruction
(Branch-Level Statistic)**

*Definition*

This is a count of the number of users instructed and the hours of instruction offered in the use of information technology or resources obtainable using information technology in unstructured sessions, at the impromptu request of users.

**Figure 4-3
Weekly formal user instruction tally sheet.**

| Library: | | Date Week Begins: | | |
|---|---|---|---|---|
| Date | Sponsor | Instruction Subject | # of Users | Session Length (in minutes) |
| | | | | |
| | | Totals: | | |

### Procedure

1. Select a one-week period. *Note*: Data may be collected for more than one week and averaged.

2. Prepare a written, step-by-step plan for collecting this statistic. Figure 4-4 may facilitate the capturing of informal and point-of-use training data.

3. Count the number of users and hours (measured in 5- to 15-minute increments as decided by the library) of point-of-use instruction offered during the sample week period chosen. Include *only* the informal or impromptu instruction provided in the use of information technology or resources accessible using information technology. Examples include use of the Web, Internet searching, use of public-access workstations or personal computers, and subject-based resources available on the Internet. Multiply by 52 to get an annual count.

## Summary

The preceding section presented selected e-metrics, e-metric definitions, methodological considerations and calculations, and issues associated with collecting e-metric data. Library managers, staff, and others should use that material as a basic guideline for collecting and reporting the described e-metrics. Although the *how* of collection may vary by library, due to a number of situational and organizational factors, librarians should adhere to the definitions and overall collection methodologies so as to ensure that all libraries essentially collect and report the same data.

**Figure 4-4**
**Daily point-of-use instruction tally sheet.**

| Library/Branch: | | Date/Day: |
|---|---|---|
| Session | # of Users (May be more than 1) | Session Length (in minutes) |
| **Session 1** | | |
| **Session 2** | | |
| **Session 3** | | |
| **Session 4** | | |
| **Session 5** | | |
| Totals: | | **(Total hours):** |

Clearly, not all of the presented e-metrics will matter to all libraries for decision making, management, and reporting purposes. Each library will need to determine the e-metrics data that they want through an evaluation needs assessment process (see Chapter 1), and then establish a collection and reporting structure to acquire, report, and use such data.

Also, libraries will need to review periodically the e-metric data that they collect to determine 1) their usefulness for decision making, management, and external reporting purposes; 2) the level of effort required to collect in relation to the value and utility of collected data; and 3) other data needs requirements. Libraries should continually assess the data that they collect to ensure that it meets their data needs. Over time, library managers will likely need to discontinue the collection of less useful data and begin collecting new data that is seen as more valuable in terms of expending limited resources.

## Using the E-metrics and Performance Indicators in Your Library: Some Examples

This section of the chapter provides librarians with some guidance on how to use the e-metrics and performance indicators for various types of decision making activities. The section is not exhaustive, and does not include uses of all the e-metrics and performance indicators. Rather, this section presents selected combinations of e-metrics and performance indicators, and how library managers might use these for a variety of network service resource allocation, management, creation, modification, and other endeavors. The e-metrics and performance indicators used are defined in the previous section and in Appendices 4-A and 4-B. Figure 4-5 summarizes the e-metrics and performance indicators and places them in a library decision making context.

A key task for library managers and those involved in the provision of network services is to develop standards and levels of acceptable services and resources. That is, libraries need to establish various target levels of service provision, benchmarks, quality standards, and other goals for the library's network services and resources. These will provide library managers with important metrics against which to gauge the results of the library's various network service and resource evaluation efforts. For example, library managers may want to establish a *cost per title* goal for all their licensed e-journals. Such an indicator enables a library manager to determine whether a particular journal is within the margin of cost for this particular type of resource. Another form of benchmark or target might include service and resource user satisfaction ratings (e.g., an average rating of 4, with 1 being "not at all satisfied" and 5 being "very satisfied"). In the end, it is critical for the library to determine, in advance, acceptable

**Figure 4-5**
Using e-metrics and performance indicators for decision making purposes.

| Resources, Accessibility, and Infrastructure | | | |
|---|---|---|---|
| **E-metric** | **Performance Indicators** | **Decision Making Use** | **Follow-on Evaluation** |
| (W/I) Public-access workstations<br>(W/I) Public-access workstation users<br>(W/I) Rejected sessions<br>(EM) Full-text titles available by subscription<br>(EM) E-book titles available | (W/I) Number of workstation hours available per capita<br>(W/I) Population per public-access workstation<br>(W/I) Percentage of rejected sessions<br>(EM) Percentage of serial titles offered in electronic form<br>(EM) Percentage of book titles available in electronic form | Identification of capacity:<br>■ Can be used to determine the need for additional capacity in the areas of workstations, e-journals, databases, and licensing. | Service quality approaches to determine user perceptions of quality of the library's infrastructure and capacity of services and resources. |
| **Use** | | | |
| **E-metric** | **Performance Indicators** | **Decision-Making Use** | **Follow-on Evaluation** |
| (I) Formal user IT instruction<br>(I) Point-of-use IT instruction<br>(SV) Electronic document delivery<br>(SV) Virtual visits<br>(SV) Virtual reference transactions | (I) Number of user attendances at electronic service training lessons per capita<br>(SV) Percentage of virtual visits to total visits<br>(SV) Percentage of information requests submitted electronically | Determine licensing, service, resource provision, allocation, and future needs:<br>■ Given the level of use of the resource or service, should the library continue to fund, develop, or support the service or resource? Perhaps there is a need to engage in a marketing campaign to promote the service or resource. | Service quality approaches to determine user perceptions of quality of the library's network services and resources, particularly:<br>■ Online databases<br>■ E-journals<br>■ Instructional services |

(Continued)

**Figure 4-5 (Continued)**
**Using e-metrics and performance indicators for decision making purposes.**

| | | Use | |
|---|---|---|---|
| **E-metric** | **Performance Indicators** | **Decision-Making Use** | **Follow-on Evaluation** |
| (U) Commercial services sessions<br>(U) OPAC sessions<br>(U) Commercial services searches<br>(U) Library collections searches<br>(U) OPAC searches<br>(U) Library collection full-content units examined<br>(U) Commercial services full-content units examined<br>(U) Library collection descriptive records examined<br>(U) Commercial services descriptive records examined<br>(U) OPAC descriptive records examined | (SV) Percentage of population reached by electronic services<br>*(SV) Total reference activity*<br>*(SV) Percentage of virtual reference to total reference activity*<br>*(SV) Percentage of documents delivered electronically*<br>(U) Percentage of remote OPAC sessions<br>(U) Number of documents downloaded per session<br>*(U) Percentage of remote commercial services sessions*<br>*(U) Percentage of electronic materials use to total library material use*<br>*(U) Total library material use*<br>(W/I) Workstation use rate | ▪ Determine whether the level of use requires additional service or resource provision:<br>  ▶ More training sessions, to include additional topics<br>  ▶ Continued Web development and digitization of library holdings<br>  ▶ Enhancements to the library's digital reference services<br>  ▶ More staff in particular areas of instruction, web development, and digital reference<br>▪ Given the searches conducted by users, the library might highlight and/or make available aspects of its existing holdings to better meet the information needs of users. Or perhaps the library might acquire various resources that fulfill the information needs of users (libraries may consider reviewing interlibrary loan requests, in combination with the items searched in the various library electronic holdings). | ▪ Digital reference website and services. Outcomes assessment to determine various changes in user knowledge, skills, and behavior due to the use of library-provided collections, particularly:<br>  ▪ Online databases<br>  ▪ E-journals<br>  ▪ Instructional services<br>  ▪ Digital reference<br>  ▪ Website and services<br>Need to link library network services and resources to specific impacts on the service and resource users. |

## Cost Efficiency

| E-metric | Performance Indicators | Decision Making Use | Follow-on Evaluation |
|---|---|---|---|
| (F/E) Electronic materials expenditures<br>(F/E) Electronic network expenditures | (F/E) Cost per database session<br>(F/E) Cost per document downloaded | Determination of the cost effectiveness and efficiency of licensed resources. Can assist library managers in making resource allocations based on cost and use:<br>■ Does the use of the e-journal, e-book, or database justify its cost?<br>■ Does the e-journal, e-book, or database meet the library's pre-determined cost benchmarks? | Outcomes assessment approaches that help the library determine the extent to which an e-journal, e-book, or database (or other network service or resource) facilitates community economic development, education, scholarship, the securing of external funding, or other measures of service community impacts. |

## Potentials & Development

| E-metric | Performance Indicators | Decision-Making Use | Follow-on Evaluation |
|---|---|---|---|
| (I) Formal staff IT instruction | (F/E) Percentage of expenditure on information provision spent on the electronic collection<br>(I) Number of attendances at formal IT and related training lessons per staff member<br>(SV) Percentage of library staff providing and developing electronic services | Assists library managers in assessing the extent to which library staff are engaging in continual education efforts; have the necessary skills to engage in various network services and resources provision; can engage in service and resource evaluation efforts; and possess a number of related skills (e.g., web design, web development, etc). In particular, library managers can: | Outcomes assessment to determine the changes in technology skills, knowledge, and behavior of staff, and how that enables the provision of and/or enhances the library's ability to provide various network services and resources. |

(Continued)

**Figure 4-5 (Continued)**
**Using e-metrics and performance indicators for decision making purposes.**

| | Potentials & Development | | |
| E-metric | Performance Indicators | Decision-Making Use | Follow-on Evaluation |
|---|---|---|---|
| | | ■ Conduct a training needs assessment in various areas of network service and resource provision (or more broadly across the library's areas of operation)<br>■ Review specific courses staff have taken over time<br>■ Determine gaps in training by service and resource needs<br>■ Develop a continuing education effort for library staff<br>(see, for example, http://clp.mylibraryservice.org, which is a continuing education site that the Southeast Florida Information Network (SEFLIN) developed for its member libraries, based on various training needs assessment efforts. | |

**W/I = Workstations/Infrastructure U = Usage EM = Electronic Materials F/E = Finances/Expenditures SV = Services I = Instruction**

E-metric source: National Information Standards Organization. (2003). *Z39.7-2002 draft standard–Information services and use: Metrics and measures for libraries and information providers.* Available at http://www.niso.org/emetrics. Accessed December 15, 2003.
Performance indicator source: International Standards Organization. (2003). *Technical Report 20983: Information and documentation–performance indicators for electronic library services.* International Standards Organization.

Those e-metrics/performance indicators presented in *italics* are from Bertot, McClure, & Ryan (2001); Shim, et al. (2001); and ICOLC (2001).

levels of service and resource provision so as to facilitate the interpretation of the evaluation effort results and to use those results in the future planning of the service and resource.

## Resources: Are They "Enough?"

A common question that faces library managers and staff as they provide network services and resources is: Are we providing enough? This question pervades a number of services and resources such as public-access workstations, e-journal titles, databases, and e-books. Library managers can use a number of e-metrics and performance indicators to answer this question. These include:

- E-metrics
  - Public-access workstations;
  - Public-access workstation users;
  - Rejected sessions;
  - Full-text titles available by subscription; and
  - E-book titles available.
- Performance indicators
  - Number of workstation hours available per capita;
  - Population per public-access workstation;
  - Percentage of rejected sessions;
  - Percentage of titles available in electronic form; and
  - Percentage of book titles available in electronic form.

By using the public-access workstation e-metrics and performance indicators, in combination with library-established service and resource goals, library managers can better determine the extent to which the library provides enough public-access workstations (number of workstations, workstations per capita) and enough access to public-access workstations (hours available). For licensed resources, it is important to determine whether the library has acquired enough simultaneous-use licenses for licensed resources. Library managers can accomplish this through analyzing the number and percentage of rejected sessions. Finally, by using the titles and percentage of titles available in electronic form, library managers can determine the overall balance of the library collection and the need to restructure the collection to meet user needs (particularly when combined with the various forms of user assessment discussed in Chapter 3).

## Resources: Are They Being Used?  In What Way?

As libraries provide specific network services and resources (e.g., licensed databases, e-books, and e-journals; instruction; digital reference), a central question becomes: Are the services and resources being used?  Secondary questions include by whom, how often, and in what way(s).  There are a number of e-metrics and performance indicators by service or resource type that can assist library managers in answering these questions.  These include:

- E-metrics, licensed resources
  - ▶ Commercial services sessions;
  - ▶ Commercial services searches;
  - ▶ Commercial services full-content units examined; and
  - ▶ Commercial services descriptive records examined.
- Performance indicators, licensed resources
  - ▶ Number of documents downloaded per session;
  - ▶ Percentage of remote commercial services sessions;
  - ▶ Percentage electronic materials use is of total library material use; and
  - ▶ Total library material use.
- E-metrics, Web services and resources
  - ▶ Virtual visits;
  - ▶ Virtual reference transactions;
  - ▶ Library collection full-content units examined; and
  - ▶ Library collection descriptive records examined.
- Performance indicators, Web services and resources
  - ▶ Percentage of population reached by electronic services;
  - ▶ Percentage of virtual visits to total visits;
  - ▶ Total visits;
  - ▶ Percentage of information requests submitted electronically;
  - ▶ Total reference activity; and
  - ▶ Percentage of virtual reference activity to total reference activity.
- E-metrics, instruction
  - ▶ Formal user IT instruction; and
  - ▶ Point-of-use IT instruction.
- Performance indicators, instruction
  - ▶ Number of user attendances at electronic service training lessons, per capita.

Library managers who are interested in assessing their licensed resources can use a number of e-metrics that describe the use of those resources, e.g., number of sessions, searches, and items examined. In addition, library managers can assess the extent to which those uses come from within the library or remotely, the amount of resources accessed per user session, and what percentage of library materials use is electronic, rather than print. Combined with additional user-based methods identified in Chapter 1, library managers can develop an overall picture of what licensed resources are used, with what frequency, and from where, along with the extent to which service and resource users find the service and resource to be of high quality, and the extent to which the service or resource changed a user's skills, knowledge, and behavior.

In terms of Web-based resources and services, the aforementioned e-metrics and performance indicators enable library managers to know how many visitors use library services and resources remotely (visitors), what resources users are accessing while on line, the extent to which digital/virtual reference services are being used, and aggregate measures of network services and resources (e.g., total visits, total reference activities, and percentages of virtual visits/digital reference transactions compared to total visits and reference transactions). These data provide managers with a sense of how the library is being used—both electronically and traditionally. Such data enable library managers to determine (a) resource allocation to in-building versus network services, (b) the proportion of allocations, and (c) to what extent the library should support both types of services.

Finally, the foregoing measures provide an overall indication of the extent to which the library is reaching its service population through such indicators as training sessions attended per capita and total number of visitors (a composite of virtual and walk-in visitors). These measures provide an overall sense of the library's service and resource reach within the community it library serves. Although it is not always possible to separate virtual visits from those outside the library's population service area, this is no different than the traditional visits-per-capita measures that libraries currently use for walk-in visitors. Libraries assume that visitors to the library are from the service population, but this is not always the case.

## Is it Cost-Effective?

A key question facing library managers is: What are we getting for our investments in technology and network services and resources? This is a complex question that involves a number of different factors. By way of example, this section focuses on licensed resources. The relevant e-metrics and performance indicators available to library managers are:

- E-metrics
  - Electronic materials expenditures.
- Performance indicators
  - Cost per database session;
  - Cost per document downloaded; and
  - Cost per e-journal title (see Chapter 6).

These e-metrics and indicators inform library managers as to the total cost of electronic materials (e.g., licensed databases, e-journals, e-books) and the costs per use of such resources. Combined with predetermined cost goals, a library manager can determine the cost effectiveness of a library's negotiated resource rates and the extent to which it is appropriate to continue the licensing of a particular resource or set of resources.

## Looking Across E-metrics: Developing a Picture

There are various ways to use the e-metrics and performance indicators for decision making and other purposes. Selecting use, availability, and cost effectiveness measures can help library managers determine whether they want to continue to develop and/or support certain services and resources. As an example, a library manager could use the following e-metrics and performance indicators regarding licensed resources:

- Commercial services sessions;
- Commercial services searches;
- Commercial services full-content units examined;
- Turnaways;
- Electronic materials expenditures;
- Cost per database session;
- Cost per document downloaded; and
- Cost per e-journal title (see Chapter 6).

By using these e-metrics and indicators, library managers know how much their electronic materials cost, how often and in what way they are used, what the resources cost on a per-item (session, download, title) basis, and whether the library has enough capacity to meet user demands for licensed resources (e.g., turnaways). When combined with previously determined benchmark data, library managers can determine the overall cost effectiveness and efficiency of each of the library's resources. Moreover, as discussed in Chapter 6, library managers can use such data for the purpose of negotiating with vendors regarding licensed resource costs.

Another example involves the *visitor* suite of e-metrics and indicators. These e-metrics and indicators include virtual visits; the percentage of virtual visits to total visits; and total visits. With these, library managers can determine the number of visitors to the library who are not physical visitors, to what extent library use is changing, and what strategies the library might employ to promote certain desired forms of library use (e.g., bring more people into the buildings, offer more services and resources electronically).

## Beyond E-metrics and Performance Indicators

Although the e-metrics and performance indicators identified can assist library managers with a number of resource allocation, planning, and other decisions or activities, they do not provide any sense of service and resource assessment by users. Thus, library managers who want to have data regarding the extent to which users are satisfied with such services and resources (e.g., online journals, databases), or the outcomes of such services and resources (e.g., library website services), will need to engage in the types of evaluation strategies identified in Chapter 2.

The combination of e-metrics and performance indicator data, along with user-based assessment of network services and resources, can be extremely powerful. In essence, these are two sides of a coin: One side provides library managers and staff with resource and service use data, as well as various measures of efficiency and effectiveness; another side provides library managers and staff with feedback regarding the utility, quality, and outcomes of the services and resources.

## Concluding Comments

E-metrics and performance indicators can provide library managers and staff with important data regarding the uses, cost effectiveness, and general effectiveness and efficiency of library network services and resources. They cannot, however, provide library managers with data regarding users' perceptions and assessments of service and of resource quality and outcomes. Both forms of data are important, and library managers and staff need to engage in both e-metrics and user-based forms of data collection.

## Notes

1. Library "systems" that function as autonomous independent libraries (e.g., federated library systems and special libraries on university campuses, such as law libraries, medical libraries, science libraries, etc.) will need to work out a collection and reporting system that accounts for this structure.

## References

Bertot, John Carlo; McClure, Charles R.; & Davis, Denise M. (2002). *Developing a national data collection model for public library network statistics and performance measures: Final report.* Washington, DC: Institute of Museum and Library Services. Available at http://www.ii.fsu.edu/Projects/IMLS/final.report.natl.model.pdf. Last accessed November 17, 2003.

Bertot, John Carlo, McClure, Charles R., & Ryan, Joe. (2001). *Statistics and performance measures for public library network statistics.* Chicago, IL: American Library Association.

Brophy, P., Clarke, Z., Brinkley, M., Mundt, S., & Poll, R. (2000). *EQUINOX library performance measurement and quality management system performance indicators for electronic library services.* Available at http://equinox.dcu.ie/reports/pilist.html. Last accessed November 18, 2003.

Counting Online Usage of Networked Electronic Resources (COUNTER). See http://www.projectcounter.org/. Last accessed March 11, 2004.

International Coalition of Library Consortia (ICOLC). (1998). Guidelines for statistical measures of usage of Web-based indexed, abstracted, and full-text resources. *Information Technology and Libraries,* 17(4): 219–221. See also http://www.library.yale.edu/consortia/webstats.html. Additional ICOLC documents are available at http://www.library.yale.edu/consortia/statementsanddocuments.html. Last accessed March 11, 2004.

International Standards Organization. (1998). *ISO/CD 11620 information and documentation: Library performance indicators.* Stockholm, Sweden: Swedish General Standards Institute.

International Standards Organization. (2003). *ISO/CD 11620/AMD. 1 information and documentation: Library performance indicators.* Stockholm, Sweden: Swedish General Standards Institute.

International Standards Organization. (2003). *ISO/CD 11620 information and documentation: Library performance indicators technical report 20983.* Stockholm, Sweden: Swedish General Standards Institute.

International Standards Organization. (2003). *ISO/CD 2789 information and documentation: International library statistics.* Stockholm, Sweden: Swedish General Standards Institute.

National Information Standards Organization (NISO). (2003). *NISO Z39.7-200X Draft. Information services and use: Metrics & statistics for libraries and information providers–Data Dictionary.* Bethesda, MD: National Information Standards Organization. Available at http://www.niso.org/emetrics/. Last accessed March 11, 2004.

Shim, Wonsik; McClure, Charles R.; Fraser, Bruce T.; & Bertot, John Carlo. (2001). *Data collection manual for academic and research library network statistics and performance measures.* Washington, DC: Association of Research Libraries.

Appendix 4-A. Library E-Metrics Comparison across Library Standards and Other Selected Initiatives.

## *Information Use Management and Policy Institute*
### School of Information Studies, Florida State University

## Library Network Statistics Definitions:
## A Selected Comparison across Initiatives and Standards

By:

John Carlo Bertot, Associate Director and Associate Professor
bertot@lis.fsu.edu

Manimegalai M. Subramaniam, Research Associate
mm02n@garnet.acns.fsu.edu

September 1, 2003

NOTE: The information presented in this report is subject to change as the standards and initiatives fin
their documentation.

School of Information Studies
Florida State University
Information Use Management and
Policy Institute
Tallahassee, FL 32306-2100
http://www.ii.fsu.edu

## PURPOSE OF COMPARISON

The table presented below seeks to compare the two major library statistics standards, International Standards Organization (ISO) Standard 2789 and National Information Standards Organization (NISO) Standard Z39.7, to each other as well as two additional key initiatives – those from members of consortia as presented by the International Coalition of Library Consortia (ICOLC) and those from members of the publisher community as presented by Project COUNTER. In particular, this document:

- Compares terms and definitions directly where possible across the ISO, NISO, ICOLC, and COUNTER initiatives; and
- Includes additional terms and definitions that do not exist across all initiatives so to have a comprehensive listing of all terms and definitions.

The document contents are current as of September 1, 2003. Readers should note that the wording in the definitions can change over time. This is particularly the case with the NISO Z39.7 language, as that standard continues its review and comment period.

## LIBRARY STATISTICS DEVELOPMENT

Many of the terms and definitions contained within the selected initiatives are based on the following research efforts and reports:

- Bertot, John Carlo, McClure, Charles R., and Ryan, Joe. (2001). *Statistics and performance measures for public library network statistics.* Chicago, IL: American Library Association.
- Bertot, John Carlo, McClure, Charles R., and Davis, Denise M. (2002). Developing a national data collection model for public library network statistics and performance measures: Final report. Washington, D.C.: Institute of Museum and Library Services. Available at http://www.ii.fsu.edu/Projects/IMLS/final.report.natl.model.pdf, last accessed June 17, 2003.
- Brophy, Peter, Clarke, Zoë, Brinkley, Monica, Mundt, Sebastian, and Poll, Roswita Poll (2000). *EQUINOX library performance measurement and quality management system performance indicators for electronic library services.* Available at http://equinox.dcu.ie/reports/pilist.html, last accessed June 18, 2003.
- Project COUNTER, http://www.projectcounter.org.
- Shim, Wonsik, McClure, Charles R., Fraser, Bruce T., and Bertot, John Carlo. (2001). *Data collection manual for academic and research library network statistics and performance measures.* Washington, D.C.: Association of Research Libraries.

Readers who wish to have more in-depth insight into the methodologies for developing and field-testing the various network statistics and performance measures should consult these resources directly.

| Element | ISO | NISO | Counter | ICOLC |
|---|---|---|---|---|
| **Electronic Materials** | **3.2.12 Electronic collection** All resources in electronic form in the library collection. Note: The electronic collection includes databases, electronic serials and digital documents. Free internet resources which have been catalogued by the library in its OPAC or a database should be counted separately. | **4.10 Other Materials-- Electronic** An electronic document or item. Includes e-books, databases, Internet resources and other digital documents. Electronic Collection All resources in electronic form in the library collection. Note: The electronic collection includes databases, electronic serials, and digital documents. Free Internet resources which have been catalogued by the library in its OPAC or a database should be counted separately. | | |
| | **3.2.1 Abstract & Indexing Database** Collection of bibliographic references analyzing and presenting on a continuous basis periodical and/or other titles that usually relate to a common discipline or geographic area. Note: This includes electronic reference and indexing tools which in print form would be counted as periodicals. Databases primarily containing full text are excluded. | **4.10.1 Abstract & Indexing Databases** Collection of bibliographic references analyzing and presenting on a continuous basis periodical and/or other titles that usually relate to a common discipline or geographic area. This includes electronic reference and indexing tools which in print form would be counted as periodicals. Databases primarily containing full text are excluded. | | |

129

| Element | ISO | NISO | Counter | ICOLC |
|---|---|---|---|---|
| **Electronic Materials (continued)** | **3.2.7 Compact Disk Read–Only Memory (CD-ROM)** Computer based information storage and retrieval medium based on laser technology that contains data in text and/or multimedia formats. Note: CD-ROMs are counted according to their contents as database, digital document, electronic serial. | **4.10.2 Compact Disk Read–Only Memory (CD-ROM)** Computer based information storage and retrieval medium based on laser technology that contains data in text and/or multimedia formats. CD-ROMs are counted according to their contents as database, digital document, electronic serial. **4.10.3 Computer Files** The number of pieces of computer-readable disks, tapes, CD-ROMs, and similar machine-readable files comprising data or programs that are locally held as part of the library's collections available to library clients. Examples: U.S. Census tapes, sample research software, locally mounted databases, and reference tools on CD-ROM, tape or disk. Does not include bibliographic records used to manage the collection (i.e., the library's own catalog in machine-readable form), library system software, and microcomputer software used only by the library staff. | | |

| Element | ISO | NISO | Counter | ICOLC |
|---|---|---|---|---|
| **Electronic Materials (continued)** | **3.2.8 Database**<br>Collection of electronically stored data or unit records (facts, bibliographic data, texts) with a common user interface and software for the retrieval and manipulation of the data. Note 1: The data or records are usually collected with a particular intent and are related to a defined topic. A database may be issued on CD-ROM, diskette, or other direct access method, or as a computer file accessed via dial-up methods or via the Internet. Note 2: Licensed databases are counted separately even if access to several licensed database products is effected through the same interface. | **4.10.4 Databases**<br>Collection of electronically stored data or unit records (facts, bibliographic data, texts) with a common user interface and software for the retrieval and manipulation of the data. Notes: The data or records are usually collected with a particular intent and are related to a defined topic. A database may be issued on CD-ROM, diskette, or other direct access method, or as a computer file accessed via dial-up methods or via the Internet. Licensed databases are counted separately even if access to several licensed database products is effected through the same interface. | **3.1.1.11 Database**<br>A collection of electronically stored data or unit records (facts, bibliographic data, texts) with a common user interface and software for the retrieval and manipulation of data (NISO)<br><br>**3.1.2.7 Database record**<br>An individual record in a standard format, the collection of which in a form that can be processed by a computer constitutes a database. | |

| Element | ISO | NISO | Counter | ICOLC |
|---|---|---|---|---|
| **Electronic Materials (continued)** | **3.2.14 Full-text database** Collection of original texts (monographs, reports, journal articles, etc.), printed music, cartographic or graphic documents. Note 1: Patents and electronic serials are excluded. Note 2: A database with a mixture of full texts, moving images or sound and other items should be counted as a full-text database.<br><br>**3.2.24 Other database** Database containing descriptive information or numeric data that is usually consulted for specific pieces of information rather than read consecutively, e.g. directories, encyclopedias, dictionaries, statistical tables and figures, and/or collections of scientific formulae. | | | |

| Element | ISO | NISO | Counter | ICOLC |
|---|---|---|---|---|
| **Electronic Materials (continued)** | **3.2.9 Digital document** Information unit with a defined content that has been digitized by the library or acquired in digital form as part of the library collection. Note 1: This includes eBooks, electronic patents, networked audiovisual documents and other digital documents, e.g. reports, cartographic and music documents, preprints, etc. Databases and electronic serials are excluded. Note 3: A digital document may be structured into one or more files. | **4.10.5 Digital Documents** Information unit with a defined content that has been digitized by the library or acquired in digital form as part of the library collection. This includes eBooks, electronic patents, networked audiovisual documents and other digital documents, e.g. reports, cartographic and music documents, pre-prints etc. Databases and electronic serials are excluded | | |

133

| Element | ISO | NISO | Counter | ICOLC |
|---|---|---|---|---|
| **Electronic Materials (continued)** | **3.2.11 eBook** Digital documents, licensed or not, where searchable text is prevalent, and which can be seen in analogy to a print book (monograph). Note 1: The use of eBooks is in many cases dependent on a dedicated device and/or a special reader or viewing software. Note 2: eBooks can be lent to users either on portable devices (eBook readers) or by transmitting the contents to the user's PC for a limited time period. Note 3: Doctoral dissertations in electronic format are included.<br><br>**3.2.13 Electronic serials** Serials published in electronic form only or in both electronic and other format. Note: Comprises serials held locally and remote resources for which access rights have been acquired, at least for a certain period of time. | **4.10.6 eBooks** Digital documents, licensed or not, where searchable text is prevalent, and which can be seen in analogy to a print book (monograph). The use of eBooks is in many cases dependent on a dedicated device and/or a special reader or viewing software. Note 1. eBooks can be lent to users either on portable devices (eBook readers) or by transmitting the contents to the user's PC for a limited time period. Note 2. Doctoral dissertations in electronic format are included.<br><br>**4.10.7 Electronic serials** Serials published in electronic form only or in both electronic and other format. Note: Comprises serials held locally and remote resources for which access rights have been acquired, at least for a certain period of time. | | |

| Element | ISO | NISO | Counter | ICOLC |
|---|---|---|---|---|
| **Electronic Materials (continued)** | **3.3.27 Website** Electronic service that has a unique domain on the Internet and consists of a collection of digital documents. Note 1: The pages of a web site are usually interconnected by the use of hypertext links. Note 2: Excludes documents that fit the definitions of electronic collection and external Internet resources that may be linked from the library website. | **4.10.8 Free Internet Resources** The number of links to unique free Internet resources (digital documents, databases, electronic journals, etc.) which have been catalogued by the library in its OPAC or a database | | |
| | **3.2.25 Other digital documents** Digital documents other than an e-book, networked audio-visual document or electronic patent, e.g. report, pre-print, cartographic or music document etc. in electronic format. | **4.10.9 Other digital documents** Digital documents other than an e-book, networked audio-visual document or electronic patent, e.g. report, pre-print, cartographic or music document etc. in electronic format. | | |

| Element | ISO | NISO | Counter | ICOLC |
|---|---|---|---|---|
| **Electronic Materials (continued)** | **3.2.22 Multimedia document** Document combining different information media, text, graphics, photos, video, audio, in digital format. Note: Multimedia documents are counted according to their main features or purposes e.g. as a database, an electronic serial or a digital document. | **4.9.3 Multi Media Documents** Documents combining different information media – text, graphics, photos, video, audio – in digital format. Note: Multimedia documents are counted according to their main feature or purpose e.g. as database, electronic serial or digital document | | |

| Element | ISO | NISO | Counter | ICOLC |
|---|---|---|---|---|
| **Finances / Expenditure** | **3.5.2 Operating expenditure / Ordinary expenditure** Expenditure incurred in the running of a library. Note: Money spent on staff and on resources that are not used and replaced regularly. This includes expenditure on employees, rent, acquisitions and licensing, binding, computer network (operations and maintenance), telecommunication, building maintenance, etc. May also be termed 'current' or 'recurrent' expenditure. When applicable, local and national sales / purchase taxes (e.g. Value Added Tax (VAT) are included). | **6.2.8 Electronic Access Expenditures** All operating expenditures from the library budget associated with access to electronic materials and services. Include computer hardware and software used to support library operations, whether purchased or leased, mainframe and microcomputer. Includes expenditures for maintenance. Includes expenditures for equipment used to run information service products when that expenditure cannot be separated from the price of the product. Includes expenditures for services provided by national, regional, and local bibliographic utilities, networks, consortia and commercial services. Includes all fees and usage costs associated with such services as OCLC FirstSearch or electronic document delivery. Note: Excludes capital expenditures. | | |

| Element | ISO | NISO | Counter | ICOLC |
|---|---|---|---|---|
| **Finances / Expenditure (continued)** | | **6.2.9 Electronic Materials Expenditures** Expenditures for electronic documents or items. Includes eBooks, databases, Internet resources and other digital documents.<br><br>**6.2.10 Electronic Network Expenditures** Expenditures for services provided by national, regional, and local bibliographic utilities, networks, and consortia. | | |

| Element | ISO | NISO | Counter | ICOLC |
|---|---|---|---|---|
| Services | **3.3.5 Electronic service** Electronic library service, which is either supplied from local servers or accessible via networks. Note: Electronic library services include the OPAC, the library web site, the electronic collection, electronic document delivery (mediated), electronic reference service, user training on electronic services and Internet access offered via the library. | **7.3.1 Virtual Reference Transactions** Virtual reference transactions conducted via e-mail, website, or other network-based medium designed to support virtual reference. (ARL E-metrics; Bertot, McClure, Ryan). Note: Includes questions either received or responded to. | | |
| | **3.3.25 Virtual visit** User's request on the library website from outside the library premises, regardless of the number of pages or elements viewed. | **7.9.1.5 Virtual Visits**. A user's request of the library web site from outside the library premises regardless of the number of pages or elements viewed. (ISO 2789, 3.3.25) Excludes web site visits from within the library. Ne: This statistic is the equivalent of a session for a library's website. As such, there is a need to exclude various actions (e.g., hits, downloads) by users during any given visit. | | |

| Element | ISO | NISO | Counter | ICOLC |
|---|---|---|---|---|
| **Services (continued)** | **3.3.4 Electronic Document Delivery, mediated** Electronic transmission of a document or part of a document from the library collection to a user, mediated by library staff, not necessarily via another library. Note 1. Electronic transmission of documents to members of the population to be served is included. FAX transmission is excluded. Note 2: May be split up as to transmission with or without charge to the user. | **7.4.1 Electronic Document Delivery** Electronic transmission of a document or part of a document from the library collection to a user, mediated by library staff, not necessarily via another library. Note 1. Electronic transmission of documents to members of the population to be served is included. FAX transmission is excluded. Note 2: May be split up as to transmission with or without charge to the user. | | |

| Element | ISO | NISO | Counter | ICOLC |
|---|---|---|---|---|
| Services (continued) | **3.3.6 External Document Supply** Document or part of it in print or electronic form delivered from outside the library collection by non-library suppliers (not through interlibrary lending) with the library being involved in the transaction and/or the payment. Note: It is irrelevant whether a number of individual transactions is paid per view or a certain number of transactions have been prepaid. | **7.4.2 External Document Supply** Document or part of it in print or electronic form delivered from outside the library collection by non-library suppliers (not through interlibrary lending) with the library being involved in the transaction and/or the payment. Note: It is irrelevant whether a number of individual transactions is paid per view or a certain number of transactions have been prepaid. | | |

| Element | ISO | NISO | Counter | ICOLC |
|---|---|---|---|---|
| Workstations | **3.4.6 Workstation** Computer that may stand alone or be networked, or a dumb terminal. | **7.8 Public Access Workstations** Library owned public access graphical workstations that connect to the Internet for a dedicated purpose (to access an OPAC or specific database) or multiple-purposes. | | |

| Element | ISO | NISO | Counter | ICOLC |
|---|---|---|---|---|
| Workstations (continued) | | **7.8.1 Number of Public Access Workstations** Annual count of the total number of library owned public access graphical workstations that connect to the Internet for a dedicated purpose (to access an OPAC or specific database) or multiple-purposes. This statistic is counted and collected for each participating branch, if applicable. **(Branch Level Statistic)** Note: Computers in computer labs used for public instruction if graphical and connected to the Internet should be counted. Public access graphical workstations that connect to the Internet that are used by both staff and the public should be counted if the workstation is used by the public for at least half of the hours during an average week that the library is open to the public. Reference desk computers used by staff to assist the public should not be counted. | | |

143

| Element | ISO | NISO | Counter | ICOLC |
| --- | --- | --- | --- | --- |
| **Workstations (continued)** | | **7.8.2 Number of Public Access Workstation Users**<br>Annual count of the number of users of all of the library's graphical public access workstations connected to the Internet computed from a one-week sample. **(Branch Level Statistic)** | | |

| Element | ISO | NISO | Counter | ICOLC |
|---|---|---|---|---|
| Usage | **3.3.7 Information request** Information contact that involves the knowledge / use of one or more information sources (printed& non-printed materials, machine-readable databases, the library's own and other institutions' catalogues) by library staff. 1): Adapted fromANSI/NISOZ39.71995. 2):May also involve recommendations, interpretation, or instruction in the use of such sources. 3):The request can be delivered personally or by means of telephone, regular mail, fax or electronic media 4):It is essential that libraries do not include directional and administrative inquiries, e.g. for locating staff / facilities, regarding opening times or about handling equipment. 5): Inquiries excluded, if asked for the purpose of locating items of stock that have already been identified bibliographically | **7.3 Information Requests** An information contact that involves the use, knowledge, recommendations, or interpretation, or instruction in the use of one or more information sources by a member of the library staff. The term includes information and referral service. Information sources include: Printed and non-printed materials, Machine-readable databases (including computer-assisted instruction), the library's own catalogs and other holdings records, other libraries and institutions through communication or referral, persons both inside and outside the library. | | |

145

| Element | ISO | NISO | Counter | ICOLC |
|---|---|---|---|---|
| **Usage (continued)** | **3.3.15 Record downloaded** Catalogue record or database entry fully displayed during a session on a database or the OPAC | **7.9.1.1 Units/Records Examined** Content in the electronic collection that is delivered to a user. The sub-categories that follow provide for a detailed breakdown by type of content delivered (full-content unit, or descriptive record) and system delivering the content (Library Collection, Commercial Service or OPAC). | **3.1.2.9 Item requests** Number of items requested by users. User requests include viewing, downloading, emailing and printing of items, where this activity can be recorded and controlled by the server rather than the browser. Turn aways will also be counted. | **Number of Menu Selections** Categorized as appropriate for the vendor's system. If display of data can be accomplished by browsing (the use of menus), this measure must be provided. (e.g. an electronic journal site provides alphabetic and subject-based menu options in addition to a search form). The number of searches and the number of alphabetic and subject menu selections should be tracked. |
| | **3.3.3 Document downloaded** Full text of a document, or a part of a document, in the electronic collection that is delivered to the user. | **7.9.1.1.1 Library Collection Full-Content Units Examined** Number of full-content units from library electronic collection examined, downloaded, or otherwise supplied to a user. Exclude OPAC or commercial services (i.e., online databases). | **3.1.2.10 Successful request** For web-server logs successful requests are those with specific return codes, as defined by NCSA. | **Number of full-content units** Examined, downloaded, or otherwise supplied to user, to the extent these recordable and controlled by the server rather than the browser. |

| Element | ISO | NISO | Counter | ICOLC |
|---|---|---|---|---|
| Usage (continued) | | **7.9.1.1.2 Commercial Services Full-Content Units Examined** Number of subscription service full-content units examined, downloaded, or otherwise supplied to user, to the extent that these are recordable and controlled by the server rather than the browser. (ICOLC Guidelines, December 2001). Note 1: Journal articles – by journal title with ISSN and title listed. Note 2: Ebooks – by book title with ISBN and title listed. Note 3: Reference materials – by content unit appropriate to the resource (e.g., dictionary definitions, encyclopedia articles, biographies, etc.). Note 4: Non-textual resources – by file type as appropriate to resources (e.g., image, audio, video, etc.). (ICOLC Guidelines, December 2001) | | Journal articles – by journal title with ISSN and title listed. Note 2: Ebooks – by book title with ISBN and title listed. Note 3: Reference materials – by content unit appropriate to the resource (e.g., dictionary definitions, encyclopedia articles, biographies, etc.). Note 4: Non-textual resources – by file type as appropriate to resources (e.g., image, audio, video, etc.). |

| Element | ISO | NISO | Counter | ICOLC |
|---|---|---|---|---|
| Usage (continued) | | **7.9.1.1.3 Library Collection Descriptive Records Examined** Number of descriptive records concerning the library's electronic collection delivered to a user. Note 1: Determined by the record type appropriate to the resource, e.g., abstract, archive, index. Note 2: Exclude OPAC or commercial services (i.e., online databases). | | |
| | | **7.9.1.1.4 Commercial Services Descriptive Records Examined** Number of descriptive records concerning the library's commercial services delivered to a user. Note 1: Determined by the record type appropriate to the resource, e.g., abstract, archive, index. Note 2: Exclude OPAC or library collection descriptive records (i.e., library website services and collections). | | |

148

| Element | ISO | NISO | Counter | ICOLC |
|---|---|---|---|---|
| Usage (continued) | **3.3.12 Online Public Access Catalogue (OPAC)** Database of bibliographic records describing the collection usually of one particular library or library system. Note: It allows searching by name, title and subject and offers online access through public terminals. | **7.9.1.1.5 OPAC Descriptive Record Examined** Number of descriptive records from the library's online catalog delivered to a user. Note 1: Exclude commercial services or library collection descriptive records (i.e., library website services and collections). | | |

| Element | ISO | NISO | Counter | ICOLC |
|---|---|---|---|---|
| Usage (continued) | **3.3.20 Search (query)** Unique intellectual inquiry in a database or the OPAC. Note: A search (query) is recorded each time a search request is submitted to the server. | **7.9.1.2 Searches/Menu Selections (Queries)** A search is defined as intending to represent a unique intellectual inquiry whether conducted through a search form submitted to the server or through the use of menu selections (e.g. browsing a list of subjects.) | **3.1.2.8 Search** A specific intellectual query, typically equated to submitting the search form of the online service to the server. | **Number of queries (searches)** A search is intended to represent a unique intellectual inquiry. Typically a search is recorded each time a search form is send/submitted to the server. Subsequent activities to review or browse among the records retrieved or the process of isolating the correct single item desired do not represent additional searches, unless the parameter (s) defining the retrieval set is modified through resubmission of the search form, a combination of previous search sets, or some other similar technique. Immediately repeated duplicate searches, double clicks, or other evidence indicating unintended user behavior should be counted. |

150

| Element | ISO | NISO | Counter | ICOLC |
|---|---|---|---|---|
| Usage (continued) | | **7.9.1.2.1 Library Collection Searches (Queries)** A search is defined as intending to represent a unique intellectual inquiry. Typically a search is recorded every time a search request is submitted to the server. (ISO 2789, Annex A) Note 1: Limited to library electronic collection services. Note 2: Exclude spider/crawler searches. Note 3: Include menu selection searches.<br><br>**7.9.1.2.2 Commercial Services Searches (Queries)** A search is defined as intending to represent a unique intellectual inquiry. Typically a search is recorded every time a search request is submitted to the server. Note 1: Limited to commercial services. Note 2: Mistyped search strings do not represent unique intellectual inquiries. Note 3: Exclude spider/crawler searches. Note 4: Include menu selection searches | | **Number of menu selections** If display of data can be accomplished by browsing (the use of menus), this measure must be provided (e.g. an electronic journal site provides alphabetic and subject-based menu options in addition to a search form). The number of searches and the number of alphabetic and subject menu selections should be tracked. |

| Element | ISO | NISO | Counter | ICOLC |
|---|---|---|---|---|
| Usage (continued) | | **7.9.1.2.3 OPAC Searches (Queries)** A search is defined as intending to represent a unique intellectual inquiry. Typically a search is recorded every time a search request is submitted to the server. Note 1: Limited to the library online catalog service. Note 2: Exclude spider/crawler searches. Note 3: Include menu selection searches. | | |

| Element | ISO | NISO | Counter | ICOLC |
|---|---|---|---|---|
| **Session Access** | **3.3.21 Session** Successful request of a database or the OPAC. Note 1: A session is one cycle of users activities that typically starts when a user connects to a database or the OPAC and ends with explicit (by leaving the database through log-out or exit) or implicit (time out due to user inactivity) termination of activities in the database. The average timeout period would be 30 min. If another time period is used, this should be reported. Note 2: Sessions on the library website are counted as virtual visits. Note 3: Requests of a general entrance or gateway page should be excluded. Note 4: If possible, requests by search engines should be excluded. **3.3.22 Session Time** Duration of a session. Note: This will usually be the period of time between a lo-in to and an implicit or explicit log-off from a database or the OPAC. | **7.9.1.3 Sessions** A session is defined as a successful request of an online service or library's online catalog. It is one cycle of user activities that typically starts when a user connects to the service or database and ends by terminating activity that is either explicit (by leaving the service through exit or log-out) or implicit (timeout due to user inactivity). **7.9.3.5 Session Time**. Duration of a session. Note: This will usually be the period of time between a log-in and an implicit or explicit log-off from a database or the OPAC. | **3.1.5.2 Session** Same as NISO **3.2.1 Start time** Records the time a user's session begins (first login or IP authentication), to the nearest second, using UTC (Co-ordinated Universal Time, formerly GMT). **3.2.2. End time** Records the time a user's session ends or timeouts, to the nearest second, using UTC (Co-ordinated Universal Time, formerly GMT). **3.2.3. Duration** Records the time a user's session lasts, to the nearest second. **3.2.4. Total activity** Total number of views or downloads of items per session. **3.1.5.3 Timeout** Automatic termination of a session due to a period of user inactivity. The average timeout setting would be 30 minutes. If another timeout period is used this should be reported. (NISO) | **Number of sessions** Must be provided in order to satisfy reporting requirements of government agencies and professional organizations. ICOLC recognizes that the definition, collection, and reporting of this measure are subject to interpretation. In the stateless web environment, statistics gathered as sessions can provide only a rough indication of the number of actual sessions conducted, thus limiting the overall meaningfulness of this particular indicator. |

| Element | ISO | NISO | Counter | ICOLC |
|---|---|---|---|---|
| **Session Access (continued)** | | **7.9.1.3.1 OPAC Sessions**<br>A session is defined as a successful request of the library's online catalog. It is one cycle of user activities that typically starts when a user connects to the OPAC and ends by terminating activity in the OPAC that is either explicit (by leaving the database through log-out or exit) or implicit (timeout due to user inactivity). In some cases, e.g. OPAC use inside the library, several users one after the other might make use of the same workstation, and sessions could not be separated. In most systems, a session is cut off after a specified time of non-use, thus avoiding part of the problem. The average timeout setting would be 30 minutes. If another timeout period is used this should be reported. Browser/proxy cashing will be likely to reduce the number of requests registered in log files | | |

154

| Element | ISO | NISO | Counter | ICOLC |
|---|---|---|---|---|
| **Session Access** (continued) | | **7.9.1.3.1 OPAC Sessions**<br><br>A session is defined as a successful request of the library's online catalog. It is one cycle of user activities that typically starts when a user connects to the OPAC and ends by terminating activity in the OPAC that is either explicit (by leaving the database through log-out or exit) or implicit (timeout due to user inactivity). In some cases, e.g. OPAC use inside the library, several users one after the other might make use of the same workstation, and sessions could not be separated. In most systems, a session is cut off after a specified time of non-use, thus avoiding part of the problem. The average timeout setting would be 30 minutes. If another timeout period is used this should be reported. Browser/proxy cashing will be likely to reduce the number of requests registered in log files | | |

155

| Element | ISO | NISO | Counter | ICOLC |
|---|---|---|---|---|
| **Session Access (continued)** | | **7.9.1.3.2 Commercial Services Sessions (continued)** In most systems, a session is cut off after a specified time of non-use, thus avoiding part of the problem. The average timeout setting would be 30 minutes. If another timeout period is used this should be reported. Browser or proxy cashing will be likely to reduce the number of requests registered in logfiles. | | |
| | **3.3.17 Rejected Sessions (Turnaways)** Unsuccessful request of a database or the OPAC because of requests exceeding simultaneous user limit. Note: Rejection through entry of wrong passwords is excluded. | **7.9.1.4 Rejected Sessions (Turnaways)** A rejected session (turnaway) is defined as an unsuccessful log-in to an electronic service by exceeding the simultaneous user limit. (ISO 2789, Annex A) Note: Failure of log-in because of wrong passwords is excluded. | **3.1.5.4 Turnaway (Rejected session)** A turnaway (rejected session) is defined as an unsuccessful log-in to an electronic service by exceeding the simultaneous user limit. | **Number of Turnaways** Peak simultaneous users, any other indicator relevant to the pricing model applied to the library and consortium. |

| Element | ISO | NISO | Counter | ICOLC |
|---|---|---|---|---|
| **Session Access** (continued) | **3.3.9. Internet Session** Internet access by a user from a workstation provided on the library premises Note: Internet sessions can only be counted if users have registered or authenticated themselves when accessing the Internet. | **7.9.3 Internet Access** Internet access by a user from a workstation provided on the library premises or remotely.<br><br>**7.9.3.1 Internet Session** Internet sessions can only be counted if users have registered or authenticated themselves when accessing the Internet. | | |

| Element | ISO | NISO | Counter | ICOLC |
|---|---|---|---|---|
| **User Orientation & Training** | **3.3.24 User training** Training program set up with a specified lesson plan, which aims at specific learning outcomes for the use of library services. Note 1: User training can be offered as a tour of the library, as a library tuition, or as a web-based services for users. Note 2: The duration of lessons is irrelevant. | **7.10.2 Formal User Information Technology Training** A count of the number of users instructed and the hours of instruction offered in the use of information technology, or resources obtainable using information technology in structured sessions – either delivered in the library using a computer lab or other instructional setting or delivered electronically through online-based instruction. (Bertot, McClure, Davis). **7.10.4 Point-of-Use Information Technology Training** A count of the number of users instructed and the hours of instruction offered in the use of information technology or resources obtainable using information technology in unstructured sessions at the impromptu request of users. | | |

Appendix 4-B. Historical Evolution of E-metrics.

# *Information Use Management and Policy Institute*
School of Information Studies, Florida State University

## Historical Evolution of Network Statistics:
## A Selected Comparison across Initiatives and Standards

By:

John Carlo Bertot, Associate Director and Associate Professor
bertot@lis.fsu.edu

.

Manimegalai M. Subramaniam, Research Associate
mm02n@garnet.acns.fsu.edu

**September 1, 2003**

School of Information Studies
Florida State University
Information Use Management and
Policy Institute
Tallahassee, FL  32306-2100
http://www.ii.fsu.edu

- 424 -

## PURPOSE OF COMPARISON

This table compares historical evolution of the network statistics by analyzing some previously used standards such as Equinox, Association of Research Libraries (ARL), ICOLC, and American Library Association (ALA) (Bertot, McClure & Ryan, 2001). This table:

- Facilitates the understanding of network statistics across the known major developmental initiatives;
- Provides an at-a-glance view of the similarities and differences in data elements, definitions, and focus of the initiatives; and
- Demonstrates the differences and similarities that can occur with network statistics over time due to factors such as technology change, situational context, and measurement intend.

The table is a useful resource for those interested in reviewing the initiatives that developed the network statistics and those bodies that seek to incorporate the statistics into various standards.

## LIBRARY STATISTICS DEVELOPMENT

Many of the terms and definitions contained within the selected initiatives are based on the following research efforts and reports:

- Bertot, John Carlo, McClure, Charles R., and Ryan, Joe. (2001). *Statistics and performance measures for public library network statistics*. Chicago, IL: American Library Association.
- Bertot, John Carlo, McClure, Charles R., and Davis, Denise M. (2002). Developing a national data collection model for public library network statistics and performance measures: Final report. Washington, D.C.: Institute of Museum and Library Services. Available at http://www.ii.fsu.edu/Projects/IMLS/final.report.natl.model.pdf, last accessed June 17, 2003.
- Brophy, Peter, Clarke, Zoë, Brinkley, Monica, Mundt, Sebastian, and Poll, Roswita Poll (2000). *EQUINOX library performance measurement and quality management system performance indicators for electronic library services*. Available at http://equinox.dcu.ie/reports/pilist.html, last accessed June 18, 2003.
- Shim, Wonsik, McClure, Charles R., Fraser, Bruce T., and Bertot, John Carlo. (2001). *Data collection manual for academic and research library network statistics and performance measures*. Washington, D.C.: Association of Research Libraries.

Readers who wish to have more in-depth insight into the methodologies for developing and field-testing the various network statistics and performance measures should consult these resources directly.

# LIBRARY NETWORK STATISTICS COMPARISON

| Element | EQUINOX | ALA | ARL | ICOLC |
|---|---|---|---|---|
| Electronic Materials | **Database**<br>Collection or file of electronically stored data or unit records with software for the retrieval and manipulation of the data. (ISO/DIS 2789)<br><br>**Document**<br>Recorded information or material object which can be treated as a unit in a documentation process. (ISO/FDIS 5127) [NOTE: Documents can differ in their physical form and characteristics.]<br><br>**Electronic Library Materials**<br>Every document in electronic form which needs special equipment to be used. [NOTE: Electronic resources include digital documents, electronic serials, databases, patents in electronic form and networked audiovisual documents.] ISO/DIS 2789 | | **R2 – Number of Electronic Reference Resources**<br>Number of electronic reference resources & aggregation services – by individual institution or consortia licensing<br><br>**R3 – Number of Electronic Books**<br>Number of full-text monographs – by individual institution or consortia licensing. | |

| Element | EQUINOX | ALA | ARL | ICOLC |
|---|---|---|---|---|
| Electronic Materials (continued) | **Library Collection** All documents provided by a library for its users. [NOTE 1: Comprises documents held locally and documents on remote resources for which access rights have been acquired at least for a certain period of time. NOTE 2: Access rights may be acquired by the library itself, by a consortium and/or external funding. NOTE 3: Acquisition is to be understood as deliberately selecting a document, securing access rights and including it in the OPAC or other databases of the library. Interlibrary lending and document delivery and excluded. NOTE 4: Does not include links to Internet resources for which the library has not secured access rights by license or other contractual agreement. ISO/DIS 2789 | | **P3 – Percentage of Electronic Books to All Monographs** Percentage of the number of e-books available to all monographs available; **D1 – Size of Library Digital Collection** Digital materials created or converted by the library & made available electronically. Includes – e-theses, special collections, maps, sound recordings, films – not purchased. | |

| Element | EQUINOX | ALA | ARL | ICOLC |
|---|---|---|---|---|
| Finances / Expenditure | **PI 5: Cost per session for each electronic library service**<br>The cost of each electronic library service made available by the library divided by the number of sessions on that ELS (Electronic Library Services) during the specified time period.<br>Note: The cost of each ELS is the acquisition, subscription, licensing or pay-per-view costs to the library for that service. Infrastructural costs such as hardware and software are not included.<br><br>**PI 6: Cost per document or entry (record) viewed for each electronic library service**<br>The cost of each electronic library service made available by the library divided by the number of documents or entries (records) viewed from that ELS during the specified time period. Note: Same as above | | **C2 – Cost of Electronic Reference Sources**<br>Expenditures for electronic reference sources & aggregate services. Include annual access fees & other service costs paid directly to vendor or through consortia arrangements. | |

163

| Element | EQUINOX | ALA | ARL | ICOLC |
|---|---|---|---|---|
| **Finances / Expenditure (continued)** | **PI 11: Percentage of total acquisitions expenditure spent on acquisition of electronic library services** <br> The library's expenditure on acquisition, subscription, license and pay-per-view charges for electronic resources expressed as a percentage of total acquisitions expenditure. | | **C1 – Cost of Electronic Full-Text Journals** <br> Expenditures for electronic full-text journal subscriptions. Include initial purchase cost, membership fees, annual licenses paid directly or as part of consortia. <br><br> **C3 – Cost of Electronic Books** <br> Expenditures for electronic full-text monographs. Include annual purchase costs & membership fees, annual access & service fees paid directly to vendor or through consortia arrangements. | |

164

| Element | EQUINOX | ALA | ARL | ICOLC |
|---|---|---|---|---|
| Finances / Expenditure (continued) | | | **C4 – Library Expenditures for Bibliographic Utilities, Networks & Consortia** Expenditures for services provided by national, regional & local bibliographic utilities, networks, & consortia (OCLC, RLG); exclude fees paid for client database access – which should be reported in C1 through C3.<br><br>**C5 – External Expenditures for Bibliographic Utilities, Networks & Consortia** Expenditures paid by external agencies, on the library's behalf for access to computer files, e-journals or search services through a centrally funded system or consortia arrangements. (Examples – VIVA – Virginia, CNSLP – Canada, U-Cal Cal Digital Library Expenditures). | |

| Element | EQUINOX | ALA | ARL | ICOLC |
|---|---|---|---|---|
| **Finances / Expenditure (continued)** | | | **D3 – Cost of Digital Collection Construction and Management** Direct costs (personnel, equipment, software, contracted services) to create digital materials or to convert; include expenditures related to digitization, OCR, any creation, preparation, data storage & copyright clearance; exclude costs for resources purchased externally. | |

| Element | EQUINOX | ALA | ARL | ICOLC |
|---|---|---|---|---|
| Services | **Electronic Library Services**<br>A service which is either supplied from local servers or accessible via networks. [NOTE: Electronic library services comprise the OPAC, the library website, electronic resources, electronic document delivery and internet access offered via the library.] **ISO/DIS 2789** [NOTE: referred to as ELS throughout]<br><br>**Population to be served** Number of individuals for whom the library is set up to provide its services and materials. **ISO 11620** [NOTE: For public libraries this will normally be the population of the legal service area; for academic libraries this will normally be the total of academic and professional staff plus students. Each library must decide who to include in its population to be served and this must be carefully recorded to facilitate benchmarking.] | | | |

167

| Element | EQUINOX | ALA | ARL | ICOLC |
|---|---|---|---|---|
| Services (continued) | **Target Population**<br>Groups of actual and potential users appropriate to an individual library as the object of a specific service or as the primary users of specific materials.<br>**ISO 11620**<br>[NOTE: The target population may be the population to be served by the library, a specific group within that population, or some other group that the library is aiming to serve. The target population must be defined by the library in each instance and carefully recorded to facilitate benchmarking.] | | | |

| Element | EQUINOX | ALA | ARL | ICOLC |
|---|---|---|---|---|
| Services (continued) | | **Number of virtual reference transactions (p.7)** Annual count of the number of reference transactions using the Internet. A transaction must include a question received electronically (e.g. via e-mail, WWW form, etc.) and responded to electronically (e.g. e-mail). | **U1 – Number of Electronic Reference Transactions** Number of electronic reference transactions – via e-mail, WWW form, etc | |
| | | | **P1 – Percentage of Electronic Reference Transactions of Total Reference** Percentage of annual e-reference transactions to total reference transactions; has to be electronic; exclude phone & fax; includes counts for any local or national project – DigiRef or LC's CDRS. | |
| | | **Number of virtual visits to networked library resources (p.8)** Count of visits to the library via the Internet. A visit occurs when an external user connects to a networked library resource for any length of time or purpose (regardless of the number of pages/elements viewed) | **U5 – Virtual Visits to Library's Website and Catalog** Number of client visits to the library's website or catalog from outside the physical library premises without regard to the number of pages viewed. As some may be misleading, this is an estimate only. | |

| Element | EQUINOX | ALA | ARL | ICOLC |
|---|---|---|---|---|
| **Services (continued)** | | **Number of staff hours spent servicing information technology (p.7)** Annual count of the staff hours spent in servicing information technology in public service areas based on a one-week sample. | **P2 – Percentage of Virtual Visits of All Library Visits** Number of virtual library visits out of all library visits; A virtual visit is when a client is visiting the library's website or catalog from outside the physical plant of the library; Exclude use of electronic resources; this measure is an estimate due to management issues. | |

| Element | EQUINOX | ALA | ARL | ICOLC |
|---|---|---|---|---|
| Workstations | **Library Computer Workstation**<br>Public access networked and stand alone computers, provided in the library, though not necessarily by the library, offering access to electronic library services<br><br>**PI 8: Library computer workstation (LCW) use rate**<br>The number of LCW used during a specified time period as a percentage of the number of library computer workstations provided during that time period. LCW provided includes all LCW that are on open access and in working order or otherwise available for use. | **Number of public access Internet workstations (p.7)**<br>Annual count of the number of library owned public access graphical workstations that connect to the Internet for a dedicated purpose (to access an OPAC or specific database) or multiple purposes.<br><br>**Number of public access Internet workstation users (p.7)**<br>Annual count of the number of users of all the library's graphical public access workstations connected to the Internet computed from a one-week sample.<br><br>**Maximum speed of public access Internet workstations (p.7)**<br>Indication of the maximum bandwidth of public Internet access, e.g., less than 56kbps, 128kbps, 1.5mbps, etc. | | |

| Element | EQUINOX | ALA | ARL | ICOLC |
|---|---|---|---|---|
| Workstations (continued) | **PI 9: Number of library computer workstation (LCW) hours available per member of the population to be served** The number of LCW provided by the library multiplied by the number of hours the library is open in the specified time period and divided by the total number of persons in the population to be served. The time period will normally be one week. LCW provided includes all open access LCWs that are in working order and otherwise available for use. | | | |

| Element | EQUINOX | ALA | ARL | ICOLC |
|---------|---------|-----|-----|-------|
| Usage | **PI 1: Percentage of the population reached by electronic library services**<br>The percentage of the library's total population to be served who are actually using electronic services offered by the library.<br><br>**PI 4: Number of documents and entries (records) viewed per session for each electronic library service**<br>The number of documents viewed from each ELS during a specified time period divided by the number of sessions on each service during that time period.<br><br>**Document or record viewed**<br>Any full text of a digital document or electronic resource that is uploaded, or any catalogue record or database entry that is fully displayed during a search. [NOTE: Visits to the library website are excluded.] ISO/DIS 2789 | **Number of items examined using subscription services (p.7)**<br>Count the number of views to each entire host to which the library subscribes. A view is defined as the number of full-text articles / pages, abstracts, citations, and text only, text/graphics viewed. | **D2 – Use of Library Digital Collection**<br>Number of times digital collections titles and files are accessed; number of searches conducted during reporting period.<br><br>**U4 – Number of Items Requested in Electronic Databases**<br>Number of items requested in all of the library's electronic resources. Can include journal articles, e-books, and other type of materials – may be citation, abstract, TOC, full-text. | |

| Element | EQUINOX | ALA | ARL | ICOLC |
|---|---|---|---|---|
| Usage (continued) | **PI 7: Percentage of information requests submitted electronically** The number of information requests submitted electronically during a specified time period as a percentage of the total number of information requests received during the same period.<br><br>**PI 14: User satisfaction with electronic library services** The average rating, on a five-point scale, from 1-5 with 1 as the lowest value, given by users to the library's electronic library services. | | | **Number of Menu Selections** Categorized as appropriate for the vendor's system. If display of data can be accomplished by browsing (the use of menus), this measure must be provided. (e.g. an electronic journal site provides alphabetic and subject-based menu options in addition to a search form). The number of searches and the number of alphabetic and subject menu selections should be tracked. |

| Element | EQUINOX | ALA | ARL | ICOLC |
|---|---|---|---|---|
| Usage (continued) | | **Number of full-text titles available by subscription (p.7)** Count the number of full-text titles that the library subscribes to and offers to the public computed one time annually. | **R1: Number of Electronic Full-text Journals** Number of electronic full-text journal subscriptions – by individual institution or consortia licensing. | **Number of full-content units** Examined, downloaded, or otherwise supplied to user, to the extent these recordable and controlled by the server rather than the browser. Journal articles – by journal title with ISSN and title listed. Note 2: Ebooks – by book title with ISBN and title listed. Note 3: Reference materials – by content unit appropriate to the resource (e.g., dictionary definitions, encyclopedia articles, biographies, etc.). Note 4: Non-textual resources – by file type as appropriate to resources (e.g., image, audio, video, etc.). |

| Element | EQUINOX | ALA | ARL | ICOLC |
|---|---|---|---|---|
| Usage (continued) | | **Number of database queries / searches (p.7)** Total count of the number of searches conducted in the library's online databases. Subsequent activities by users (e.g. browsing, printing) are not considered part of the search process. | **U3 – Number of Queries (Searches) in Electronic Databases** Number of user initiated queries (searches) in licensed electronic resources. Usually a search is recorded each time a search request is submitted to the server. | **Number of queries (searches)** A search is intended to represent a unique intellectual inquiry. Typically a search is recorded each time a search form is send/submitted to the server. Subsequent activities to review or browse among the records retrieved or the process of isolating the correct single item desired do not represent additional searches, unless the parameter (s) defining the retrieval set is modified through resubmission of the search form, a combination of previous search sets, or some other similar technique. Immediately repeated duplicate searches, double clicks, or other evidence indicating unintended user behavior should be counted. |

| Element | EQUINOX | ALA | ARL | ICOLC |
|---------|---------|-----|-----|-------|
| Usage (continued) | | | | **Number of menu selections** If display of data can be accomplished by browsing (the use of menus), this measure must be provided (e.g. an electronic journal site provides alphabetic and subject-based menu options in addition to a search form). The number of searches and the number of alphabetic and subject menu selections should be tracked. |

177

| Element | EQUINOX | ALA | ARL | ICOLC |
|---|---|---|---|---|
| Usage (continued) | **Information requests** Information contact that involves the knowledge or use, or recommendations, interpretation or instruction in the use of, one or more information sources (printed and non-printed materials, machine-readable databases, the library's own and other institutions' catalogues) by library staff. May also involve recommendations, interpretation or instruction in the use of such sources. Note 1: The request can be delivered personally or by means of telephone, regular mail, fax / electronic media. Note 2: It is essential that libraries do not include directional or administrative enquiries: for locating staff or facilities, regarding opening times or about handling equipment such as reader printers and computer terminals. NOTE 3: Enquiries are also excluded if asked for the purpose of locating items of stock that have already been identified bibliographically. | | | |

| Element | EQUINOX | ALA | ARL | ICOLC |
|---|---|---|---|---|
| **Session Access** | **Session**<br>An established connection to an electronic service, usually by a log-in.<br>[NOTE 1: Connecting to a website is regarded as a session if the referring link is external to the website. NOTE 2: Connections to a general entrance or gateway page should be excluded.] **ISO/DIS 2789**<br><br>**PI 2: Number of sessions on each electronic library service per member of the target population**<br>The total number of sessions on each ELS by members of the target population during a specified time period divided by the number of persons in the target population.<br><br>**Remote session**<br>Session established from outside the library building | **Number of database sessions**<br>Total count of the number of sessions (logins) initiated to the online databases. | **U2 – Number of Logins (Sessions) to Electronic Databases**<br>Number of user initiated sessions in licensed electronic resources. Starts at connection & ends with explicit termination (timeout or logout). | **Number of sessions**<br>Must be provided in order to satisfy reporting requirements of government agencies and professional organizations. ICOLC recognizes that the definition, collection, and reporting of this measure are subject to interpretation. In the stateless web environment, statistics gathered as sessions can provide only a rough indication of the number of actual sessions conducted, thus limiting the overall meaningfulness of this particular indicator. |

179

| Element | EQUINOX | ALA | ARL | ICOLC |
|---|---|---|---|---|
| **Session Access (Continued)** | **PI 3: Number of remote sessions on electronic library services per member of the population to be served**<br>The total number of sessions on ELS established from outside of the library building by members of the population to be served during a specified time period divided by the number of persons in the population to be served.<br><br>**PI 10: Rejected sessions as a percentage of total attempted sessions**<br>The number of attempted sessions on electronic library services that are rejected expressed as a percentage of the total number of attempted sessions on electronic library services. Total number of attempted sessions is calculated by adding the total number of rejected sessions and the total number of successful sessions. | | | **Number of Turnaways**<br>Peak simultaneous users, any other indicator relevant to the pricing model applied to the library and consortium. |

| Element | EQUINOX | ALA | ARL | ICOLC |
|---|---|---|---|---|
| **User Orientation & Training** | **PI 12: Number of attendances at formal electronic library service training lessons per member of the population to be served**<br>The number of attendances at formal ELS training lessons divided by the total number of persons in the population to be served. | **User information technology instruction (p.8)**<br>A count of the number of users instructed and the hours of instruction offered in the use of information technology or resources obtainable using information technology in structured, informal, and electronically delivered instruction sessions conducted or sponsored by the library) | | |
| | **PI 13: Library staff developing, managing and providing ELS and user training as a percentage of total library staff**<br>Number of library staff (full-time equivalent) providing, maintaining and developing ELS and training users expressed as a percentage of the total full-time equivalent number of library staff. | **Staff information technology instruction (p.8)**<br>Annual count of the total number of staff instructed and the number of hours of formal instruction in the management or use of information technology or resources obtainable using information technology. | | |

**Appendix 4-C**
**ISO Library Performance**
**Indicators.**

| | Resources, Accessibility, and Infrastructure | |
|---|---|---|
| **Performance Indicator** | **Source** | **Definition** |
| Number of workstation hours available per capita | TR 20983 B.1.6.1 | The number of hours that a workstation is available for a member of the population to be served during a year. Workstations reserved exclusively for the use of staff are excluded. |
| Population per public-access workstation | TR 20983 B.1.6.2 | The ratio of the population to be served to the number of publicly accessible workstations. Workstations reserved exclusively for the use of staff are excluded. Libraries may wish to calculate separately the number of workstations connected to the Internet. |
| Percentage of rejected sessions | TR 20983 B.1.3.4 | The percentage of rejected sessions of the total attempted sessions for each licensed database during a specified time period. Sessions by library staff and for user training should be included. Sessions rejected because of incorrect passwords or user IDs are not included. |

## Use

| Performance Indicator | Source | Definition |
|---|---|---|
| Number of documents downloaded per session | TR 20983 B.1.3.1 | The number of documents and entries downloaded in part or in whole from each electronic resource, divided by the number of sessions on each service during a specified time period. |
| Percentage of population reached by electronic services | TR 20983 B.1.1.1 | Use of electronic resources by library staff and for user training is included in the number of sessions, as well as in the number of documents and entries downloaded. The percentage of the population to be served who have used any of the electronic services provided by the library during a specified time period. |
| Percentage of virtual visits to total visits | TR 20983 1.3.6 | The number of visits to the library's web site from outside the library's physical premises during a specific time period, divided by the sum of the number of visits to the website and the number of physical visits to the library during the same period. |
| Percentage of remote OPAC sessions | TR 20983 B.1.3.5 | The percentage of sessions on the OPAC which originated from outside the library during a specified time period. |
| Percentage of information requests submitted electronically | TR 20983 B.1.4.1 | The number of information requests submitted electronically during a specified time period as a percentage of the total number of information requests received during the same period. |
| Workstation use rate | TR 20983 B.1.6.3 | The percentage of workstations in use at the time of investigation. Workstations exclusively for the use of staff are not included. |
| Number of user attendances at electronic service training lessons per capita | TR 20983 B.1.5.1 | The number of attendances at user training on electronic services during a specified time period, divided by the population to be served. |

(Continued)

**Appendix 4-C (Continued)**
**ISO Library Performance Indicators.**

| | Cost Efficiency | |
|---|---|---|
| **Performance Indicator** | **Source** | **Definition** |
| Cost per database session | TR 20983 B.1.3.2 | The cost of each database divided by the number of sessions during a specified period. The cost of a database is the acquisitions, subscription or licensing costs paid by the library. Pay-per-view costs are not included in this definition, as the costs per session are evident. This indicator applies only to priced databases. |
| Cost per document downloaded | TR 20983 B.1.3.3 | The costs of each electronic resource divided by the number of documents or entries downloaded in part or in whole from that electronic resource during a specified period. The cost of an electronic resource is the acquisitions, subscription or licensing cost paid by the library for that resource. "Pay per download" costs are not included in this definition as the costs per download are evident. For the purpose of this indicator, an entry in an electronic resource or database is a downloadable information entity consisting of one or more data files, the essential information usually being full text. Downloading is achieved by requesting a document from a server, usually by means of a web browser. |

## Potentials and Development

| Performance Indicator | Source | Definition |
|---|---|---|
| Percentage of expenditure on information provision spent on the electronic collection | TR 20983 B.1.2.1 | The percentage of the library's total expenditure on information provision spent on the electronic collection. The electronic collection includes digital documents, electronic serials, electronic books, and databases. Expenditure on the electronic collection-for the purpose of this indicator-includes the library's acquisition, subscription and licensing costs. As an alternative, a library might decide to include pay-per-view and electronic document delivery costs with the costs of collection building. This should be stated clearly when publishing or comparing scores. Total acquisitions expenditure would exclude expenditure on binding.Expenditure on infrastructure, such as hardware, software or networking, and on digitization of documents should not be included. Value-added taxes, sales and service taxes, or other local taxes are included. Their inclusion may affect international comparisons. |

(Continued)

**Appendix 4-C (Continued)**
**ISO Library Performance Indicators.**

| | Potentials and Development | |
|---|---|---|
| Performance Indicator | Source | Definition |
| Number of attendances at formal IT and related training lessons per staff member | TR 20983 B.3.1.1 | The number of attendances of staff members at formal IT and related training lessons, divided by the total number of library staff (number of persons, not FTE). In the sense of this indicator, IT and related training covers the development, use, and management of library-related software and hardware, and of electronic library services. Training is organized in preplanned lessons that can be held either in-house or externally and hosted by library staff or external experts. The indicator also assesses the number of attendances at training lessons. |
| Percentage of library staff providing and developing electronic services | TR 20983 B.3.2.1 | Number of library staff (FTE = full-time equivalent) planning, maintaining, providing and developing IT services and technically developing and improving the library's Web-based services, divided by the total number of library staff (FTE). Staff in information and help services, in user training dealing with electronic library services, and in content-related work on the library's Internet services are excluded. |

*Source:* International Standards Organization. (2003). *ISO/CD 11620 information and documentation-Library performance indicators technical report 20983.* Stockholm, Sweden: Swedish General Standards Institute.

# CHAPTER 5

# Needs Assessment

**Denise M. Davis**

## Networked Services: Definition and Scope

In 2001, the work of 20 individuals appeared in an edited book, *Evaluating Networked Information Services: Techniques, Policy and Issues* (McClure & Bertot). Although there had been much discussion since mid-1990 about networked information services, this was the first attempt to compile into one volume seminal work in this area. Among the issues mentioned in this book is that there was no consensus on definitions for networked services and resources, nor was there agreement on methods of measurement that reflected the use and uses of such services and resources.

In the three years since this work was published, research has continued in these areas. John Carlo Bertot, Chuck McClure, Denise Davis, Joe Ryan, Jeff Shim, and others have been working on behalf of a few organizations. The American Library Association (ALA) has introduced electronic metrics (e-metrics) into one of its surveys, the Public Library Association annual survey of its member libraries.[1] The Association of Research Libraries (ARL) introduced e-metrics into its annual Supplemental Survey of its members as part of ARL's New Measures Initiative.[2] The International Coalition of Library Consortia (ICOLC) developed core criteria for electronic metrics that have been embraced by the library and publishing communities, and upon which a variety of additional metrics have been developed.[3] The National Center for Education Statistics (NCES), through its library statistics program, has introduced core electronic metrics to its annual State Library Agency Survey, and has modified some expenditure data reporting in its annual Federal-State Cooperative Survey of Public Library Data and its biennial Academic Library Survey.[4] The National Information Standards Organization (NISO) revised its Library Statistics Standard, Z39.7, to incorporate electronic metrics. There is more about this later in this chapter, as well as in Chapter 4.[5] Project COUNTER, a collaborative project between publishers and information users to develop a code of practice, has incorporated the existing work of the authors and the U.S. and international library statistics communities.[6] And the International Organization for Standardization (ISO) accepted recommendations from the U.S. representatives to Subcommittee 8, Library Statistics, to include electronic metrics and methods of measurement to further the comparable data collection and assessment of networked services.[7] More details on each of these initiatives is available in Chapter 4.

As a result of these U.S. and international initiatives, the information community is approaching consensus on what comprises network services and resources, and the methods of measurement are aligning with reasonable consistency. Challenges remain, however, in regard to the depth of data collection and interpretation.

The scope and range of services and the measurement options allow for considerable latitude among libraries and the information community. The majority of improvement in the last four years has been in bringing the vendor and library communities closer together as to which e-metrics provide the greatest value to assessment. Although the business models for publishers, database vendors, and libraries are different, there is a middle ground of network service and resource e-metrics upon which there is agreement. The costs associated with collecting and reporting these data to and by libraries, publishers, and content vendors is significant.

At present, although basic network services and resource usage data have comparable value across library types, there is a growing division between public and academic libraries in regard to search-based usage data. In particular, more detailed usage data that feed into performance indicators are being required of publishers and database vendors by academic and special libraries. These data include subject-level search data, typically derived from the indexing of articles by keyword and subject. Although detailed data are not prevalent, Project COUNTER is working with academic and research libraries to determine the level of detail that may be required of these libraries in the future.

The extent to which the vendor-delivered e-metrics and the library-supplied e-metrics meld depends largely upon the information technology infrastructure in place at the library. Challenges remain with the comparability of metrics depending upon the infrastructure of each installation of networked service, e.g., the configuration of hardware and software upon and through which services are delivered. Please refer to the Chapter 4 material on e-metrics and performance indicators, and see Chapter 9 regarding vendor database usage statistics.

The range of terms developed over the past several years to describe and measure network services and resources is extensive. The most comprehensive list is available from the NISO Standard on Library Statistics, Z39.7, *Information Services and Use: Metrics & statistics for libraries and information providers--Data Dictionary* (http://www.niso.org/emetrics). The e-metrics compiled as of November 2003, just prior to the standard's release for voting by the NISO membership, appear in Fig. 5-1. In addition to e-metrics, standard input and output data may also be needed. These include overall and specialized staffing, expenditures, overall collection data, services including reference, and general infrastructure data (hours open, number of workstations for staff and the public, Internet service information including costs, etc.). See Chapters 7 and 8 for a discussion of evaluation frameworks and methodologies regarding e-metrics.

Methods of measurement for standard input and output metrics, as well as for e-metrics, vary—from precise counts of transaction-level data, generally collected through log file analysis, to more heuristic measures of use per typical week. Each method is reasonably valid, provided it is consistently applied. Libraries rely on publishers and vendors to do this, although some library staff are becoming better able to use the data even when it is not fully comparable. This typically occurs through labeling data transaction data and linking them to comparable traditional library transaction data, such as circulation, library use, interlibrary loan, and reserves. The importance of consistency of measurement cannot be overstated. To begin a needs assessment process without understanding the necessity for adequate and reliable input and output data only makes the process more difficult. Additional information on methods of measurement is excerpted from the NISO *Library Statistics Standard* Appendixes A and B, and appears as Figs. 5-2 and 5-3 (NISO, 2003). There is quite a number of electronic metrics to choose from, and these are the components of further work, especially by Project COUNTER and the ARL's New Measures Initiative. Many of these e-metrics have already been built into needs assessment and outcomes-based analysis activities of public, academic, and special libraries in the United States.

## Assessing Change: The Value of Needs Assessment

The purpose of any needs assessment is to understand the impact of change on an organization, in terms of both investment and value. It further helps libraries understand the short- and long-term implications of change. Through a well-designed needs assessment, libraries can identify small and large areas for continuous improvement, even if that improvement suggests ending a service.

All of the data items discussed briefly earlier in this chapter, along with those included in Chapter 9 of this book, feed into a needs assessment project. The scope of a needs assessment may be to determine the viability of a new service; to enhance, re-engineer, or discontinue an existing service; or simply to assess the impact of a service on a library's infrastructure, including staff. Don't interpret needs assessment to mean purely *need*. The *assessment* component is equally valuable. The core components of any assessment will help you understand short- and long-range requirements for developing or sustaining a service. Depending upon the depth of the assessment, it is possible to scrutinize at a micro level the value of network services and resources. This is extremely effective in understanding the true cost of network services and resources to the organization, and the value of the service to the target community being served. Chapter 6 discusses e-metrics evaluation and assessment issues, planning, and strategies.

## Components of Needs Assessment

It may be useful to think of needs assessment of networked information services as you would an onion—many layers that sometimes bring tears to your eyes. There are, however, some fairly consistent components of a needs assessment for network services and resources. These include service goals (what and why), target population (who), infrastructure (how), and implementation (how and when).

In a 1997 report prepared for the U.S. National Commission on Libraries and Information Science, Bertot and McClure outlined the core issues limiting the information community from gathering timely and reliable network statistics. In *Policy Issues & Strategies Affecting Public Libraries in the National Networked Environment: Moving Beyond Connectivity*, Bertot and McClure stated (p. 12),

> The networked environment, however, is much more complex than such data collection activities reflect. Indeed, research by the authors (Bertot & McClure, 1996) shows that a network is a multi-dimensional entity that encompasses minimally the following:
>
> • **Technical infrastructure:** The hardware, software, equipment, communication lines, and technical aspects of the network;
>
> • **Information content:** The information resources available on the network;

- **Information services:** The activities in which users can engage and the services that users may use to complete various tasks;

- **Support:** The assistance and support services provided to help users better use the network; and

- **Management:** The human resources, governance, planning, and fiscal aspects of the network. Data collection activities, therefore, must begin to reflect this multi-dimensionality of electronic networks.

Bertot and McClure further describe some data collection requirements necessary to discover networked resources extensiveness, efficiency, effectiveness, service quality, impact, usefulness, and adoption. Working from the broader perspective of service goals, target population, infrastructure, and implementation, it is important to consider elements of quality of service during the needs assessment process. The elements identified by Bertot and McClure provide a valid and reliable starting point, and they are further described in Chapter 1.

## Understanding the Service Goals

Beginning with service or resource goals may present the most effective starting point in a needs assessment. Understanding service or resource goals—the *what* and *why* of the network services and resources—helps you focus on the questions to pose while keeping the customer or end user in mind. Defining what service is currently provided, or the network service to be provided, is the first step. To do this, consider the types of network services provided.

Does your library currently provide, or plan to provide:

- Web-based connectivity and access, or access to a closed intranet (point-to-point) to subscription services or an online catalog;

- Online subscription services, including full-text content (including images), with live links to additional content (periodical databases, encyclopedias, etc.);

- Still images, either in a locally mounted database or from a source where access rights have been negotiated (photo archives, genealogy services, medical or other scientific image databases, etc.);

- Sound (audio) capabilities, either from locally provided resources or from Web-based services, and streaming video, including dimensional imaging resources; or

- Teleconferencing, including satellite feed.

The reason for thinking about the kinds of services and resources that you are making available, or plan to make available, is that they not only have service implications—indeed, they also impact the hardware, software, and telecommunications infrastructure that your library develops or enhances. This is especially the case if the library is participating in a multilibrary project as a partner or consortia member, or even a multistate networked services acquisition project.

Licensing issues must also be considered in any needs assessment. Service goals may not be met if licensing requirements limit access to or distribution of subscribed content. Other license issues arise with computer-based licensing of network software, file management software, and computer application software, including image viewers and word or data processing applications. Cost, number of users, term of license, and updates or upgrades also must be considered in the assessment.

Outsourcing of network development or support, if applicable, should be included in the assessment. Although it is generally the case that localized support will be more prevalent, and therefore may be more easily defined and assessed, outsourcing or subcontracting for services should be considered. It may be determined during the needs assessment process that economies of scale are achieved when the library contracts with another library or libraries, or a service provider, to provide technical support, acquire content or negotiate licenses, or provide long-range telecommunications support to the networked services of the library. Consortia, often not seen as an outsourcing mechanism, may play such a role. Through membership in, or participation with, a consortium of libraries it may be possible to develop networked services, or to enhance existing services in ways not possible for the individual institution. These developed services, or enhancements, may be improved by preferred pricing, or simply by the time saved in getting a service up and running. Consider these aspects of service goals during the needs assessment process.

Decision points for outsourcing include:

- Staff shortages;
- Lack of adequate technical support, and no evidence that support will become available without outsourcing;
- Economies of scale on purchasing, and network services are better supported through outside resources than through in-library resources (e.g., providing 24/7 access by moving the server to another department, agency, or service); and/or
- A mandate from library administration or a parent organization, such as what has been happening with federal and state government agencies.

Thus, there are a number of factors that can contribute to a library's decision to outsource a network service or resource.

For larger libraries, library organizations, and consortia, local content development and ongoing support will need to be part of the needs assessment of service goals. Not only does this level of input into network services content impact a range of staff, it also impacts the infrastructure of the services overall. As technology changes, local content may need enhancements to remain compatible within the improved hardware, software, and telecommunications infrastructure. This component alone requires a separate needs assessment, which then should be integrated into additional assessments. Without the necessary internal support of such content and collections, service goals will be more difficult to achieve.

## Understanding the Service or Target Population

Simple and straightforward questions need to be asked about the population served, or expected to be served, through network services and resources. Key questions include:

- **Who are the customers?** Have the customers for the service or resource changed since the service or resource was initially offered?
- **Where are the customers?** Has the location of the customers changed over time? Will developing technology affect the access point(s) or mechanism(s) of users to network services and resources?

To help address the *who* question, it is best to refer to the library's mission statement and service goals. For some libraries, the service or target population may be governmentally mandated. If the library plans to expand the service or target population, it is best to articulate that change as part of the needs assessment in order to ensure adequate gathering of anecdotal information or data to inform the process.

Table 5-1 provides a quick view of service populations by location of service, either internal or external to the library. As part of the assessment, understanding the extent to which users fall into these categories will help outline the extent of technical support users need, as well as the hardware, software, and telecommunications requirements to deliver services and resources to those users. The extent to which the library can answer questions about change, either before or during the needs assessment process, will further inform the need for enhanced service support in the technical infrastructure and information support areas of networked services. It is also important to understand the NISO Z39.7 Committee makes the distinction of internal and external users to

**Table 5-1**
**Service or target population, internal and external to library.**

| Service or Target Population | |
| --- | --- |
| **Internal to library** | **External to library** |
| In-library patrons | Eligible remote users |
| | Contact library by telephone, fax, email |
| **Both internal and external users** | |
| Educators, including teachers, faculty, administrators, students | |
| Public library staff and customers | |
| Academic library staff and customers, including faculty, administrators, and staff from partner institutions (consortium members, etc.) | |
| Special (staff, researchers, doctors, lawyers, etc.) | |

demonstrate that some internal use assumes anyone can use a service or networked resource from within the library building. It may be the case that a particular library's contract restricts use, and that restriction should be identified during the assessment process so as to determine the full extent of providing services to target populations.

## Understanding the Infrastructure that Supports Networked Services

One of the most significant elements in determining the extent to which libraries are able to gather the necessary data to undertake a needs assessment of network services and resources is the hardware and software infrastructure of the network itself. In 1996–1997 the notion of *redeployment of library resources* was already being analyzed nationally. In two independent studies, one by Bertot, McClure & Zweizig (1996) and another by Bertot & McClure (1997), the researchers reported figures from public library information technology (IT) budgets that reflected an increase in expenditures for Internet-related costs of more than 10 percent between 1996 and 1997. The authors noted that libraries were anticipating annual IT cost increases of more than 5 percent. Among the categories of network services and IT-related expenditures reported, libraries anticipated seeing continued cost increases for hardware, software, telecommunications fees, facilities upgrades, training, content and resource development, program planning and management, staffing, and maintenance. Something that has changed little since the 1996–1997 studies is the flat or contracting level of library budgets. Libraries have not seen significant increases in operating budgets, and their ability to maintain acquisition levels and service levels has negatively impacted overall expenditures for network services and resources, as well as other library services.

Within this context, Bertot and McClure suggest five areas of infrastructure assessment:

1. *Hardware and software* includes all the computers, printers, servers, and desktop or network software that the library has in place, or expects to acquire. Assessment of hardware and software needs entails not only identifying the expenditures for acquiring new computers, servers, or software, but also the costs associated with the existing hardware and software. To the extent that you can identify and cost out the existing hardware and software environment, the easier it will be to describe and assess future needs. The library may wish to isolate staff from public-access computers, especially if funds allocated to purchase hardware and software were specifically targeted to one or the other, such as the Bill and Melinda Gates Foundation grants.

2. *Telecommunications support* refers to any Internet or network service support the library pays for. This support may be in-house, from library paid staff or contract staff assigned to the library—which may be the case with universities with centralized IT support to departments, or with public or school libraries that rely on city, county, or district IT support. Typically, this represents staff support, but it may also include technical support to remote or virtual users of the library services.

3. *Remote and local access* is an area of assessment in which it may be difficult to derive adequate or accurate data to assess. Generally, the library either supports or wishes to support in-library, in-network (a campus network, a city or county government network, etc.), or remote or out-of-network access. The ability to identify adequate and accurate data on access to library networked services is determined by the network design and the presence of data log files for the services. Generally, libraries use commercial transaction log software (e.g., *eIQ LogAnalyzer, WebLog,* or *Analog*) or program transaction log compilers to collect the number of users to various library networked services and the Internet Protocol (IP) address from which the request originated. By doing this, libraries can sort network use by local users (on a campus or within local government) from the remote user coming to the library services from a commercial Internet Service Providers (ISP). In addition to getting log transaction files locally, libraries may also have these data reported by the ISP or the database vendor under contract to deliver content to the library, such as Proquest,

OCLC, Elsevier, etc. These logs are typically user-authentication logs to the services provided by the publisher or vendor. Once the user is successfully logged on to a service, additional use data are available from vendors regarding searches, full-text views of the content, etc., as outlined in Fig. 5-1. Examples of transaction logs are available in Chapter 8, as well as on the book's companion website, http://www.ii.fsu.edu/neteval.

4. *Staffing* is one of the more critical areas of the needs assessment. The presence of, or access to, qualified staff to develop and maintain the infrastructure of networked service, both technical and content, is essential. Areas of staff assessment include the number of staff, whether they are library staff or contract, the number of hours assigned to support networked services, and the annual cost of staffing.

5. *Building and facility* are the brick-and-mortar aspects of the assessment. This category includes furniture, network telecommunications wiring or wireless infrastructure, electricity, lighting, and similar components of the building. The authors have positioned the assessment of network telecommunications wiring or wireless infrastructure in this category, because installing or upgrading it is as much about the building as it is about the hardware and software.

Together, these areas are the core infrastructure that requires consideration in a network service and resource needs assessment process.

### Understanding Implementation

It is often joked that you should multiply a project timeline by three to more accurately estimate project completion. This is certainly the case with network services and resources. It is one thing to design on paper a network services or resources implementation and quite another thing to actually do it. Areas of assessment already described assist in developing the tools to assess need. These categories of assessment are also focus points in the design and implementation of network services and resources.

The authors recommend that libraries establish teams to accomplish the work required in a needs assessment. Representation from the various areas of the library under review is best—public service, selection or acquisitions, IT, administration (including the budget analyst and the facilities manager), and representatives from any branch libraries participating in the assessment.

Remember that you must answer the *what, why, who,* and *how* of the implementation. An early question to ask, after the initial needs assessment is complete, is which components of networked services will be managed internally and which will be outsourced. Outsourcing is not such a negative concept as it once was. It may be in the best interest of the library to contract for support, rather than to absorb the start-up and ongoing staff and training costs required to maintain certain services. Facility, infrastructure, staffing, training (staff and the public), individual library projects, consortia projects, and statewide or multistate projects are all components of implementation that need to be assessed. Keeping the network services and resources project operational is another area of assessment. The extent to which the library has control over staffing and services will impact the assessment. This is the case whether the project is fully supported within the individual library or system, or if the project depends upon cooperative participation, as may be the case in a consortium or other partner project.

## Methods of Assessment

This section presents methods associated with conducting network service and resource needs assessment activities. Chapter 3 presents methods for assessing network services and resources in general.

A variety of methods have been used successfully to solicit user expectation and get feed-back on new library services. These include questionnaires and surveys, administered with direct human contact with the user or through Web-based pop-up survey instruments. One approach has been to position Web-based surveys at the end of searches, or e-mail them to users within a certain interval of time after network service or resource use. The ability to target surveys to specific users requires an infrastructure that captures user identification information and can link it to a patron record. Although this method more accurately targets any user, whether in-library or remote, it may be more difficult for smaller libraries to implement. The author suggests reviewing the Association of Research Libraries project on service quality measures, LibQUAL™, to learn more about methods of targeted user surveys (http://www.libqual.org).

Internal analysis of staffing and expenditures is a necessary component of networked services needs assessment. For some libraries, staffing level and expenditure information is readily available. In other cases, it may take more time to determine full-time equivalent (FTE) staffing levels due to outsourced work or staff that are a shared resource in or to the library. Remember to report staffing figures in terms of full-time equivalents (e.g., 3.5 FTE). This allows you to deal more effectively with resource analysis. Rather than focusing on hours of staff time spent supporting networked services, the focus is on total staff involved. Expenditure data may also be difficult to collect, especially if you are comparing start-up costs with current costs. The years between start-up and today may mean those figures are more difficult to locate. Another expenditure that may be difficult to derive is for shared networked services. Remember to report expenditure data in whole units of currency, e.g., dollars. You will find rounding up to the next dollar makes the process easier to manage. Also, convert expenditures to the library's primary unit of currency.

Usage logs, which may include transaction log analysis, internal and vendor-provided logs, user sign-ups to use networked services, staff logs of information, and reference transactions associated with networked services, are all important data for the needs assessment. The extent to which these data cover a period of time, especially years, will aid in developing the parameters of the assessment.

Additional information about methods of measurement and definitions, beyond those noted in Figs. 5-1, 5-2 and 5-3, are available from the National Information Standards Organization standard Z39.7-2002, Library Statistics, at http://www.niso.org/emetrics.

## Planning Calendar

In developing a planning calendar for undertaking a needs assessment for networked services, it is important to identify independent activities and concurrent activities of the project. For instance, if the library is undertaking a full-scale needs assessment of its networked services, and those services include four facilities with a total of 11 service sites, 17 staff, and 24 subscription products under review, there will be segments of the assessment that can go on independently of others. Using this example, Fig. 5-4 outlines the independent and concurrent activities.

In this example, the library system has a centralized human resources department in the main library that will determine employee cost based on independent analysis of FTEs per library. The main library pays for all hardware and software, telecommunications, and furniture, except for Library 4, which has a departmental lab in the library. IT staff at the main library will work with staff at Library 4 to determine expenditures for hardware, software, and furniture. The library system also has centralized materials acquisition that will determine database expenditures based on concurrent analysis of database access. The date completed should be reasonable and achievable, while keeping in mind the ultimate deadline for the assessment.

Building on the planning grid in Figs. 5-4, 5-6 and 5-7 provide additional detail on categories of needs assessment. These are meant to help you begin to articulate elements of needs assessment and are not comprehensive.

## Service Goals

Library XYZ is the only library on a small liberal arts campus in upstate Wisconsin. The library is part of a regional resource-sharing network, and is a member of a statewide consortium that purchases databases for its members. Library XYZ has decided to undertake an 18-month needs assessment process to improve networked services.

Library XYZ has three service goals: Goal 1 is to increase the use of existing networked services; Goal 2 is to increase staff support of user training; and Goal 3 is to provide after-hours user support. Needs assessment tasks identified for Goal 1 appear in Fig. 5-5.

A component of needs assessment in Fig. 5-5 is materials evaluation, with the purpose of reapportioning funds to improve content delivered within the library's networked services. Figure 5-6 outlines possible steps in conducting a networked services content evaluation and acquisition analysis.

Two components of the overall needs assessment process are implementation planning and equipment life-cycle issues. From the surveys and focus groups, the library has determined the key areas for improving networked services. Included in any modification of networked services is an implementation plan, within which equipment life-cycle issues should be addressed. Figure 5-7 presents some key issues to consider.

## Conclusion

Assessment of networked services is being mainstreamed with the regular evaluation of overall library services. The author presented in this chapter a *tool kit* of assessment resources offering a range of baseline methods and models. These methods of assessment are further reinforced and enhanced by the continued integration of e-metrics into a range of surveys, including those supported by the ALA and ARL, and the NCES-sponsored surveys of public, academic, and state libraries. In addition to U.S. efforts in assessing networked services, there is worldwide attention paid to the subject through the work of the ISO and publisher initiatives such as Project COUNTER. The combined value of the continued improvement of such methods and analysis and the integration of e-metrics into regularized surveys of libraries contributes to more reliable data reporting and more replicable assessment models in the future.

**Figure 5-1**

NISO Standard Z39.7–E-metrics summary.

| E-metric | Detailed E-metric | Definition |
|---|---|---|
| **Collections** | *# Full text titles available by subscription* | Number of titles. |
| | *# E-book titles available by subscription* | Number of E-book titles. |
| **Units/ Records Examined** | | Content in the electronic collection that is delivered to a user. The sub-categories that follow provide for a detailed breakdown by type of content delivered (full-content unit, or descriptive record) and system delivering the content (Library Collection, Commercial Service or OPAC). Note: Please see 7.6: Loans and Document Delivery. |
| | *Library Collection Full-Content Units Examined* | Number of full-content units from library electronic collection examined, downloaded, or otherwise supplied to a user. Exclude OPAC or commercial services (i.e., online databases). |
| | *Commercial Services Full-Content Units Examined* | Number of subscription service full-content units examined, downloaded, or otherwise supplied to user, to the extent that these are recordable and controlled by the server rather than the browser. (ICOLC Guidelines, December 2001). Note 1: Journal articles–by journal title with ISSN and title listed. Note 2: Ebooks–by book title with ISBN and title listed. Note 3: Reference materials–by content unit appropriate to the resource (e.g, dictionary definitions, encyclopedia articles, biographies, etc.). Note 4: Nontextual resources– by file type as appropriate to resources (e.g, image, audio, video, etc.). (ICOLC Guidelines, December 2001). |
| | *Library Collection Descriptive Records Examined* | Number of descriptive records concerning the library's electronic collection delivered to a user. Note 1: Determined by the record type appropriate to the resource, e.g, abstract, archive, index. Note 2: Exclude OPAC or commercial services (i.e., online databases). |

(Continued)

Figure 5-1 (Continued)

NISO Standard Z39.7–E-metrics summary.

| E-metric | Detailed E-metric | Definition |
|---|---|---|
| | *Commercial Services Descriptive Records Examined 7.9.1.* | Number of descriptive records concerning the library's commercial services delivered to a user. Note 1: Determined by the record type appropriate to the resource, e.g., abstract, archive, index. Note 2: Exclude OPAC or library collection descriptive records (i.e., library website services and collections). |
| | *OPAC Descriptive Records Examined* | Number of descriptive records from the library's online catalog delivered to a user. Note 1: Exclude commercial services or library collection descriptive records (i.e., library website services and collections). |
| **Searches/ Menu Selections (Queries)** | | A search is defined as intending to represent a unique intellectual inquiry, whether conducted through a search form submitted to the server or through the use of menu selections (e.g., browsing a list of subjects). |
| | *Library Collection Searches (Queries)* | A search is defined as intending to represent a unique intellectual inquiry. Typically a search is recorded every time a search request is submitted to the server. (ISO 2789, Annex A) Note 1: Limited to library electronic collection services. Note 2: Exclude spider/crawler searches. Note 3: Include menu selection searches. Note 4: Excludes OPAC searches. |
| | *Commercial Services Searches (Queries)* | A search is defined as intending to represent a unique intellectual inquiry. Typically a search is recorded every time a search request is submitted to the server. (ISO 2789, Annex A) Note 1: Limited to commercial services. Note 2: Mistyped search strings do not represent unique intellectual inquiries. Note 3: Exclude spider/crawler searches. Note 4: Include menu selection searches. |
| | *OPAC Searches (Queries)* | A search is defined as intending to represent a unique intellectual inquiry. Typically a search is recorded every time a search request is submitted to the server. (ISO 2789, Annex A) Note 1: Limited to the library online catalog service. Note 2: Exclude spider/crawler searches. Note 3: Include menu selection searches. |

(Continued)

**Figure 5-1 (Continued)**

**NISO Standard Z39.7–E-metrics summary.**

| E-metric | Detailed E-metric | Definition |
|---|---|---|
| | **# Virtual reference transactions** | Number of transactions. |
| | **# Virtual visits to networked library resources** | Number of resources. |
| **Sessions** | | A session is defined as a successful request of an online service or library's online catalog. It is one cycle of user activities that typically starts when a user connects to the service or database and ends by terminating activity that is either explicit (by leaving the service through exit or log-out) or implicit (timeout due to user inactivity). |
| | **OPAC Sessions** | A session is defined as a successful request of the library's online catalog. It is one cycle of user activities that typically starts when a user connects to the OPAC and ends by terminating activity in the OPAC that is either explicit (by leaving the database through log-out or exit) or implicit (timeout due to user inactivity). (ISO 2789, Annex A; modified to exclude commercial services). Note 1: In some cases, e.g. OPAC use inside the library, several users one after the other might make use of the same workstation, and sessions could not be separated. In most systems, a session is cut off after a specified time of non-use, thus avoiding part of the problem. The average timeout setting would be 30 minutes. If another timeout period is used this should be reported. Browser or proxy cashing will be likely to reduce the number of requests registered in logfiles. |

(Continued)

**Figure 5-1 (Continued)**

| NISO Standard Z39.7–E-metrics summary. | | |
|---|---|---|
| E-metric | Detailed E-metric | Definition |
| | *Commercial Services Sessions* | A session is defined as a successful request of a commercial service (e.g., online database). It is one cycle of user activities that typically starts when a user connects to a database and ends by terminating activity in the database that is either explicit (by leaving the database through log-out or exit) or implicit (timeout due to user inactivity). (ISO 2789, Annex A, modified to exclude OPAC sessions). Note 1: For multiple databases compiling several individual databases, further information should be provided as to the separate databases hosted. Note 2: In some cases, e.g., database use inside the library, several users one after the other might make use of the same workstation, and sessions could not be separated. In most systems, a session is cut off after a specified time of nonuse, thus avoiding part of the problem. The average timeout setting would be 30 minutes. If another timeout period is used this should be reported. Browser or proxy caching will be likely to reduce the number of requests registered in log files. |
| | *Rejected Sessions (Turnaways)* | A rejected session (turnaway) is defined as an unsuccessful log-in to an electronic service by exceeding the simultaneous user limit. (ISO 2789, Annex A) Note: Failure of log-in because of wrong passwords is excluded. |
| | *Virtual Visits* | A user's request of the library website from outside the library premises, regardless of the number of pages or elements viewed. (ISO 2789, 3.3.25) Excludes website visits from within the library. Note: This statistic is the equivalent of a session for a library's website. As such, there is a need to exclude various actions (e.g., hits, downloads) by users during any given visit. |
| | *Public service time spent servicing information technology* | Time spent. |

(Continued)

Figure 5.1 (Continued)

NISO Standard Z39.7–E-metrics summary.

| E-metric | Detailed E-metric | Definition |
|---|---|---|
| | *Formal user information technology instruction* | Number of instructions. |
| | *Point-of-use information technology instruction* | Number of instructions. |
| Hardware | *# Public-access workstations* | Number of workstations. |
| | *# Public-access workstation users* | Number of workstation users. |
| | *Maximum speed of public-access Internet workstations* | Range of speeds (dial-up, T-1, T-3, etc.). |

(Continued)

**Figure 5.1 (Continued)**

## NISO Standard Z39.7–E-metrics summary.

Figure 1 shows the data on use of the library's electronic services that are considered necessary and useful for collection by libraries.

| | From inside the library | From elsewhere inside the institution | From outside the institution |
|---|---|---|---|
| Number of sessions, OPAC | X | X | X |
| Number of sessions, commercial services | X | X | X |
| Number of rejected sessions (turnaways) | X | X | X |
| Number of searches (queries), library collection | X | X | X |
| Number of searches (queries), commercial services | X | X | X |
| Number of searches (queries), OPAC | X | X | X |
| Number of units/records examined, library collection full-content units | X | X | X |
| Number of units/records examined, commercial services full-content units | X | X | X |
| Number of units/records examined, library collection descriptive records | X | X | X |
| Number of units/records examined, commercial services descriptive records | X | X | X |
| Number of units/records examined, OPAC descriptive records | X | X | X |
| Number of virtual visits | | X | X |
| Number of menu selections | | X | X |
| Number of virtual reference transactions | X | X | X |

**Figure 5-2**
**Excerpts from NISO Z39.7 Appendix A: Methods of Measurement.**

### Expenditures

Report funds expended by the library in the fiscal year being measured (regardless of when received) from its regular budget and from all other sources; e.g., research grants, special projects, gifts and endowments, and fees for services. If items in this section are not paid from the library budget but can be easily identified in other parts of the institution's budget, report them here. Expenditures should be reported for the 12-month period which corresponds to your library's fiscal year between the calendar period June 1 to September 30. All expenditures should be reported in whole dollars in the most appropriate category to provide an unduplicated count of expenditures. DO NOT REPORT ANY EXPENDITURES MORE THAN ONCE.

### Gate Count in a Typical Week

Report the number of persons who physically enter library facilities in a typical week. It is understood that a single person may be counted more than once.

### Hours Open in a Typical Week

Report an unduplicated count of hours open in a typical week for both main library and branches using the following method. If a library is open from 9 a.m. to 5 p.m., Monday through Friday, it should report 40 hours per week. If several of its branches are also open during those hours, the figure remains 40 hours per week. Should Branch A also be open one evening from 7:00 to 9:00, the total hours during which users can find service becomes 42. If Branch B is open the same hours on the same evening, the total remains 42, but if it is open two hours on another evening, or from 5:00 to 7:00 on the evening when Branch A is open later, the total becomes 44 hours during which users can find service.

### Infrastructure Measurements

Infrastructure measurements are related to the following categories: 5.1 Gross Measured Area ; 5.2 Net Usable Area ; 5.3 Net Usable Area by Function ; 5.4 Physical Facilities, 5.4.1 Mobile Facilities, 5.4.2 Physical Facilities; 5.5 Seating Capacity ; 5.6 Workstations, 5.6.1 Available Workstations, 5.6.2 Available Internet Workstations. Methods of measurement within these categories include square footage, linear feet, cubic feet, and physical item count. The FSCS survey of public library data reports square footage of facilities, and a definition is available from the NCES website. The U. S. National Archives & Records Administration (NARA) and the Society of American Archivists (SAA) provide useful information on these methods. NARA has developed a Lifecycle Data Requirements Guide for their internal use.

(Continued)

**Figure 5-2 (Continued)**
Excerpts from NISO Z39.7 Appendix A: Methods of Measurement.

**Infrastructure Measurements**

To request guidance from NARA on methods of measuring collection size, capacity, and the like, please submit a question to them through the "Contact NARA" link at http://www.archives.gov/global_pages/contact_us.html. Additionally, refer to the Glossary for Archivists, Manuscript Curators, and Records Managers, Lewis J. Bellardo and Lynn Carlin. This edition is currently available for purchase from the SAA website at http://www.archivists.org/catalog/. A revision is underway and will be online and searchable from the SAA website. The anticipated publication date is 2004.

**Reference Transactions in a Typical Week**

Report the total number of reference transactions in a typical week. A reference transaction is an information contact that involves the knowledge, use, commendation, interpretation, or instruction in the use of one or more information sources by a member of the library staff. Information sources include printed and non-printed materials, machine-readable databases (including assistance with computer searching), catalogs and other holdings records, and, through communication or referral, other libraries and institutions, and persons both inside and outside the library. Include information and referral services. If a contact includes both reference and directional services, it should be reported as one reference transaction. When a staff member utilizes information gained from a previous use of information sources to answer a question, report as a reference transaction, even if the source is not consulted again during this transaction. Duration should not be an element in determining whether a transaction is a reference transaction.

**Total Annual Number of Items Examined Using Subscription Services**

Count the number of views to each vendor subscription (OCLC, Gale, etc.) to which the library subscribes. A view is defined as the number of full-text articles/pages, abstracts, citations, and text only or text/graphics viewed.

**Total Annual Number of Database Queries/Searches**

Total count of the number of searches conducted in the library's online databases. Subsequent activities by users [e.g., browsing, printing] are not considered part of the search process. Check with your database vendor for this data.

(Continued)

**Figure 5-2 (Continued)**
**Excerpts from NISO Z39.7 Appendix A: Methods of Measurement.**

### Total Circulation

The total annual circulation of all library materials of all types, including renewals. Note: Count all materials in all formats that are charged out for use outside the library. Interlibrary loan transactions included are only items borrowed for users.

### Total Full-Time Equivalent Employees (FTE)

Report the number of filled or temporarily vacant FTE positions paid from funds under library control during the Fall of the fiscal year being reported. To compute FTEs of part-time employees and student assistants, take the TOTAL number of hours worked per week by part-time employees IN EACH CATEGORY and divide it by the number of hours CONSIDERED BY THE REPORTING LIBRARY TO BE A FULL-TIME WORK WEEK (e.g., 60 hours per week of part-time work divided by 40 hours per full-time week equals 1.50 FTE). Data should be reported to two decimal places.

### Total Number of Materials Held at End of Fiscal Year

Report the total number of each category held at the end of the fiscal year. To get this figure, take the total number held at the end of the previous fiscal year, add the number added during the fiscal year just ended, and subtract the number withdrawn during that period.

### Total Unduplicated Population of Legal Service Areas

This is the total unduplicated population of those areas in your state that receive library services. The population of unserved areas is not included in this figure. Note: A state's actual total population of legal service areas may be different.

### Typical Week

A typical week is a time that is neither unusually busy nor unusually slow. Avoid holidays, vacation periods, and days when unusual events are taking place in the community or in the library. Choose a week in which the library is open its regular hours.

(Continued)

**Figure 5-2 (Continued)**
**Excerpts from NISO Z39.7 Appendix A: Methods of Measurement.**

| |
|---|
| **E-metrics** |
| Four core datasets have been identified which should, if possible, be collected for all services—separately for each service as well as summed for all services: |
| ■ Number of sessions; |
| ■ Number of searches (queries); |
| ■ Number of units or descriptive records examined (including downloads); and |
| ■ Number of virtual visits. |
| In addition to these core datasets that provide basic information on the use of electronic services, some additional data have been found relevant and should be collected when possible and appropriate: |
| ■ Number of rejected sessions (turnaways); |
| ■ Number of menu selections; and |
| ■ Number of virtual reference transactions. |
| All data refer to the use of the library collection, the library's website, the OPAC, and Internet access via the library—not to users' accessing documents on the Internet that are publicly available and free via the Internet access in the library. |
| **Sessions** |
| A session is defined as a successful request of a database or the OPAC. It is one cycle of user activities that typically starts when a user connects to a database or the OPAC and ends by terminating activity in the database or OPAC that is either explicit (by leaving the database through log-out or exit) or implicit (timeout due to user inactivity) (see ISO 2789, 3.3.21 and Annex A)   Note: For multiple databases compiling several individual databases, further information should be provided as to the separate databases hosted. In some cases, e.g., OPAC use inside the library, several users one after the other might make use of the same workstation, and sessions could not be separated. In most systems, a session is cut off after a specified time of nonuse, thus avoiding part of the problem. The average timeout setting would be 30 minutes. If another timeout period is used this should be reported. Browser or proxy caching will be likely to reduce the number of requests registered in log files. |
| (Continued) |

209

Figure 5-2 (Continued)
Excerpts from NISO Z39.7 Appendix A: Methods of Measurement.

**Sessions**

**Rejected Sessions (Turnaways)**

A rejected session (turnaway) is defined as an unsuccessful log-in to an electronic service by exceeding the simultaneous user limit (see ISO 2789, 3.3.17 and Annex A) Note: Failure of log-in because of wrong passwords is excluded. The number of sessions exceeding the simultaneous user limit cannot always be differentiated from other rejections, e.g., missing or mistyped passwords.

**Document Downloaded**

Full text of a document or part of a document in the electronic collection that is delivered to a user. (ISO 2789, 3.3.3)

**Documents or Records Viewed**

Some electronic services (e.g., OPAC, reference database) do not typically require downloading, as simply viewing documents (abstracts, titles) is normally sufficient for users' needs. Viewing documents is defined as having the full text of a digital document or electronic resource downloaded, or having any catalog record or database entry fully displayed during a search. (ISO 2789, Annex A). Note: Documents viewed and downloading transactions can be compared to the following steps in the traditional use of open-access collections: browsing at the shelves and taking documents to a working place or to the issue desk.

**Number of Menu Selections**

Number of user-initiated searches through the use of alphabetic and subject menu selections. (ICOLC) Note: Categorized as appropriate for the vendor systems, if display data can be accomplished by browsing (e.g., the use of menus).

**Number of Searches (Queries)**

A search is defined as intending to represent a unique intellectual inquiry. Typically, a search is recorded every time a search request is submitted to the server (see 2789, 3.3.20 and Annex A) [applies to licensed database services] Note: Mistyped search strings do not represent unique intellectual inquiries. In practice, however, libraries will have difficulty differentiating these unintended searches from intended, but unsuccessful searches. Also, libraries will need to exclude spider/crawler searches.

(Continued)

**Figure 5-2 (Continued)**
Excerpts from NISO Z39.7 Appendix A: Methods of Measurement.

| **Full-Content Units Examined (licensed resources)** |
| --- |
| Number of full-content units examined, downloaded, or otherwise supplied to users, to the extent that these are recordable and controlled by the server rather than the browser. (ICOLC Guidelines, December 2001). Note:(1) Journal articles–by journal title with ISSN and title listed; (2) E-books – by book title with ISBN and title listed; (3) Reference materials–by content unit appropriate to the resource (e.g., dictionary definitions, encyclopedia articles, biographies, etc.); (4) Nontextual resources–by file type as appropriate to resources (e.g., image, audio, video, etc.). (ICOLC Guidelines, December 2001 |
| **Total Annual Virtual Visits to Networked Library Resources** |
| A visit occurs when an external user connects to a networked library resource for any length of time or purpose [regardless of the number of pages or elements viewed]. Examples of a networked library resource include a library OPAC or a library web page. In the case of a user visit to a library website, a user who looks at 16 pages and 54 graphic images registers one visit on the Web server. |
| **Number of Public-Access Workstations** |
| Annual count of the total number of library-owned public- access graphical workstations that connect to the Internet for a dedicated purpose (to access an OPAC or special database) or multiple purposes. Collect and report this statistic for each participating branch, if applicable. (Branch Level Statistic). Computers in computer labs used for public instruction, if graphical and connected to the Internet, should be counted. Public-access graphical workstations that connect to the Internet and that are used by both staff and the public should be counted, if the workstation is used by the public for at least half of the hours during an average week that the library is open to the public. Reference desk computers used by staff to assist the public should not be counted. |

(Continued)

**Figure 5-2 (Continued)**
**Excerpts from NISO Z39.7 Appendix A: Methods of Measurement.**

## Number of Public-Access Workstation Users

Annual count of the number of users of all of the library's graphical public-access workstations connected to the Internet, computed from a one-week sample. (Branch Level Statistic). Note: Select a one-week period during the test period. One week equals the number of hours the library is open over a consecutive seven-day period. Note: Data may be collected for more than one week and averaged, but report this change in procedure when submitting the data to the project website. Count each user that uses the graphical public access workstations connected to the Internet, regardless of the amount of time spent on the computer. A user who uses the library's workstations three times a week would count as three users in the count. Internet use includes all types of usage including WWW, e-mail, telnet, chat, etc. The study team recognizes the potential difficulty of determining whether a user on a multipurpose (CD-ROM access, word processing, etc.) workstation is using the Internet. Do not include staff use of these workstations. Obtain a total figure of users for the week (or an average weekly use figure if you counted users over a two-week period) and report that number for each participating branch, if applicable. If you collect the user data over a two-week period, for example, and during the first week 70 users were counted and 80 users were counted the second week, then the average number of users would be 75 (obtained and reported by adding week one's users to week two's [70 + 80 = 150] and dividing by the number of weeks surveyed [150÷2 = 75]).

## Virtual Reference Transactions

Virtual reference transactions conducted via e-mail, website, or other network-based medium designed to support virtual reference. (ARL E-metrics; Bertot, McClure, Ryan). Combined definition to create a new one. Note: Include a question either received or responded to electronically.

**Figure 5-3**
Excerpts from NISO Z39.7 Appendix B: Measuring the Use of Electronic Library Services, B.2 and B.3

| B.2. Issues of Measuring the Electronic Collection |
|---|
| In contrast to conventional resources, electronic resources often have no physical form and boundaries, and this will affect the measurement of both collection and use. For example: |
| ■ Documents can consist of several files or elements (text, image, multimedia), and be embedded in Web frames. Also the same document may look different when viewed through different Web browsers. Furthermore, the contents of electronic resources (whether individual full texts or those in databases) can undergo changes over time. Uniform Resource Identifiers (URI) are becoming more widespread and support the clear identification of documents. |
| ■ Databases can be configured to combine and sort information so that every search command may constitute a new object (document). Active Server Page (ASP) technology, for example, allows the generation of a Web page out of a number of database entries upon each request. These cannot be counted as documents prior to their generation, and it is difficult to measure use. |
| ■ As abstract and indexing, full-text, and other databases begin to merge into complex database products, it becomes increasingly difficult to differentiate between them. Therefore subdivision is only proposed as an optional measure in Annex B. In the future, many differences between electronic serials and full-text databases will be likely to diminish as well. A precise count of their number will therefore become difficult. |
| ■ Many resources (electronic serials, databases, or digital documents) can be accessed free on the Internet, and libraries may catalog and index some of these. This is dealt with in the main standard (see ISO 2789, 6.2.14). |

| B.3. Issues of Measuring Use |
|---|
| Communication on the Internet can be described as stateless and transaction-based. Each Web server will record some significant parameters of these transactions. Depending on individual settings, the statistical information will be gathered in one or more *log files*. In their standard setting—called Common Log file Format (CLF)—seven basic parameters are recorded. Among these are the requesting IP address (unique Internet Protocol number attached to each Internet computer); authentication information; a time stamp; the transfer success status; and the transfer volume. The CLF can be extended by two more parameters, i.e., the referring link and the computer's browser and operating system. Log files therefore only collect statistical data on transactions between Internet computers; time-based data (e.g., search time, or time of document or resource exposure) can only be assessed if Web log mining tools are being operated to analyze site or server traffic. |

(Continued)

213

**Figure 5-3 (Continued)**
**Excerpts from NISO Z39.7 Appendix B: Measuring the Use of Electronic Library Services, B.2 and B.3**

In order not to affect the usability of electronic collections, libraries rarely implement personal authentication. Use by members of the population to be served, however, can only be determined if some identification information is being recorded. For the purpose of measurement, a request is therefore regarded as being originated by a member of the population to be served if the IP address belongs to the library or institution/legal service area. The access to paid-for electronic library services (e.g., acquired or licensed databases, serials, etc.) is usually authenticated for lists or blocks of IP addresses. It must therefore be presumed that members of the population to be served will have originated all successful requests. Requests of free services (e.g., OPAC and library website), however, are impossible to validate in total. While access from inside the institution (identified by IP addresses) is assumed to originate from members of the population, remote use (e.g., from computers at home) will generally be anonymous. Furthermore, individual IP addresses using the same proxy server will not be recognizable, because only the IP address of the proxy will be recorded in the log file.

At the time of this writing a wide range of software tools are available to extract and analyze descriptive statistical information from log files, and a number of online statistics suppliers offer professional guidance in collecting and presenting log data. It must be recognized, however, that the quality and precision of statistics for web-based electronic collections will vary in a number of areas:

- Many paid-for electronic collections must be accessed on remote (supplier) servers. Although an increasing number of suppliers nowadays present use statistics of electronic resources in accordance with a variety of guidelines (including ICOLC and others), libraries are dependent on suppliers for the completeness and quality of the data made available to them, and results are difficult to compare.

- Most Internet providers use proxy servers, and users can activate local cache files in their browsers to store copies of documents that have previously been accessed. In a proxy server environment, repeat requests for a document are supported within caches/proxies instead of through the document server, thereby shortening the time of transmission. Because these requests will not reach the document server, no statistical entry will be recorded in the log file, and the number of requests counted will underestimate the amount of real use. Individual browser cache settings can add more complication, however, because some professional web analysis tools—many of them developed to measure web advertising—can induce computers to ignore the stored copy and instead newly request the document.

- Not all requests of a page can be regarded as use: search engines will usually request websites for indexing purposes, and library website administrators will access their pages because most of them are subject to frequent maintenance. The number of requests counted will therefore overestimate the amount of real use. These entries can be removed if the requesting IP address is being recorded in the file. If no automatic filtering is available, the total count must be diminished manually by these page requests.

214

**Figure 5-4**
**Needs assessment—independent and concurrent activities.**

| Assessment category | Library 1 (Main) | | | Library 2 (branch) | | | Library 3 (branch) | | | Library 4 (branch) | | |
|---|---|---|---|---|---|---|---|---|---|---|---|---|
| | Independent | Concurrent | Date | Independent | Concurrent | Date | Independent | Concurrent | Date | Independent | Concurrent | Date |
| Staffing (FTE) | x | | MM/DD/YR | x | | | x | | | x | | |
| Databases (24) | x | | | x | | | x | | | x | | |
| User input, questionnaire | x | | | x | | | x | | | x | | |
| Focus groups | x | | | x | | | x | | | x | | |
| Database exit survey | x | | | NA | | | NA | | | x | | |
| **Expenditures** | | | | | | | | | | | | |
| Staffing | x | | | NA | | | NA | | | NA | | |
| Hardware/software | x | | | NA | | | NA | | | x | | |
| Telecom | x | | | NA | | | NA | | | | x | |
| Furniture | x | | | NA | | | NA | | | | | |
| Utilities | x | | | | | | | | | | | |
| Databases | x | | | | | | | | | | | |
| Memberships (OCLC, consortia, etc.) | x | | | | | | | | | | | |

Figure 5-5
**Sample service goals task table.**

| Goal 1: Increase use of existing networked services | | | | |
|---|---|---|---|---|
| Assessment Components | Resources Required | Cost | Completion Date | Library Considerations |
| Conduct user surveys to evaluate the value of current networked services to the customer. | Assign two staff to develop survey. Staff from public services and IT. | Staff, no added cost. Reduce desk schedule to accommodate project. | 4 weeks | 1. Staff skill, availability, and interest in conducting user surveys. |
| | Survey development support from Sociology Dept. | Pro bono | 2 days | 2. Participation and responsiveness of external department in supporting library development of survey instrument. |
| | Timeline for survey field test, actual survey, and summary of results. | No added cost | 1 day | |
| | Database exit survey development | $300 to campus computing student | 5 days | 3. (a) Campus computing response time in completing web-based database exit survey. |
| | Conduct surveys | Database exit survey – $350 server space | 14 days | (b) Costs exceeding budgeted amount. |
| | | User survey, in-library– $75 printing | 6 intervals per day for in-library survey | 4. Usable results issues. |
| | Summary of results | Staff, no added cost | 5 days | |
| | Handoff to assessment committee | | Simultaneous with date summary report completed | |

(Continued)

216

**Figure 5-5 (Continued)**
**Sample service goals task table.**

| | | | | |
|---|---|---|---|---|
| **Goal 1: Increase use of existing networked services** | | | | |
| Assessment Components | Resources Required | Cost | Completion Date | Library Considerations |
| Improve public technology area | Assess existing equipment and furniture, including lighting | Staff and campus maintenance, no added cost | 5 weeks | 1. Funding issues with improvements.<br><br>2. Availability of campus maintenance to implement improvement. |
| Reapportion materials funds to database acquisition | Analyze existing expenditures by subject, compare over the last 4 years | Staff, no added cost<br><br>Reports from consortium part of membership fee | 8 weeks | Skill of staff to analyze expenditures based on reports provided. |
| Marketing | Review exiting networked services marketing materials, web pages, and campus outreach efforts | Staff, no added cost | 4 weeks | Staff availability to complete marketing enhancements. |

**Figure 5-6**
Content evaluation and acquisition.

| Reapportion materials funds to database acquisition | | | |
|---|---|---|---|
| Assessment Components | Resources Required | Cost | Completion Date |
| Analyze existing expenditures by subject, compare over the last 4 years | Staff: 1 acquisitions 2 materials selectors 1 student assistant | Staff, no added cost. Reports from consortium part of membership fee. | 8 weeks |
| Focus group with faculty | Staff: 2 reference 1 circulation 1 acquisitions 1 IT  share goal, cost analysis, user survey results | Staff, no added cost. Refreshments—$200 | 5 weeks concurrent with student focus groups |
| Focus group with students | Staff: 2 reference 1 circulation 1 acquisitions 1 IT  Share user survey results, goal, cost analysis | Staff, no added cost. Refreshments—$200 | 5 weeks concurrent with faculty focus groups |

(Continued)

**Figure 5-6 (Continued)**
**Content evaluation and acquisition.**

**Reapportion materials funds to database acquisition**

| Assessment Components | Resources Required | Cost | Completion Date |
|---|---|---|---|
| Summary of focus group discussions | Staff: 2 reference 1 circulation 1 acquisitions 1 IT | Staff–no added cost | 8 weeks |
| Additional cost analysis from faculty and student recommendations | Staff: 1 acquisitions 2 materials selectors | Staff–no added cost; contact with consortium to verify group pricing for some titles | 2 weeks |
| Distribute report to Assessment Committee | Subcommittee chair post to library network/web page | No added cost | 1 week |

**Figure 5-7**
**Implementation and life cycle issues.**

| | Resources | Replacement or upgrade cycle | Cost | Completion Date |
|---|---|---|---|---|
| Legacy hardware or other systems components | 6 public computers | Stagger over 36 months, then begin again | $10,000 per year | Interval #1–12 months |
| | 2 networked public printers | Public printers every 4 years, repair as required | $1,000 per year, carry over unspent revenue | As needed |
| | 12 staff computers | Stagger over 48 months, then begin again | | Interval #1–12 months |
| | 4 staff printers 3 staff networked printers | Staff printers replaced only as needed | $500 per year | As needed |
| Network upgrade | Servers | Purchase upgraded server in year one of networked services enhancements. Stagger other server replacement on 36- month cycle, or as needed. | $5,000–$8,000 | As soon as possible |
| | High-speed telecommunications | Upgrade as needed, with campus upgrades | $20,000 reserve each year. Do not carry over. | As needed |
| | Wireless nodes | Purchase hardware and software in year two of networked services enhancements | $25,000 one-time funds, annual license fees of $1,200 | To be determined |
| Furniture | Public service area: 2 tables 4 seats | NA | $1,400 | NA |
| | Staff area: 1 system furniture unit, fully wired | | $1,100 | |

# Notes

1. American Library Association, Office for Information Technology Policy, Washington, D.C. Available at http://www.ala.org/Content/Navigation Menu/Our_Association/Offices/ALA_Washington/OITP_(Office_for _Information_Technology_Policy)/OITP_(Office_for_Information _Technology_Policy).htm. Last accessed November 1, 2003.
2. Association of Research Libraries, New Measures Initiative. Available at http://www.arl.org/stats/newmeas/newmeas.html. Last accessed November 1, 2003.
3. International Coalition of Library Consortia. Available at http://www .library.yale.edu/consortia. Last accessed November 2, 2003.
4. National Center for Education Statistics, Library Statistics Program. Available at http://www.nces.ed.gov/surveys/libraries/. Last accessed November 1, 2003.
5. National Information Standards Organization. Available at http://www .niso.org. Last accessed November 1, 2003.
6. Project COUNTER. Available at http://www.projectcounter.org/. Last accessed November 1, 2003.
7. International Organization for Standardization (ISO). Available at http://www .iso.ch/iso/en/ISOOnline.frontpage. Last accessed November 1, 2003.

# References

Bertot, J.C., & McClure, C.R. (1997). *Policy issues and strategies affecting public libraries in the national networked environment: Moving beyond connectivity.* Washington, DC: U.S. National Commission on Libraries and Information Science.

Bertot, J.C., & McClure, C.R. (2001). Evaluating networked information services: Techniques, policy, and issues. Medford, NJ: Information Today, Inc.

Bertot, J.C., McClure, C.R., & Zweizig, D.L. (1996). *The 1996 national survey of public libraries and the Internet: Progress and issues.* Washington, DC: National Commission on Libraries and Information Science.

National Information Standards Organization (NISO). (2003). *NISO Z39.7-200X draft. Information services and use: Metrics & statistics for libraries and information providers—Data Dictionary.* Bethesda, MD: National Information Standards Organization. Available at http://www.niso.org/emetrics. Last accessed March 11, 2004.

# CHAPTER 6

# Requests for Proposals, Licenses, and Contracts: Assessing Negotiated Agreements for Network-Based Collections and Services

Denise M. Davis

## Introduction

As libraries develop broader network-based collections and services, the significance of content acquisition takes center stage. Libraries use a variety of means to acquire materials and services, and the methods used to acquire electronic databases and related services evolved through the historic methods–direct procurement, subscription services, and one-year contracts. As technology evolved and content delivery platforms changed, methods for acquiring fairly expensive materials and services shifted away from individual library direct purchasing. The procurement methods used to acquire technology, equipment, and replacement-based goods and services became valuable to libraries for networked resources and services.

The range of procurement methods available to libraries includes direct licensing; leveraging negotiated contractual pricing for groups (regional and statewide cooperatives and consortia, and networks like

PALINET, SOLINET, BCR, etc.); and requests for information (RFI) or requests for proposals (RFP). Depending upon local procurement requirements, a library may be able to leverage one or more of these methods to acquire networked resources and services.

The decision making process for acquiring networked resources spans simple to elaborate, depending on the procurement options for the library. Network-based services metrics (e-metrics) and detailed pricing information support libraries in making sound decisions on the value of networked resources and services. More and more libraries are looking carefully at content cost, service performance, and overall value. Even more libraries are requiring networked resource publishers and vendors to supply use statistics and related e-metrics as part of the negotiated license. The extent to which libraries leverage e-metrics to evaluate resource and service value enhances their ability to make sound and reasoned procurement decisions for very expensive resources.

This chapter outlines the variety of network-based collection and service acquisitions models, issues to consider, and the role of network-based performance measures in assessing database value. The author refers readers to related chapters elsewhere in this book in order to reinforce methods of measurement and best practices for materials acquisitions.

## Purchasing Networked Resources and Services: RFIs, RFPs, Contracts, and Licenses

Many libraries contract for networked resources directly with publishers and database vendors. However, since the mid-1990s the trend to leverage group purchasing has provided many libraries the opportunity to participate in regional and statewide database and network services licensing agreements. The variety of opportunities to subscribe to or purchase licensed rights to collections and services is complicated, at best. The decision to take one procurement path over another may have as much to do with finances, or with what entity can sign license agreements, as with the actual content being purchased. Depending on the governance structure of the library, a library may be limited in its ability to leverage the most cost effective method for delivering networked services and content to its users.

For many libraries the most effective method of purchasing, subscribing to, or licensing network-based collections and services is by negotiating contracts directly with publishers, vendors, and service providers. The process used depends on local procurement requirements, perhaps outlined by city or county government. In other cases, the library follows generally recognized procurement and business rules in developing a content acquisition and purchasing process. This model emphasizes local control over purchasing decisions.

In addition to the local purchasing model, libraries may also participate with regional or statewide cooperatives or consortia in acquiring network-based collections and services as needed. In this case, the library has the opportunity to identify the best-value model. In some cases, contracts exceeding a certain dollar amount require review and approval by a governing body or the community purchasing agent. Consult with the library's budget manager to confirm procurement rules. Additionally, the author strongly recommends that all contracts be reviewed by an attorney before signing.

There are a variety of methods for learning about, and acquiring, networked resources and services. The most prevalent methods are direct contracting, requests for information (RFI), and requests for proposals (RFP). An RFI or RFP may be required for contracts exceeding a specific dollar amount, or when more than one library is soliciting pricing on particular network resources or services.

An RFI process is most typically used when libraries are still in the planning and investigation stages of implementing a new service or technology infrastructure. The purpose of an RFI is to solicit information from a range of sources to determine parameters, especially pricing, for the new service or infrastructure. RFIs are used primarily for planning purposes.

Requests for proposals (RFP) are formal solicitations for goods or services, and are often used when procuring networked resources for a group of libraries, such as a consortium, or for statewide access. RFPs may also be required if a contract cost exceeds the spending authority of a library. For instance, a library may be authorized to sign single contracts up to $100,000. A database license that exceeds this amount may require a competitive bid process, and may require a purchasing office to handle the procurement activity.

For libraries that benefit from statewide or regional and cooperative negotiated contracts, the RFI or RFP process may not be necessary. A lead library in a regional cooperative may take responsibility for handling contract negotiations and participant licenses. In the case of a legally established consortium or cooperative, direct purchasing on behalf of members may be possible without an RFI or RFP process.

After a database license or network service agreement has been negotiated, a contract typically is signed. This contract may be referred to as a *license*. The contract binds the purchaser (the library) to the terms of the negotiated agreement. The contract sets the annual price and the term (duration) of the contract, and sets parameters for terminating a contract. It is important that all contracts be reviewed by a lawyer to ensure that neither party is agreeing to unnecessary liability, and that the terms are acceptable to each library participant and to the database or network services supplier.

Libraries participating in group sales agreements still are required to contract for access, either with the consortium or with the lead library. In fact, for many libraries the same agreement between the publisher or vendor and the cooperative or consortium is signed by each participating member library. If signing the full database license agreement or vendor contract is not required, cooperatives, consortia, or statewide database administrators typically implement any of the following *in lieu of* legal agreements to ensure understanding of and compliance with the parent contract, as well as any additional requirements imposed by the group as part of the negotiated price program. These agreements include, but are not limited to, resource sharing agreements, memoranda of understanding, intergovernmental agreements, and interagency agreements. The author advises consultation with an attorney or individual responsible for negotiating contracts and agreements on behalf of the library to determine the appropriate *in lieu of* document.

Orbis Cascade Alliance, an Oregon-based multistate consortium of higher education institutions, engages in *in lieu of* agreements with its members. This arrangement streamlines the database enrollment process for members and provides Orbis Cascade Alliance with a legal contract, with each participating member accessing specific electronic resources. The general membership memorandum of understanding is available at http://libweb.uoregon.edu/orbis/MOU.html. For additional information regarding specific *in lieu of* agreements with members, please contact Orbis Cascade Alliance directly.[1]

## Key Components of an RFP, Proposal Review, and Award Recommendation

Each RFP process is different, but there are similar components of the solicitation document and process. Solicitation documents begin with an introductory statement outlining the purpose of the solicitation, who is requesting the solicitation, a list of terms used in the RFP, mandatory requirements and desirable elements of the solicitation, pricing requirements (especially if there are limited funds), evaluation criteria, response specifications, and a solicitation and procurement calendar. Standard contract terms and conditions are typically prescribed by the purchasing agent, and often include invoicing, payment, late fees, warranties, legal compliance requirements for the contractor, intellectual property indemnity, and the like.

In addition to standard contract terms and conditions, there may be a need to include *special* contract terms and conditions. These may include guidance on the initial contract term and renewals, extensions, price adjustments, billing information, and any special restrictions. Special restrictions might include a penalty for withdrawing content from a database without sufficient notice to the library, or if the withdrawal significantly diminishes the value of the database a penalty would be imposed on the content provider or publisher. A list of proposer references is typically required with any RFP.

The substantive portion of the RFP is the specific requirement of the network service or resource being solicited. The evaluation criteria and scoring components must be incorporated into the RFP. All proposers must know how they are being evaluated, and all evaluations must be conducted using the same criteria and point allocation.

If a proposal does not meet the mandatory requirements of the RFP, the proposal is declined. Only those proposals that meet the mandatory requirements are reviewed and scored based on desirable features, pricing, or other evaluation criteria. An example of evaluation criteria and point allocation is noted in Fig. 6-1. These were taken from the Oregon State Library statewide database solicitation in 2004.[2]

Proposal reviews are based on evaluation of desirable features, pricing, and usually a field test of resources or services. Each component of the evaluation represents a percentage of the total proposal score. For instance, desirable features may constitute 30% of the total score, pricing 50%, and field test comments 20%. In this example, pricing is clearly the priority, representing half of the total weighted score of each proposal.

A timeline must be included in the RFP to alert potential respondents of deadlines. The calendar must be mapped out, including dates for releasing an RFP, any type of pre-bid hearing to respond to proposers' questions, the deadline for responses, an evaluation period, negotiating within the competitive range of proposals, and the final contract negotiation and award. The calendar should be flexible, and the RFP should clearly state that the dates are approximate and may change.

An evaluation or review team should be established. It is important to have a variety of reviewers, especially people directly affected by the network service or resource acquisition. The group also should include people knowledgeable of the services or resources under consideration. The evaluation criteria and directions for evaluation should be clear to all taking part in the review. Any interactions with proposers during the RFP process, especially during the review period, are strictly taboo, and this should be made clear to all reviewers. Setting up a closed listserv for that group may prove valuable. It allows a communication mechanism, while retaining the security of the review process. Be sure to leave adequate time for evaluation, and for discussion of reviews.

**Figure 6-1**
**Sample network resource evaluation criteria.**

| Desirable Feature | Points | Evaluation Criteria and Point Allocation |
|---|---|---|
| Number of full-text titles in the database | 40 points | 40 => 3,101<br>30 2,801–3,100<br>20 2,301–2,800<br>10 1,801–2,300<br>0 = 1,800 |
| Number of embargoed titles. What is the shortest embargo period? What is the longest embargo period? | 10 Points | 10 = 0 titles and 0 time<br>5 = <=50 titles and <=30 days<br>0 = >50 titles and >30 days |
| Statistics for Individual Libraries:<br>It is desired to have individual library database usage statistics. Describe availability and methods to provide routine and customized management reports, and how you assist libraries in retrieving usage reports.<br>Are the statistics reported compliant with National Information Standards Organization (NISO) Z39.7, as listed in http://www.niso.org/emetrics or with Project COUNTER, as listed in http://www.projectCounter.org? | 2 Points | 2 = Yes<br>0 = No |
| Usage Constraints, ILL, and Digital Reference Services:<br>It is desired that customers understand usage constraints, including ILL and digital reference. Describe whether or not customers have any constraints on viewing, downloading, and printing for noncommercial use by authorized users, other than normal copyright considerations. Describe whether or not the proposer's products can be used to fill normal Interlibrary Loan (ILL) requests. A normal ILL request would come from a library that does not have access to the resources to fill a patron's request. Depending on the loaning library's ILL practice or policy, the request may come from inside or outside Oregon. Libraries would not loan access to the entire electronic database product. Libraries would use electronic products to provide occasional access for normal ILL activities. Also, describe whether or not the proposer's products can be used to perform digital reference services. | 6 Points | 6 = Yes<br>(no constraints)<br>0 = No<br>(one or more constraints) |
| Price increase per annum:<br>It is desired that annual price increases remain as low as possible. Proposers are to indicate their proposed annual price increase. Annual price increase shall not exceed 3%. | 10pts possible | 10 pts = < 2% price increase<br>5 pts = >2%, but less than 3% price increase<br>0 pts = 3% price increase |

228

Finally, the reviewers' comments and evaluation will be compiled and discussed. Scores will be reviewed and the group will make its final recommendation. It may be that a rank order of proposals will result, or a clear leader will emerge. It is from this point that contract negotiations begin. Upon successful completion of the negotiation a contract will be signed.

## Statewide Network-Based Collection and Service Procurement Models

Other libraries may operate within procurement regulations that specifically outline the process used, thereby prescribing what purchasing methods may be leveraged and which may not. This is often the case with statewide database programs, such as those seen in Ohio, Georgia, Indiana, Washington, Montana, and Wisconsin. Varying from state to state, procurement requirements may be set at the state level. For some, the statewide procurement model assigns responsibility to a separate governing council or organization. These groups determine the process for evaluation and acquisition of the statewide resources.

In other statewide procurement arrangements, the state library administers the program and, as a direct arm of state government, often is required to follow state procurement regulations. In other states, the statewide program resides with higher education and follows procurement practices associated with that group. Figure 6-2 is illustrative of the range of implementations of statewide networked resources programs throughout the United States. On closer inspection of these library and organization websites, the reader will discover that there are a variety of implementations of leveraged large-group sales for a variety of resource-sharing technologies and collections. This figure reflects only a few of the thousands of cooperative arrangements in place in the United States. Included in Fig. 6-2 are governance structures and procurement models in place at the time this book was written.

## Assessment Models: Input for Effective Resource Acquisition

The evaluation of (1) technical requirements and efficiencies, (2) the content made available through networked resource agreements, (3) cost analysis of those resources, and (4) the overall use of networked services is critical in determining the overall value of networked services. The following section will take each evaluation component and outline methods for implementing a reliable and sustainable networked resource and service assessment process.

**Figure 6-2**
**Statewide database licensing programs: governance and funding.**

| Statewide Program Administration | Administrative Unit | Governing Structure | Financing for Statewide Program | Contract Negotiation Model |
|---|---|---|---|---|
| Alaska | SLED–Statewide Library Electronic Doorway<br><br>Originally developed through the cooperation of the University of Alaska, the State Library, and libraries statewide<br><br>http://www.library.state.ak.us/dev/internet.html | SLED Advisory Group | Supported by the State Legislature | RPF, direct negotiations on behalf of Alaska libraries |
| Maryland | State Library of Maryland, Division of Library Development, Sailor Network staff<br>http://www.sailor.lib.md.us/sailor/welcome.html | State Library of Maryland and Sailor Governance Board | State funds, local funds provided by libraries, Federal LSTA | RFP, direct negotiations on behalf of public libraries in Maryland |
| Massachusetts | Massachusetts Library Information Network (MLIN)<br>http://www.mlin.org/flash3.html<br>http://www.mlin.lib.ma.us/mblc/index.shtml | Massachusetts Board of Library Commissioners | State and local funding provided by libraries; Federal LSTA | RFP, direct negotiations on behalf of Massachusetts libraries |
| OhioLINK | Ohio Board of Regents (higher education)<br>http://www.ohiolink.edu/about/what-is-ol.html | OhioLINK Governing Board | State Library of Ohio and OhioLINK Governing Board | RFP, direct negotiations on behalf of higher education institutions in Ohio |

(Continued)

**Figure 6-2 (Continued)**
**Statewide database licensing programs: governance and funding.**

| Statewide Program Administration | Administrative Unit | Governing Structure | Financing for Statewide Program | Contract Negotiation Model |
|---|---|---|---|---|
| Orbis Cascade Alliance (Oregon and Washington) | Orbis Cascade Alliance Staff and Council; Executive Committee. http://libweb.uoregon.edu/orbis/ | Multistate, membership organization | Membership organization shared pricing | RFP, direct negotiation on behalf of membership. Negotiated price model. Intergovernmental agreements with members and administrative organization; Memoranda of Understanding. |
| Washington | Washington State Library http://www.statelib.wa.gov/  http://www.statelib.wa.gov/libraries/projects/sdl/ | Statewide Database Licensing Committee | Federal LSTA; state and local funding provided by libraries | RFP, direct negotiations on behalf of Washington libraries, "best price" model |
| Wyoming | Wyoming Library Database Network (WYLD) WYLD Network Governing Board http://will.state.wy.us/wyld/ http://will.state.wy.us/wyld/wyldco.html | Wyoming State Library and libraries in Wyoming | Wyoming State Library and libraries in Wyoming | Connectivity fees subsidized by State Library; costs assessed annually and set by Governing Board |

Oregon State Library: Statewide Database License Program. Available at http://www.osl.state.or.us/home/libdev/osdlp/index.html (last accessed February 22, 2004).

A series of e-metrics are noted in Chapter 4 of this book, along with methodological considerations regarding the collection and use of selected e-metrics. The detail provided about which e-metrics currently are provided by database publishers and vendors, and which can be determined by the library or network administrator, will help you identify those e-metrics most valuable to individual assessments. Following the model presented in Chapter 4, there are four instruments for achieving compliance for networked resources performance measures: definitional, reporting, methodological, and data instruments.

Database publishers have worked collaboratively with libraries to develop a common definitional guide for describing network resource statistics. The difficulty with normalizing the definitions falls to the method of access and content transmission for network resources to the customer, in other words, the technology. Although the technology is more standardized, it is not normalized across publishers or libraries. The lack of normalization impacts the data reported about information transactions. Although transaction level data are collectable, they may not be meaningful with regard to other networked resources.

The continued challenge remains in how use figures are reported to customers, the inherent methodology behind capturing and reporting network usage both by publishers and by libraries, and the data output itself. The assessment models proposed in this chapter focus on method for commercial resources, rather than OPACs and other networked services provided by libraries. This analysis relies on readily available database use reporting from publishers, network transaction log analysis by libraries, and cost analysis. For guidance on preparing your library to collect network statistics, please consult Chapter 3 of this book.

To fully understand the value of networked resources and services, an assessment process must be undertaken. Chapter Four of this book details the full range of e-metrics, methods for collecting data, and data analysis. For the purposes of illustration, this section focuses on preparing an assessment model for commercial networked resources and services. Figure 6-3 presents selected e-metrics from Chapter 4 that are relevant to this assessment model. It is important to note the level of data collection, e.g., system level or vendor level. In addition to these e-metrics, the assessment model requires detailed pricing information and, to the extent possible, detailed content information about each networked resource (e.g., complete database title counts, full-text title counts, and—as required—peer reviewed title counts).

**Figure 6-3**
Commercial networked resources and services e-metrics.

| E-metric | Definition |
|---|---|
| **Virtual Visits**<br>**(System Level Statistic)** | A user's request of the library Web site from outside the library premises, regardless of the number of pages or items viewed. Excludes Web site visits from within the library. Note: This statistic is the equivalent of a session for a library's Web site. As such, there is a need to exclude various actions (e.g., hits, downloads) by users during any given visit.<br>Count of visits to the library via the Internet with a breakdown by:<br><br>■ # Internal virtual visits: Visits while library users are in the library using public access Internet workstations (excludes library staff and staff workstations);<br>■ # External virtual visits: Visits while library users access the library remotely (excluding the visits made by library users within the library using the public access Internet workstations);<br>■ Total # virtual visits: A total count of both internal and external virtual visits.<br><br>Report *only* the number of *external* virtual visits, however. |
| **Rejected Sessions (Turnaways)**<br>**(System Level/Vendor Statistic)** | A rejected session (turnaway) is defined as an unsuccessful log-in to an electronic service by exceeding the simultaneous user limit. Note: Failure of log-in because of wrong passwords is excluded. |
| **Commercial Services Sessions**<br>**(System Level/Vendor Statistic)** | A session is defined as a successful request of a commercial service (e.g., online database). It is one cycle of user activities that typically starts when a user connects to a database and ends by terminating activity in the database that is either explicit (by leaving the database through log-out or exit) or implicit (timeout due to user inactivity). Note 1: For multiple databases compiling several individual databases, further information should be provided as to the separate databases hosted. Note 2: In some cases, e.g., database use inside the library, several users one after the other might make use of the same workstation, and sessions could not be separated. In most systems, a session is cut off after a specified time of nonuse, thus avoiding part of the problem. The average timeout setting would be 30 minutes. If another timeout period is used, this should be reported. Browser or proxy caching will be likely to reduce the number of requests registered in log files. |

**Figure 6-3 (Continued)**
**Commercial networked resources and services e-metrics.**

| E-metric | Definition |
|---|---|
| **Commercial Services Searches (Queries)** (System Level/Vendor Statistic) | A search is defined as intending to represent a unique intellectual inquiry. Typically, a search is recorded every time a search request is submitted to the server. Limited to commercial services. Mistyped search strings do not represent unique intellectual inquiries. Include menu selection searches. Exclude spider/crawler searches. |
| **Commercial Services Full-Content Units Examined** (System Level/Vendor Statistic) | Number of subscription service full-content units examined, downloaded, or otherwise supplied to user, to the extent that these are recordable and controlled by the server rather than the browser. Note 1: Journal articles–by journal title with ISSN and title listed. Note 2: Ebooks–by book title with ISBN and title listed. Note 3: Reference materials–by content unit appropriate to the resource (e.g., dictionary definitions, encyclopedia articles, biographies, etc.). Note 4: Non-textual resources–by file type as appropriate to resources (e.g., image, audio, video, etc.). |
| **Commercial Services Descriptive Records Examined** (System Level/Vendor Statistic) | Number of descriptive records concerning the library's commercial services delivered to a user. Determined by the record type appropriate to the resource, e.g., abstract, archive, index. Exclude OPAC or library collection descriptive records (i.e., library website services and collections). |

Following the methods presented in Chapter 4, assemble database usage figures for each database being assessed and for each of the e-metrics noted. Assemble separately the detailed pricing information for each commercial networked resource being assessed and title counts. Adding pricing and title count data to the assessment formula allows for more comprehensive per-title analysis. The database titles represented in Fig. 6-3 are for illustrative purposes only.

From this assessment table it is possible to derive a variety of database costs in a context of usage. More meaningful analyses for databases with primarily periodical content may be the cost per title in a database, the cost per search, or the cost per full-content unit examined. For databases such as an author's biographical tool, it is possible to determine the number of author entries to arrive at a cost per entry, but that may be less valuable in the assessment process than a cost per search or full-content unit examined.

Now that we have these data, we can assess the relative value of a database product with the library community served. Clearly, other factors impact determining value. These might include training sessions for users, marketing of database products, availability of remote user logon, or even virtual reference assistance for networked resources, including databases. It is important to note that the intent of database content analysis is to understand the use of databases and to apply a price point to that value. If use increases over time, then you can better track networked resource adoption rates by the library community. If usage drops, it may be an indicator of disappointment with the database, or that the content is available from another resource.

Some databases will have limited use because of content or audience. This does not mean they are less valued and not worth purchasing. It does mean that the audience is limited to a specific group or groups. This may be the case with a legal database, or in finance and investing. These also may be high-cost databases. In addition, infrastructure costs are not included in this analysis, because it is presumed that the technology would be in place to access commercial databases, and the focus of assessment is on the database costs themselves.

Using the data illustrated in Fig. 6-4, and using some basic cost analysis models, the following formulas demonstrate methods for determining three data analyses: database cost per title, database cost per search, and database cost per full-content unit examined.

Although the annual cost may seem high when viewed on its own, when assessed in a context of usage and potential document delivery to library customers, the price becomes quite affordable.

Figure 6-4
Assessment model: commercial databases.

| E-metric | Reporting Period: January–December, 2003 E-metric Data | General Periodicals Premier E-metric Data | Business and Industry Full-text E-metric Data | Children's Titles Galore E-metric Data | Newspapers of the U.S. E-metric Data | Comprehensive American Author's Elite E-metric Data |
|---|---|---|---|---|---|---|
| **Virtual Visits** (System Level Statistic) | 1,723,419 | | | | | |
| **Rejected Sessions (Turnaways)** (System Level/Vendor Statistic) | 297 (not attributed to a database) | 0 | 0 | 0 | 74 | 1,385 |
| **Commercial Services Sessions** (System Level/Vendor Statistic) | | 934,501 | 247,398 | 14,365 | 397,323 | 101,147 |
| **Commercial Services Searches (Queries)** (System Level/Vendor Statistic) | | 2,895,379 | 637,441 | 47,249 | 1,000,047 | 376,921 |
| **Commercial Services Full-Content Units Examined** (System Level/Vendor Statistic) | | 7,219,004 | 1,196,302 | 52,509 | 4,012,993 | 703,002 |
| **Commercial Services Descriptive Records Examined** (System Level/Vendor Statistic) | | 9,803,441 | 1,982,549 | 67,309 | 7,091,003 | 874,320 |

(Continued)

Figure 6-4 (Continued)
Assessment model: commercial databases.

| Reporting Period: January–December, 2003 | General Periodicals Premier | Business and Industry Full-text | Children's Titles Galore | Newspapers of the U.S. | Comprehensive American Author's Elite |
|---|---|---|---|---|---|
| E-metric | E-metric Data | E-metric Data | E-metric Data | E-metric Data | E-metric Data |
| Title Count: Total | 7,208 | 2,739 | 118 | 157 | NA |
| Title Count: Full-text | 3,948 | 2,340 | 118 | 157 | NA |
| Title Count: Peer Reviewed I & A | 4,001 | 127 | NA | NA | NA |
| Title Count: Peer Reviewed Full-text | 2,369 | 127 | NA | NA | NA |
| Database Price (Annual) | $74,235 | $23,500 | $17,999 | $31,000 | $25,000 |

*Database Cost per Title, General Periodicals Premier*

**Formula:** Annual database cost ÷ title count = database cost per title

$74,235 ÷ 7,208 = $10.30 per title

*Database Cost per Search, General Periodicals Premier*

**Formula:** Annual database cost ÷ annual number of searches
= database cost per search

$74,235 ÷ 2,895,379 = $0.03

*Database Cost per Full-content Unit Examined, General Periodicals Premier*

**Formula:** Annual database cost
÷ annual full-content unites examined
= database cost per full-content unites examined

$74,235 ÷ 7,219,004 = $0.01

It is at this level of assessment that libraries can compare new database procurement efforts with existing database products. If the library is beginning the database evaluation and acquisition process, and has no current negotiated agreements, it may be possible to view sample usage data from other libraries. Some publishers and database vendors have developed methods for generalizing usage based on the library size, population served, and database products of interest. Please consult with the database sales representative, or libraries of similar size in your state that may have usage data to share.

Georgia Library Learning Online (GALILEO) is a cooperative database and resource sharing project of higher education, libraries, and K–12 education in Georgia. GALILEO provides its members with vendor product evaluation forms. At the time of this writing, the forms were located on the GALILEO website, under the heading Resources for GALILEO Librarians, Vendor Performance Assessment (http://neptune3.galib.uga.edu/cgi-bin/homepage.cgi?style=&_id=c6511a4b-1138189074-4276&_cc=1).

## Summary

The procurement guidance, service evaluation and e-metrics, and methods of assessment in this chapter provide a recipe for understanding and being successful in a network service or database resource acquisition. As noted, assessment and acquisition processes can be simple or elaborate, depending upon the procurement options for the library. Libraries are looking more carefully at content cost, service performance, and overall value, and including e-metrics and detailed pricing in service and resource evaluation supports libraries in making sound purchasing decisions. Requiring networked resource publishers and vendors to supply use statistics and related e-metrics as part of the negotiated license eases ongoing service assessment.

## Notes

1. Orbis Cascade Alliance, 1299 University of Oregon, Eugene, OR 97403-1299.

2. Oregon State Library: Statewide Database License Program. Available at http://www.osl.state.or.us/home/libdev/osdlp index. html. Last accessed February 22, 2004).

## Additional Resources

Duranceau, E.F. (2000). License tracking. *Serials Review,* 26(3), 69–74.26(3), 69–74.

Jewell, T.D. (2001). *Selection and presentation of commercially available electronic resources: Issues and practices.* Washington, DC: Digital Library Federation and Council on Library and Information Resources.

Lougee, W.P. (2002). *Diffuse libraries: Emergent roles for the research library in the digital age.* Washington, DC: Council on Library and Information Resources. Available at http://www.clir.org/pubs/abstract/pub108abst.html. Last accessed December 9, 2003.

Martin, M.S. (1995). *Collection development and finance: A guide to strategic library materials budgeting.* Chicago, IL: American Library Association.

Rounds, R. S. (1994). Budgeting practices for librarians, 2nd ed. Chicago, IL: American Library Association.

Scigliano, M. (2002). Consortium purchases: Case study for a cost-benefit analysis. *Journal of Academic Librarianship,* 28(6), 393–400.

CHAPTER 7

# Policies to Ensure Use of and Access to Network-Based Services and Resources

**Denise M. Davis and John Carlo Bertot**

## Introduction

Since the early 1990s libraries have developed detailed procedures for the selection, acquisition, and cataloging of network resources, and have also needed to develop policies on acceptable use. Much of the need for policies and procedures for these resources, and the services provided around them, was that these resources were extremely expensive items to acquire, and they had fairly wide appeal. Whereas libraries cataloged and shelved print materials using a particular organizational schema, electronic resources were accessed from computers within the library and then from outside the walls of the library as technology further developed. Librarians quickly discovered that it was critical to develop a mechanism for gathering input from the user community, not only on what to purchase, but also how best to make it available.

Libraries have long had acceptable-use policies to guide users on behavior while in the library, materials use and borrowing, and copyright. These policies often follow institutional or governmental requirements, such as university or school policy, or legal liability policies for local or county government. As adoption and integration of electronic resources and network services grew, as well as access to the Internet, libraries needed to be specific about the acceptable use of computers and related equipment, mobile phones, wireless technology, etc. Further, libraries quickly realized that policies were needed not only to protect equitable access to the resources and services purchased by the library, but also to protect the privacy of the user. It was no longer enough to make the resources available; libraries now had to provide guidance on their use, especially alternate uses of equipment for chat, e-mail, word processing, Web surfing, and other activities not related directly to the use of the resources.

## Developing Policies

Libraries develop policies out of necessity. They exist to serve a practical purpose–providing guidance on the use of the library and its services and resources. Libraries should have in place guidelines on how to develop policies, including the purpose, scope, links to other policies, frequency of review, and parameters for eliminating a policy. The American Library Association and its divisions (Public Library, College and Research, and Specialized and Cooperative) provide guidance on policies. Most notable is the work of Sandra Nelson for the Public Library Association (PLA). She has developed or revised titles in the PLA Results Series. IF in 2003, Ms. Nelson and June Garcia co-authored *Creating Policies for Results: From Chaos to Clarity.*[1] This chapter's authors recommend this text as a valuable primer for libraries evaluating processes that involve developing or revising policies. As with each of the PLA Results Series titles, it provides clear and concise guidance that applies to everyday processes.

In the case of network services and resources, policies exist to provide guidance to the library's constituents: the public, staff, governing boards, and government. For some libraries, circulation or reserves, reference, or interlibrary lending policies may be modified to accommodate network services and resources. Most typically, however, policies covering network services and electronic resources are newly formed and concern collection development, acceptable use–including intellectual freedom and privacy–and unlawful use.

### Special Needs for Different Libraries

Not all libraries need the same policies. Library policies are based on the individual library's mission, as well as on the materials and services provided to primary clientele. Later in this chapter, the authors provide a cursory "environmental scan" of network services and resources policies in public, academic, school, and state libraries. In addition, the chapter highlights the role of library consortia, associations, and other organizations in providing guidance on policy development.

When considering libraries by type, one quickly recognizes that missions may vary significantly, even within same-type libraries. Additionally, collection and service policies will vary depending upon the primary service groups. For libraries with missions to serve the public, that service mission may be narrowly focused to a specific population, even though they provide limited services to the general public. Even public libraries have limited service missions due to the population served, as defined by its taxing area. Additionally, public institutions of higher education may be required to provide services to the general public, but they are able to clearly define the scope of those services.

Public libraries have challenges when access to resources or services is restricted. This happens when libraries provide access only to eligible borrowers. Viewed by many as open institutions, public libraries that need to enforce restricted access will need to include the reason for those restrictions in their policies. Such limitations may also appear for any library when the network resource has limited use options due to the licensing agreement. For example, providing remote access to a particular network resource may be limited by the licensing agreement. It is important to articulate those limitations to users as visibly as possible, including by database access screens, instructional materials, and policy statements.

Policies developed to manage network services and resources in private libraries vary somewhat from those necessary for public or public higher education libraries. Private institutions and special libraries follow the policies of their parent organization. Access is often possible by appointment, or with special access privileges, but the use of services, collections, and electronic resources is restricted to primary users only. Policy development in these circumstances becomes fairly straightforward. Policies are developed for the primary user group, including acceptable-use and remote access policies, etc. A simple policy explaining that use of the library, its services, and its resources is restricted or limited by the mission of the organization is all that may be necessary. Private libraries, including corporate ones, often participate in cooperative assistance library-to-library, including interlibrary lending. The professional code guiding this service is outlined by the American Library Association Interlibrary Code for the United States.[2] This does not mean that networked services or electronic resources are made available or used to provide interlibrary services.

In the case of academic libraries, curriculum will drive library policies concerning materials selection, access, and user services. Funding sources and governance structures further impact policies. Private academic institutions may have restricted access to the library facility and further restrictions on who may use electronic resources subscribed to or owned by the library. Public academic institutions, although primarily serving the curriculum needs of faculty and students, may be required to provide service to the general public. By way of example, the authors provide a mock case study to demonstrate a policy review process, including outlining the institutional mission and service goals that impact library policy development.

## Case Study: The College of the City of Smith (CCS)

The College of the City of Smith (CCS) is a publicly funded four-year liberal arts college in a particularly rural area of a New England state. CCS has provided access to CD-ROM databases and Web-based services, including e-books and e-journals. The library is part of a shared catalog system with five other colleges in a three-state region. The library subscriptions to e-books and e-journals, and to one full-text general periodicals database, are made possible through a statewide licensing agreement. A few other titles are purchased from a consortium of academic, public, and school libraries in the region. Overall, CCS library subscribes to only three databases on its own.

CCS is required to provide access to its library's network services and resources to other members of the regional consortium. The general periodicals database is available to any resident of the state because it was paid for with state funds. As a publicly funded state institution of higher education, CCS answers reference questions from anyone who comes to the library, but will give preference to faculty, students, and staff of CCS. Having provided access and support services to network resources for a number of years, CCS has discovered that some of its policies need review. Recent changes in federal and state law enforcement procedures also prompted a review of service and collection policies. A committee has been formed to solicit input from faculty, students, and staff, and to work with consortium members in revising policies and procedures.

CCS library staff and administration had criteria in place for developing new library policies and reviewing existing ones. These criteria included the following:

- Was the policy essential to the library meeting its mission, goals, and objectives (e.g., provide access to the library, its services, or its resources)?
- Was the policy impacted by, or did it impact

- Another library policy?

- A college code or guideline?

- A law?

- Has there been an external request to develop or review a library policy?

- If an existing policy, has it been reviewed in the last 24 months?

Using these criteria to determine if new policies were necessary, the CCS library determined that there was no need for a new policy. Staff reviewed existing policies that impacted, or were impacted by, networked services and electronic resources and discovered seven policies that needed review and possible revision:

1. Collection Development: Electronic resources supporting CCS curriculum (rev. 1998);

2. Faculty Recommendations of Library Materials (including databases) (rev. 1993);

3. Using the Library (rev. 2001);

4. Borrowing from the College of the City of Smith (CCS) (rev. 2000);

5. Processing Library Materials (rev. 2002);

6. Acceptable-use Policies: Using the Internet at CCS Library (2001); and

7. Privacy of Patron Records (rev. 2002).

In reviewing the list, CCS library staff realized that four of the policies were influenced by the presence of network services and resources, and that three influenced the acquisition of resources and provision of service. Staff developed guidance tables as part of the review planning process. These tables are used to allocate work, determine process, and develop deadlines for completion of tasks.

Table 7-1 displays whether resources or services are impacted, and which staff will be involved in the review process. Table 7-2 displays which constituents the library will invite to participate in the review of the policy. In the case of library consortia committees, the library will inform those groups of any changes and will take consortia guidelines or policies under consideration during its review.

**Table 7-1**
Internal policy review guide.

| Library Policy | Date Developed or Revised | Staff Unit Lead Review | Electronic Resource | Networked Service |
|---|---|---|---|---|
| Collection Development: Electronic resources supporting CCS curriculum | (rev.1998) | Reference Selectors | X | X |
| Faculty recommendations of library materials (including databases) | (rev.1993) | Reference Selectors | X | |
| Using the Library | (rev.2001) | Circulation | | X |
| Borrowing from the College of the City of Smith (CCS) | (rev.2000) | Circulation | X | X |
| Processing library materials | (rev.2002) | Technical Services | X | |
| Acceptable-use Policies: Using the Internet at CCS Library | (2001) | Circulation | X | X |
| Privacy of Patron Records | (rev.2002) | All units | X | X |

Table 7-1 shows the complexity of determining which functional units of the library are most effective in leading a review and recommendation process for networked services policies. In the case of privacy of patron records, circulation and reference staff would traditionally have participated in that review. In the case of electronic resources and networked services, it was determined that all functional units would send a representative to participate in the review of that policy, even thought it was most recently revised in 2002. The implications of federal requirements under the USA Patriot Act, the Children's Internet Protection Act (CIPA), and the Foreign Intelligence Surveillance Act (FISA) directly impacted the expansion of staff participation in the review of this particular policy.

Table 7-2 shows the need for each user group to participate in the policy review process. The users are impacted directly by any policy changes, and play a useful role in the decision making process of revising these policies. Bringing users into the conversation provides an opportunity to educate them about library policies and to get input from them on how to improve policies. In addition, the campus legal staff are brought in to review the policies to ensure they are in compliance with state and federal laws, or the campus code and guidelines.

The library staff then integrates feedback from the work of the CCS policy review group to update its policies. Following faculty senate requirements, the CCS library submits suggested revisions to the faculty senate's Policy Committee for approval. CCS determined that with the collaborative review process adopted by the library, the full senate did not need to adopt policy changes, but did need to discuss and adopt new policies. The library had only policy revisions, so the process moved smoothly. Policies for review were identified, reviewed, revised, and adopted within 12 months.

In the case of policies dealing with acceptable use and patron privacy, it is important to educate members of the policy review committee about the legal implications of these particular policies. For collection development and borrowing policies, libraries have an opportunity to explain the contract requirements of subscription services, e-books, and e-journals, and any other resources the library may have access rights for but which may not be commercially produced (e.g., digital image files developed by other libraries, etc.).

## Updating Policies

Libraries should revise policies as part of the normal course of business. That is to say, libraries should develop plans for systematic review of policies to ensure they are adequate, current, and legally accurate. This avoids revisions of policies under duress—perhaps due to disputes or challenges—or major overhauls that require substantial amounts of time to complete. This is not to say that 360-degree policy reviews are not valuable, but they are time consuming.

Table 7-2
External policy review guide.

| Policy | Review Dates | | Policy Review Group | | | | |
|---|---|---|---|---|---|---|---|
| | Date Developed or Revised | Revision Completed (Date) | Staff | Faculty | Students | Consortia Committee | Campus Legal Office |
| Collection Development: Electronic resources supporting CCS curriculum | Revised 2001 | | X | X | X | | |
| Faculty recommendations of library materials (including databases) | Revised 1998 | | X | X | X | | |
| Using the Library | Revised 1993 | | X | X | X | Inform | |
| Borrowing from the College of the City of Smith (CCS) | Revised 2000 | | X | X | X | Inform | Inform |
| Processing library materials | Revised 2002 | | X | X | | | |
| Acceptable-use Policies: Using the Internet at CCS Library | 2001 | | X | X | X | Inform | Inform |
| Privacy of Patron Records | Revised 2002 | | X | X | X | Inform | Review |

## Updating Policies

Libraries should revise policies as part of the normal course of business. That is to say, libraries should develop plans for systematic review of policies to ensure they are adequate, current, and legally accurate. This avoids revisions of policies under duress—perhaps due to disputes or challenges—or major overhauls that require substantial amounts of time to complete. This is not to say that 360-degree policy reviews aren't valuable, but they are time consuming.

The case study of the College of the City of Smith demonstrates the depth and breadth a policy review may require, even when systematic revisions have taken place. Examples of policies from the Omaha Public Library are presented later in this chapter. The policies were in effect as of December 2003, but the library director indicated in an interview that the website was being updated in early 2004 and policies were being systematically reviewed. She expected changes to some policies, especially those involving restrictions to chat rooms on public computers. The reality was that the computers were being used for such activity, and the policy to restrict use was not enforceable. This reinforces the point that policies must be practical and applicable. As the use of technology changes, and as behaviors change, policies should keep up with those changes and improvements.

## Laws Impacting Library Policies

State and local laws, as well as local preference, have an impact on the development of library policies. Add to this reasonable and acceptable use policies for network services and resources, and it is clear that libraries are being pulled and pushed to ensure that all areas of requirement are represented in policies. Since the late 1990s, and especially since fall 2001, U.S. libraries have been further impacted by strenuous legal requirements set in place by the federal government as a result of the USA Patriot Act (PL 107-56). Also affecting library policy development are the Children's Online Privacy Protection Act (COPPA; Title 13, PL 105-277) and the Children's Internet Protection Act (CIPA; PL 106-554). Briefly, the USA Patriot Act requires libraries to provide access to patron borrowing records and library use information, which violates the American Library Association Bill of Rights (Jaeger, Bertot, & McClure, 2003). COPPA, which has been in and out of the courts since its passage in 1998 and is still undergoing legal challenge, requires that Internet service providers not transmit material that is "harmful to minors," if the material is for commercial purposes. CIPA requires libraries to filter Internet content if a library receives federal E-Rate, Library Services and

Technology Act (LSTA) funding, or Elementary and Secondary Education Act (ESEA) funds for Internet connectivity (Jaeger, Bertot, & McClure, 2004). Thus, libraries must make difficult decisions regarding their network services and resources, particularly if they accept federal funds that obligate the library to use filtering devices on all public and staff computers. For many libraries and communities, the struggle between following federal laws and meeting the intellectual freedom needs of the community is the most significant challenge of the early 21st century.

Since state laws and statutes, as well as local and jurisdictional laws and codes, vary so significantly, the authors will highlight only the key federal laws that have impacted libraries with regard to networked services and electronic resources.

## USA Patriot Act

The USA Patriot Act (PL 107-56) is the best-known 21st-century law that has impacted American society, and especially libraries. Enacted in October 2001 as HR 3162, during the first Session of the 107th Congress, the 131-page law entitled *USA Patriot Act (Uniting and Strengthening America by Providing Appropriate Tools Required to Intercept and Obstruct Terrorism)* has far-reaching implications for how libraries do business.[3] Libraries certainly recognize that the ultimate intent of the law was to protect homeland security. The sweeping implications of the law, however, leave libraries vulnerable to search, seizure, and possible legal action if they do not cooperate with law enforcement when requested to. It remains ambiguous, and has been interpreted differently depending upon state laws, as to whether warrants and subpoenas are the only legitimate grounds for surrendering library records and equipment to law enforcement. In reviewing the law, the authors suggest taking particular note of the following titles and sections:

### Title II–Enhanced Surveillance Procedures

Sec. 201. Authority to intercept wire, oral, and electronic communications relating to terrorism.

Sec. 202. Authority to intercept wire, oral, and electronic communications relating to computer fraud and abuse offenses.

Sec. 203. Authority to share criminal investigative information.

Sec. 204. Clarification of intelligence exceptions from limitations on interception and disclosure of wire, oral, and electronic communications.

Sec. 206. Roving surveillance authority under the Foreign Intelligence Surveillance Act of 1978.

Sec. 207. Duration of FISA surveillance of non-United States persons who are agents of a foreign power.

Sec. 210. Scope of subpoenas for records of electronic communications.

Sec. 211. Clarification of scope.

Sec. 215. Access to records and other items under the Foreign Intelligence Surveillance Act.

Title V–Removing Obstacles to Investigating Terrorism

Sec. 504. Coordination with law enforcement.

Sec. 507. Disclosure of educational records.

Sec. 508. Disclosure of information from NCES surveys.

A summary of issues related to the Patriot Act was prepared by the Congressional Research Service and may be helpful (Doyle, 2004). Also, Jaeger, Bertot, & McClure (2003) provide a discussion of the policy implications of the Patriot Act. Additional guidance on the Patriot Act is available from the American Library Association, USA Patriot Act Web page (http://www.ala.org/Content/NavigationMenu/OurAssociation/Offices/IntellectualFreedom3/IntellectualFreedomIssues/USAPatriotAct.htm); the Special Library Association, USA Patriot Act Portal (www.sla.org/content/memberservice/communication/PATRIOTAct/index.cfm); the Association of Research Libraries, Federal Relations and Information Policy website (http://www.arl.org/info/); and the American Association of Law Libraries (http://www.aallnet.org/press/press011004_a.asp).

## Children's Internet Protection Act (CIPA) and Children's Online Privacy Protection Act of 1998 (COPPA)

These acts directly impact how libraries provide Internet access to minors. COPPA (PL 105-277) does not specifically require libraries to do anything, but parents, the community, and children should be informed about Internet content. The American Library Association provides policy guidance to public and school libraries on how to educate their communities about COPPA (American Library Association, 2003).

CIPA was codified as HR 4577, printed in the Congressional Record of December 15, 2000, and enacted in 2001 as PL 106-554). The law specifically impacts public and school libraries' ability to use federal funding to implement or improve access to the Internet through Education Rate (E-Rate) discounts or Elementary and Secondary Education Act (ESEA) funds. CIPA requires public and school libraries to install filtering devices on all public workstations used by minor children, and these regulations are implemented through the Federal Communications Commission (FCC) and the Universal Service Administration Company (USAC). CIPA subsequently triggered application to Library Services and Technology Act (LSTA) funding. As of federal fiscal year 2004 (October 2003), any public or school library receiving LSTA funds to implement or improve computing services must now require Internet filtering on all staff and public computers.[4] A review of the impact of CIPA on libraries is available in Jaeger, Bertot, & McClure (2004).

### Foreign Intelligence Surveillance Act of 1978 (FISA)

The last law the authors want to bring to your attention is the Foreign Intelligence Surveillance Act of 1978 (FISA). This act was passed in 1978 as PL 95-511, 92 Stat. 1783 (codified as amended at 50 U.S.C. §§ 1801–1811, 1821–1829, 1841–1846, 1861–1862). The law was amended during the 108th Congress under S 113 to "extend the coverage of the Foreign Intelligence Surveillance Act (FISA) to non-United States persons who engage in international terrorism or activities in preparation for international terrorism, without a showing of membership in or affiliation with an international terrorist group. FISA provides a means by which the government can obtain approval to conduct electronic surveillance (wiretap) and other searches with respect to a foreign power or its agents in order to obtain intelligence related to espionage, terrorism, or other matters involving national security" (Elsea, 2003).

The impact of this law on library policy derives directly from the ability of law enforcement to secure FISA warrants and subpoenas. The Electronic Freedom Foundation (EFF) has prepared a summary of questions regarding FISA and Fourth Amendment rights.[5] There is some question as to whether such law enforcement requests can be denied under the 2003 amendment (see Jaeger, Bertot, & McClure, 2003). Academic libraries are most significantly impacted by FISA due to foreign student enrollment and visiting faculty. Public libraries and school libraries may also be affected. The authors recommend that a library confirm legal requirements with its attorney to ensure that policies are FISA-compliant.

The authors further suggest that libraries check more current resources to investigate the impact of any of the federal laws mentioned on library policies, especially given the lag between the writing of this text and its publication. Beyond the library attorney, libraries may want to consult the American Library Association, the Electronic Freedom Foundation, and the American Civil Liberties Union.

# Dealing with the Media and Law Enforcement

Libraries increasingly are being questioned about use of the Internet, as well as issues around access to patron records as those issues surface in the news. It is critical that libraries have a clear policy on working with the media, that the policy includes guidance on providing statistics related to usage of the library, its collections and services, and especially on technology. Although the library may have policies on collection development, it is also important for there to be policies on what is disclosed to the media. Any such policies should be approved in accordance with normal policy development procedures. The authors suggest the following criteria for developing a policy for dealing with the media.

1. Procedures for staff to refer media inquiries:
   (a) Get full name, telephone number, etc., of the person requesting information.
   (b) Be clear with the journalist or broadcaster that the call will be responded to as soon as possible, including information about who will respond to the inquiry (e.g., the library's public information officer, director, etc.).

2. Procedures for handling inquiries:
   (a) Develop guidelines on what media inquires will be responded to.
   (b) Consider developing standard responses to frequently asked questions (e.g., number of users, number of databases, collection policies, procedure for filing complaints with the library, etc.).
   (c) To the extent possible, respond in writing to avoid being misquoted.
   (d) Ask to review the article prior to publication.

3. Maintain a record of inquiries:
   (a) Develop a process for maintaining a log of all media inquiries, regardless of how they are received (e.g., telephone, in-person, e-mail, etc.).
   (b) Keep a record of all responses, to the extent possible.

Revise the policy on responding to media inquiries as often as required, especially if local guidance changes. This is especially true for academic, public, and school libraries.

Dealing with law enforcement officials requires the library to develop a clear policy in consultation with its lawyer(s). Regarding procedures for staff, it is important that libraries give clear instructions to staff on behavior and disclosure of the contact. Many state libraries are developing guidance for libraries in their particular state, as are state library associations. Training on USA Patriot Act-related inquiries by law enforcement was well underway at the time of this writing. The authors suggest working with an attorney, with guidance from the State Library, on developing staff procedures and public policies.

# Environmental Scan

A cursory review of existing library policies on the acceptable use of and access to networked resources and the Internet, materials selection, and disclaimers reveals some commonality, regardless of library type. Although the customers vary, core issues remain the same. Libraries value and try to protect the privacy of their users, protect the library from liability for misuse of resources, and provide clear mission statements. In many cases, libraries are clear about the consequences of misuse.

## Public Library Policies

The authors recommend the format and content of the Omaha Public Library website for public libraries. In November 2003 this library published on its website the following policies related to network service and resources.

### Mission Statement

The mission of the Omaha Public Library is to educate, inform, enlighten, enrich, and entertain.
The staff, collections, services, programs and facilities advance this mission and provide a diverse range of services which empower the citizens we serve in all facets of their life and work by our dedication to the following:

Library Card Policy

Statement on Unattended Children

Circulation Rules

Internet Policy and Disclaimer"[6]

In its Internet Policy and Disclaimer section on the website, the library provides an introduction with a blunt description of the Internet, and statements on *Filtering by Omaha Public Library; Parental Responsibilities; Internet Access by Minors: Regulations and Restrictions; General Responsibilities of the User,* and a *Disclaimer.* The introductory text follows:

The Internet, a powerful, valuable, and easily accessible medium of gathering information, has emerged and has forever changed the methods by which we as citizens of this country will gather information to educate ourselves and our children.

To fulfill our mission, the Omaha Public Library provides access to a broad range of information resources, including those available through the Internet. Use of the Internet at the Omaha Public Library is a privilege, not a right. We make the Internet service available as part of our mission to offer a broadly defined program of informational, educational, recreational and cultural enrichment opportunities for residents of Omaha and the greater Douglas County region.

The Internet is, in general, an unregulated medium of information and communication. The Omaha Public Library does not monitor and has no control over the information provided through the Internet. Information on the Internet is not necessarily current, accurate, or complete. While much valuable information is available on the Internet, some may be considered by our local community standards to be obscene, patently offensive or harmful, especially to minor children, as defined by applicable state and/or federal laws. The Omaha Public Library must attempt to balance the desire for free unrestricted access to varying informational sources against the need to avoid material that may be harmful to minors or that violates community standards as defined by applicable state law and/or is obscene. For purposes of this policy minors are defined to include all individuals under the age of eighteen years.[7]

This policy is clear and concise. Omaha Public Library does not filter its adult-access computers; does filter children's computers located in specific children's areas in each library; places responsibility with the user and his or her family; requires written permission for use by minors; is specific about the consequences of unlawful activities; and codifies this policy by noting it was approved by the Library Board of Trustees on October 21, 1998, revised January 20, 1999, and revised again on May 17, 2000.

Subscription databases also are available and are clearly listed on the Omaha Public Library website. The database list is annotated with icons for Kid Friendly (🧒) and Site Accessible with Library Card number and your PIN (▬). When users attempt to access a database they are notified it is restricted, and a library ID number is requested. The user is then validated for use and passed through to the database vendor site. There are no specific policies outlined for subscription electronic resources, except as interpreted in the Internet Policy and Disclaimer. There is a further note indicating the funding source for some databases (e.g., "… the Nebraska Library Commission and is made possible by funding from the Legislature and Governor").[8] These statements are not uncommon, and are often required in order for libraries benefiting from state or federal funds to provide access to electronic resources.

### Academic Library Policies

Academic libraries often include additional guidance beyond policies and procedures. The authors recognize four institutions with model policies: The University of Virginia Library, the University of Hawaii at Hilo Library, the University of Tennessee Libraries, and the University of Texas at San Antonio Library.[9] These are singled out for the range of policies included, as well as for the inclusion of national association guidelines and best practices on access, intellectual freedom, and privacy.

An academic library consortium—the International Coalition of Library Consortia (ICOLC)—has developed a range of guiding documents regarding the acquisition of and access to electronic resources. Among those documents are the *Statement of Current Perspective and Preferred Practices for the Selection and Purchase of Electronic Information*.[10]

### School Library Policies

Although many schools do not publish library policies to their websites, they exist. Many state departments of education provide access from their websites to state-based requirements, guidelines, and best practices for school library policies. One in particular is the California Department of Education.[11] Links are provided to sample policies at individual schools, as well as state guidance on acceptable use, intellectual freedom, and collection development. It is important to remember that local communities, school districts, and state agencies play a significant role in the policies, guidelines, and best practices of school libraries.

### State Library Policies

State libraries provide guidance to their constituents on a range of policy matters, and the authors recommend visiting state library wesites for additional—and the most current—information.[12] Among the state libraries taking a lead in providing sample library policies are those of Connecticut, Indiana, Louisiana, Ohio, and Wisconsin. The policy sections of these websites deal with such topics as behavior, intellectual freedom, materials selection, Internet access, long-range planning, unattended children, and technology planning.[13]

## Other Policy Sources

In some states regional library cooperatives compile and post library policies to their websites. One such example is the Massachusetts Regional Library System, where three regional libraries in that system provide access to their policies.[14] State library associations offer another mechanism for identifying state requirements for minimum standards of operation, sample policy statements, and best practices in developing model policies. Consult the American Library Association website link to State and Regional Chapters.[15]

Another resource is *Sample Library Policies for the Small Public Library*, compiled by the Small Library Committee of the Wisconsin Association of Public Librarians.[16] Nonlibrary entities such as the Municipal Research & Services Center of Washington (MRSC), located in Seattle, provide services to local and municipal entities within the state. This particular organization maintains a useful list of public library policies on the Web (see http://www.mrsc.org/subjects/infoserv/publiclib/libpolicy.aspx?r=1). Among the policies are behavior, materials selection, computer access, Internet use, and confidentiality.[17] A number of professional associations provide policy guidance, among them the Special Libraries Association and the Public Library Association. These associations provide guidance on policy development and key issues at the state and national levels regarding library policies, as well as publications regarding Internet policies and technology planning that may be useful in developing policies and procedures around networked services (Public Library Association, 2003).

# Creating a Records Management Policy and Practice

Given the complex nature of the technology, policy, service community, and legal environment in which libraries operate, the authors recommend that libraries develop a records management policy that governs the use and reuse of library records. Library records include, but are not limited to:

• Patron borrowing and circulation records;

• Web log files;

• Database, e-book, and e-journal use logs;

• Patron network service and resource use records (i.e., any service or resource that requires a unique patron identifier to access, such as workstation reservation, database login, e-book check out); and

• Instructional session attendance.

Each of these forms of records can link service and resource usage to a particular patron in some way, though with varying degrees of accuracy. For example, Web log files may track a website session through an IP address, which may or may not correspond to a particular patron. Licensed resources, particularly those accessed via nonlibrary locations, tend to require a specific login by a user, typically the patron's library card identification number.

Given that each of these various network service and resource use files has the potential to identify service and resource use by patrons, it is important for libraries to develop clear policies and guidelines that govern the use and reuse of these records; the requirements that libraries may have to make such records available to law enforcement agencies; the library's record maintenance and disposal policy (e.g., Web log files are destroyed annually); and any other situational factors that may affect access to and use of these records. As indicated earlier in this chapter, the library needs to develop and communicate these records through a public process to ensure that the library serves the interests of its community, but also to ensure that the community is aware of factors (e.g., the USA Patriot Act, CIPA) that may dictate some or all of the content of various policies.

## Conclusion

Policies concerned with the acquisition, use, and access to network services and resources are complex, but necessary. The changing landscape of technology development, user savvy, and laws makes it even more important to review and revise various library policies on a continual basis. Are too many policies a problem? Possibly. Are too few policies a problem? Absolutely. The strategy should be to develop policies that are necessary and legally required, to educate the public about policies, and to consult users and community organizations for input into the policies, because they will have to abide by the policies developed. The authors have provided a case study that they hope articulates best practice for policy development and review. In addition, the Environmental Scan provided real examples of policies, as did other support resources.

## Notes

1. Nelson, Sandra & Garcia, June. (2003). *Creating Policies for Results: From Chaos to Clarity.* Chicago, IL: Public Library Association. PLA Results Series. http://www.ala.org/Content/NavigationMenu/PLA/Publications_and_Reports/Publications_List/Publications_List.htm. Last accessed December 11, 2003.

2.  Interlibrary Loan Code for the United States. Prepared by the Interlibrary Loan Committee, Reference and User Services Association, 1994, revised 2001. Approved by the RUSA Board of Directors, January 2001. http:// www.ala.org/Content/NavigationMenuOur_Association/Divisions/ RUSA/Professional_Tools4/Reference_Guidelines/Interlibrary_Loan _Code_for_the_United_States.htm. Last accessed December 13, 2003.

3.  HR 3162. 107th CONGRESS. US Patriot Act (Uniting and Strengthening America by Providing Appropriate Tools Required to Intercept and Obstruct Terrorism). Permanent public access is available from http://frwebgate.access.gpo.gov/cgi-bin/getdoc.cgi?dbname=107 _cong_bills&docid=f:h3162enr.txt.pdf.

4.  For additional information about Children's Internet Protection Act (CIPA) impact on Federal grant programs, please visit the following websites: http://www.ala.org/Content/NavigationMenu/Our_Association/ Offices/ALA_Washington/Issues2/Civil_Liberties,_Intellectual_ Freedom,_Privacy/CIPA1/Legislation/Analysis.PDF.http://www.fcc.gov/ learnnet/http://www.sl.universalservice.org/.http://www.imls.gov/ whatsnew/leg/protection_act.htm

5.  Electronic Frontier Foundation. Foreign Intelligence Surveillance Act Frequently Asked Questions (and Answers). Available at http:// www.eff.org/Censorship/Terrorism_militias/fisa_faq.html. Last accessed December 10, 2003.

6.  Omaha Public Library. Statements & Policies. Available at http:// www.omaha.lib.ne.us/aboutus/policies.html. Last accessed December 6, 2003.

7.  Omaha Public Library. Omaha Public Library Internet Policy and Disclaimer. Available at http://www.omaha.lib.ne.us/ aboutus/inetpolicy.html#two. Last Accessed December 2, 2003.

8.  Ibid. Online Reference. Online Databases. Subscription Databases offered by Omaha Public Library. Available at http://www.omaha .lib.ne.us/subjects/databases.shtml. Last accessed December 6, 2003.

9.  University of Virginia Library. General Information. Library Policies. University Library Policies. Available at http://www.lib.virginia.edu/ policies/. Last accessed December 3, 2003. University of Hawaii at Hilo Library. Library Policies. Available at http://library.uhh.hawaii.edu/ lib_services/policies.htm. Last accessed December 3, 2003. University of Tennessee Libraries. Electronic Resources Collection Development Policy. Available at http://www.lib.utk.edu/~colldev/elrescd.html. Last accessed December 6, 2003. University of Texas at San Antonio Library. Policies. Available at http://www.lib.utsa.edu/About/ policies.html#web. Last accessed December 3, 2003.

10. International Coalition of Library Consortia (ICOLC). Statement of Current Perspective and Preferred Practices for the selection and purchase of electronic information (March 1998). Available at http://www.library.yale.edu/consortia/statement.html. Additional information on ICOLC policies is available at http://www.library.yale.edu/consortia/statementsanddocuments.html. Last accessed December 3, 2003.

11. California Department of Education. Available at http://www.cde.ca.gov/library/policies.html. Last accessed December 6, 2003.

12. Chief Officers of Library Agencies (COSLA). This website is recommended to identify individual state library websites. Available at http://www.cosla.org. Last accessed December 6, 2003.

13. Connecticut State Library. Policy Development Materials for Public Libraries. Available at http://www.cslib.org/poldev.htm. Last accessed December 5, 2003.

14. Massachusetts Regional Library Systems. Massachusetts Regional Library Systems Policy Collection. Central Massachusetts. Available at http://www.cmrls.org/policies/; Metrowest available at http://www.mmrls.org/libpol.html; Western available at http://www.wmrls.org/policies/index.html. Last accessed December 5, 2003.

15. American Library Association. State and Regional Chapters. Available at http://www.ala.org/Content/NavigationMenu/Our_Association/Chapters/State_and_Regional_Chapters/State_and_Regional_Chapters.htm. Last accessed December 8, 2003.

16. Sample Library Policies for the Small Public Library. Compiled by the Small Library Committee of the Wisconsin Association of Public Librarians, 2nd Edition. Revised by David L. Polodna, 1999. Converted to HTML by OWLS and posted with permission.

17. Municipal Research & Services Center of Washington (Seattle, WA) Library Policies on the Web. Available at http://www.mrsc.org/subjects /infoserv/publiclib/libpolicy.aspx?r=1. Last accessed December 6, 2003.

## References

American Library Association (2003). *Children's Online Privacy Protection Act (COPPA). **Important policy notice to libraries on children's online privacy.*** Available: http://www.ala.org/Template.cfm?Section=Childrens_Online_Privacy_Protection_Act_(COPPA)&Template=/ContentManagement/ContentDisplay.cfm&ContentID=11052. Last accessed December 11, 2003.

Doyle, C. (2002, April 18). *The USA PATRIOT Act: A sketch* [RS21203]. Washington, D.C.: Congressional Research Service, The Library of Congress.

Elsea, J. (2003, May 19). Proposed change to the Foreign Intelligence Surveillance Act (FISA) under S. 113 [RS21472]. Washington, D.C.: Congressional Research Service, The Library of Congress. Available: http://www.fas.org/irp/crs/RS21472.pdf. Last accessed December 10, 2003.

Jaeger, P.T., Bertot, J.C., & McClure, C.R. (2003). The impact of the USA Patriot Act on collection and analysis of personal information under the Foreign Intelligence Surveillance Act. *Government Information Quarterly*, 20(3): 295-314.

Jaeger, P.T., Bertot, J.C., & McClure, C.R. (2004). The effects of the Children's Internet Protection Act (CIPA) in public libraries and its implications for research: A statistical, policy, and legal analysis. *Journal of the American Society for Information Science*, 55(13): 1131-1139.

Public Library Association. (2003). Best Practices in Public Libraries. Available: http://www.ala.org/Content/NavigationMenu/PLA/Resources/Best_Practices _in_Public_Libraries.htm. Publications include Public Library Association (1999). Wired for the future: Developing your library technology plan. Chicago, IL: American Library Association. Public Library Association (1998). Children and the Internet: Guidelines for developing public library policy. Chicago, IL: American Library Association. All information and Websites last accessed December 5, 2003.

# CHAPTER 8

# Resource Allocation in the Networked Environment

## Judith Hiott and Syma Zerkow

### Introduction

The missions of libraries have changed little in the last 100 years. Connecting customers to knowledge is the same whether a toddler is learning that picture and story are related to words on a page, a researcher is discovering how infected cells travel through the body, or a lawyer is escaping a grueling day in the pages of a novel. In the networked environment, however, the *means* to these ends have changed, and they will continue to change for the foreseeable future. Simply put, gaps of time and distance have been erased, and to the extent that these advantages outweigh the old, comfortable models of accumulating knowledge, they have been adopted. It may be many years before the printed book is no longer the preferred medium, but ultimately the transformation will happen. The ease—and the fun—with which libraries help users make the transition may determine the success of libraries. Making the transition with tax-driven budgets continues to be a challenge. More and more academic institutions are increasing student fees to support library budgets, and many public libraries are pursuing dedicated tax revenues, such as special tax districts and dedicated millage rates. Grants and endowments are increasingly essential for innovative projects in all libraries, and dedicating additional time and resources to fundraising activities has become essential to library budgets.

Making budget choices between nonnetworked and networked service models requires being in transition between one model and another, knowing where you are in that transition, and understanding the service and budget impact of going too slow or too fast in the transition. It also requires a commitment to move forward or stay still, but to go back only in exceptional circumstances. A continuous strategic planning model facilitates the transition, particularly when integrated with an assessment planning process as described in Chapter 1.

The pace of change in the networked environment makes a one-year sustainability plan a necessity, particularly in times of small budgets. Conversely, the five-year plan changes with technology and is dependent upon the availability of discretionary funding at any given time. Its implementation is nonlinear and opportunistic. Although difficult to develop and articulate, a ten-year vision is helpful in the networked environment. Major changes, such as transitions to e-book technology and reallocation of staff, are both easier to budget and more amenable to staff and to users when instituted over a longer period of time. A library with an accountant, an opportunist, and a visionary who enjoy working together to move the library forward is bound to succeed. If necessary, an exceptional administrator can play all of these roles, but a variety of input is preferable. A planning and budgeting model for libraries in the networked environment might look like Fig. 8-1.

**Figure 8-1**
**Library planning and budgeting model for the networked environment.**

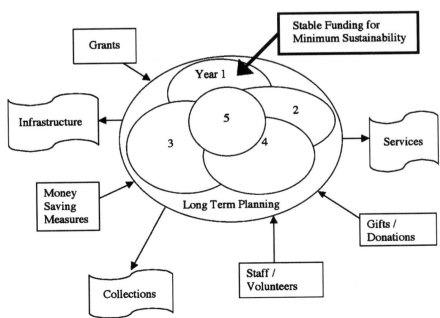

# Sustainability

To create a sustainable budget, each individual library must determine the minimum services to support and the outcomes expected from the delivery of those services. The information technology (IT) budget must include direct support of networked services and indirect support of nonnetworked services. The library's most stable funding sources should be able to support these minimum services. All other services should be prioritized and budgeted as the library identifies additional funding.

Examples of networked services and support services considered essential to many libraries include:

- Telecommunications to support increasing demands of the Web and networked services;

- Workstation replacement at a minimum replacement rate (every three to four years is optimal);

- A minimal online collection (not usually funded in the IT budget);

- A minimal Web presence; and

- Staffing to maintain the minimum level of networked services and networked support services.

These services provide a critical core infrastructure through which libraries can offer a variety of networked services and resources.

# Infrastructure

As long as telecommunications subsidies continue through such programs as the E-rate, minimum infrastructure is not difficult to sustain for most libraries, even in poor budget scenarios. The resourcefulness with which libraries identify and utilize discretionary funds determines how much and how quickly libraries are able to innovate in tough budgetary times. Sustainable innovation begins with changes in the management of everyday processes and infrastructure that increase the overall productivity of the IT department or the library as a whole. This is crucial to implementing state-of-the-art technology that permits the library to start a "hot" new service. Almost all innovations in productivity and process management require a move away from an established way of operating, but a well-researched and planned move can make a vast difference in the services a library provides.

Process management should be evolving constantly to take advantage of changing technology. For example, many libraries have stopped purchasing productivity software and electronic resources that are offered only in CD-ROM format. SimDesk Technologies is providing Web-based word processing and spreadsheet software, as well as computer storage space, to library users in metropolitan public libraries including Houston, Dallas, and Chicago. Academic institutions are supporting access to Web products such as WebCT and Blackboard. This allows libraries to discontinue non-Web-based technology infrastructure for public computers. IT staff can focus efforts on maintaining fewer and more secure platforms.

Choosing only Web-based services can be restrictive in two ways. First, there is usually a loss of software functionality in the Web environment. To avoid this, libraries should look for the most flexible and innovative Web-based products. Ask yourself if a student could create and mount a website or presentation with multimedia components using a Web-based public terminal at your library. If not, find the Web resources that will allow this. Public libraries should approach providers of the best free Web-based educational games and discuss the purchase of Web-based suites of games without advertising content. This will allow movement away from the support of separate stand-alone terminals dedicated to this single type of use. Second, many libraries have still not reached optimal network speeds or an optimal number of Internet access points. Making a commitment to totally Web-based computer services is difficult until resolution of these issues.

Streamlining terminal management varies with a library's available resources and the goals the library wants to accomplish. Standardizing the software configuration and security across computers is common to most libraries. Additional process improvements include thin client solutions and the use of systems management servers (SMS). Thin clients not only centralize terminal management but also extend the lifetime of individual public access terminals by three to four years. SMS or similar technologies allow software updates from a centralized location, saving staff time and resources, especially in multilocation libraries.

Public wireless networks in libraries allow more users to use library resources without the expense and upkeep of more workstations. An additional advantage is the positive publicity associated with being a wireless access point. Wireless carts add convenience to nonpublic applications of wireless technology, including mobile computer labs for training, remote circulation, and collection management tasks such as weeding and inventory (Breeding, 2002a).

Moving away from proprietary and nonstandards-based software saves funds at almost any level. Implementing open-source applications requires an investment in staff expertise, but large libraries that have existing staff with programming skills can manage some projects often with older equipment than most commercial software demands. For example, the Houston Public Library created a Web-based retrieval system for its central library using open-source software. This system facilitates retrieval of periodicals, books, and audio-visual items housed in closed stack areas. The system provides usage statistics by title that inform collection development decisions, and it also allows more flexibility in staffing for retrievals.

The freedom of working on a smaller scale has made open-source implementation widespread in a few medium-sized libraries. The Meadville Public Library in Pennsylvania uses open-source applications for everything from thin clients to desktop applications to digitization projects. Meadville advocates starting small and building on your success (Murdock, 2003). Similarly, Nelsonville Public Library in Ohio became the first public library to use Koha, an open-source integrated library system. Nelsonville moved to an open-source system "because the types of things we want are not going to appear in commercial library software for years" (Hedges, 2003). Lack of consistent technical support and the possibility of losing the expertise required to maintain such a system deter most libraries from moving in this direction. However, careful planning at Nelsonville has created a comfort level acceptable to staff, the freedom to develop on a library level, and the cost savings provided by open-source software.

One currently popular trend is federated searching. This allows multiple databases to be searched at one time, offering library users a more "Google-like" experience when dealing with licensed databases. Implementing federated search products is made expensive by the lack of consistent standards, both in metadata and in search and retrieval protocols. In addition, some vendors are charging for the products by the database. Therefore, the most efficient implementation for the money may be a product that searches five to ten critical databases in combination with an OpenURL resolver. Clear, consistent standards for federated searching would be a better solution and should be advocated.

## Small Underfunded Libraries

Almost all of these kinds of innovations are unattainable for most small libraries. Without the technical expertise, strategic planning direction, and funding provided by umbrella organizations—state library and state higher education support systems, larger flagship campuses, and city or county governments—sustaining networked services of any kind is impossible. The networked environment has done more to improve equity of access in libraries than any innovation since interlibrary loan. Without the support and infrastructure needed to sustain networked activities, it will not be possible to maintain and improve equal access to information, regardless of location. Advocacy on the part of all libraries for government-funded infrastructure support, collections, and services is crucial.

## Collections

According to Sandra Nelson, the only measure of success for a public library is use (Nelson, 2003). Public libraries have long been dubious about funding low-performing collections. In a 1976 article, Marvin Scilken advocates high-performing collections with a "pre-weeding" strategy (p. 69):

> When a book gets an "every library should have" review, but deep in my heart I know it won't move, we buy and file the cards but not the book. Then, if the book gets requested, we buy or borrow it.

In the networked environment, the space- and resource-saving possibilities of electronic collections, a growing user preference for remote services, and the competitive space demands of information infrastructure are pushing the print budgets toward primarily high-performance circulating collections, limited in both age and size.

For most libraries, especially public libraries, the need for ever-more stack space—a shibboleth of library planning for centuries—is no longer valid. The transformative force of this shift is networked computing, which has crushed some markets and changed others. It also has affected the way that many citizens get their information and the kind of information they want. Within this context, limiting the size of paper-based collecting is an obvious policy opportunity (Holt, 2003).

Academic libraries will continue to allocate a portion of their resources to storing the history of knowledge in its original form, but it is already clear that a few huge facilities may provide access to most of printed history in a not-too-distant future. What has not been digitized will be requested from one of these depositories, and either digitized for all to use (if it is in the public domain) or digitized and sold to the requesting library or individual, with its associated rights. Brewster Kahle's project to create a digital archive of a million books (Wolf, 2003), as well as Proquest's historical newspapers and Elsevier's plans to digitize its entire back file (Elsevier, 2003), are three examples of the direction print collections of historical value are taking. On the library front, funding the price of electronic content over the physical delivery of its print equivalent is increasingly a choice that many libraries are making (Hulsey, 2003):

After some research we switched to the article delivery service UnCover for about $250 annually, and we were able to deliver requested articles to patrons in three or four days. We now use this service only minimally, as we get all of the full-text journals available through the Michigan eLibrary (MeL). We have money and improved customer service. Also, the by-product of the reworked staff time has been dramatic.

Two budget reallocation strategies work in tandem to move libraries to the resources and services that best support their collections. They are 1) allocation of budget proportionate to use, and 2) abandonment of non-networked collection models to support networked collection models. Allocation proportionate to use presumes that a library is able to measure the use of its collections. Circulation is the traditional measure of use in the print environment and is easily collected, but measuring the use of noncirculating materials has always been a manual and staffintensive process. For this reason, such counts are rare. Fortunately, a historical measure of periodical retrievals, originally intended for staffing allocation, has provided Houston Public Library with valid information about the changes in print periodical use at its Central Library (Fig. 8-2). Even without such statistics, user preferences for the online format for homework and research are so obvious that the collection response to these trends is to continue to support and bolster electronic collections, especially in the form of aggregated periodicals databases.

**Figure 8-2**
**Print magazine retrievals for the Houston Public Library Central Library.**

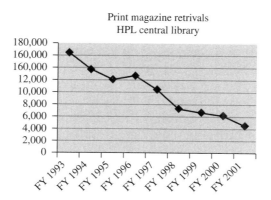

User preferences have changed even more swiftly in research libraries, particularly in the areas of science, technology, and medicine. The immediate response was to supplement print subscriptions with electronic journal subscriptions when available. According to ARL supplementary statistics for 2001–2002 (ARL, 2003):

Experimental data collected by ARL libraries over the last decade indicate that the portion of the library's materials budget that is spent on electronic materials has increased more than fivefold, from an estimated 3.6% in 1992-93 to 19.6% in 2001-02. 110 ARL university libraries reported spending more than $171 million on electronic resources in 2001-02. The vast majority of that was spent on electronic serials and subscription services, expenditures for which have increased sharply: from just $11 million when first reported on this survey in 1994-95, to more than $151 million today. Also, 48 ARL libraries reported another $20.3 million expended on their behalf through centrally funded consortia.

A few urban public libraries are attempting to follow the lead of academic libraries by purchasing e-journal subscriptions. Public library efforts are hampered by user populations that are harder to define than a university's student population. Some publishers willing to test public library markets have accommodated public libraries with reasonable early pricing, followed by adjustments for proven use.

Though librarians have known that the corresponding print collections would have to be reduced, the luxuries of state-funded consortial purchasing as well as a good economy made slow change possible until recently. Branch and small public libraries quickly converted to online indexes, popular magazines, and circulation of back issues, but public libraries with research collections have approached dropping subscriptions more cautiously. Approaches have depended on the type and amount of data available on the use of the print collection. For example, at the Seattle Public Library selecting librarians reviewed each of the library's more than 3000 periodical subscriptions for purpose, scope, focus, and subject coverage, dropping those titles that did not meet prescribed criteria (Tom Horne, personal communication, November, 2003). Houston Public Library, faced with a massive budget cut and approaching its normal periodical drop/add period, cut 30 percent from the Central Library's periodical collection. Though the library's online system for tracking print periodical use by title had been in operation for a year at the time of the cuts, the $212,000 cut reflects a much bigger view of information delivery in the online environment (Table 8-1).

The University of California has been conducting a study of the use of print and electronic journals in order to inform their collection development decisions. They have found that "on average, electronic use is more than sixteen times the rate of print use for the same journal titles" (University of California, 2003). Although the data are fairly new, the user preference for online access has made the transition to online journals much faster in academic libraries than in public libraries. Libraries are canceling print subscriptions in favor of electronic access. Duplication of print journals with full-text electronic access is often no longer affordable. The remaining concerns with canceling print journals in favor of electronic access continue to be issues surrounding availability of archival copies.

**Table 8-1**
**Periodical collection cuts.**

| Category | Number of Titles | Total Cost |
|---|---|---|
| Business Services | 10 | $ 79,418.58 |
| Magazines & Journals | 297 | $ 50,589.93 |
| Standards | 22 | $ 29,445.84 |
| Newspapers | 51 | $ 27,031.29 |
| Duplicates (Including Microform and Bindery Copies) | 75 | $ 14,664.88 |
| Indexes | 9 | $ 11,838.25 |
| **TOTAL DROPS** | | **$ 212,988.77** |

An important consideration before any library drops a print subscription in favor of an electronic journal subscription is the need for continued access to back issues in its collection. When back issues are important, libraries are seeking reasonable guarantees of back issue availability from publishers. Publishers such as Elsevier and Highwire, as well as nonprofit organizations such as JSTOR and OCLC, provide a measure of security to libraries dropping print subscriptions, but much more remains to be done in this area. As archival collections become available, libraries are especially concerned about fair pricing of these collections. Relicensing the same content annually and continued access to purchased back issues if the library is no longer a current subscriber are two of these concerns.

## Reference Collections

Online reference collections have the same advantages as online periodicals—searchable fulltext material, searching several fields at once, and access without geographic limitations—but budgeting for these collections generally means dropping print equivalents. In planning for this, administrators must address both staff acceptance and pricing issues. Staff concerns include long lines of users at computer terminals, making access to print versions faster than online versions inside the library; lingering fears of loss of access due to technical difficulties or subscription changes by the vendor; and educating users to use the online collections. These concerns are occasionally validated by careless online product development that makes print products preferable to their online counterparts.

Solving these issues will take time and will depend on staff training, customer education, and funding for continual improvements of infrastructure. As libraries are able to add workstations, provide wireless access, and improve connections, the convenience of online will overcome the dependence on print. As technology and online resources prove themselves, staff and customers will accept online reference products in the same way they do online periodical products.

Pricing issues include confused marketing on the part of publishers who are unsure whether their products would sell better as e-books or databases. Although single-title searching is not efficient, aggregating multiple titles into a single product may increase the price of the product beyond what many libraries can afford. In addition, librarians are reluctant to pay for the same content on an annual basis (license rather than purchase), and vendors are reluctant to provide wider geographic access than was previously provided by multiple print copies. Vendors continue to test different pricing models, and a variety of pricing schemes exist for different types and sizes of libraries.

Having usage statistics for print reference sources would go a long way toward facilitating the transition from print to online. Usage measures for print reference collections are not readily available, since they do not circulate. Ultimately, libraries are relying on anecdotal evidence from reference librarians that includes both an admission that only a tiny portion of the old print reference collection continues to be used, and some reluctance to move to online. When requests for specific online titles reach a critical point, budgetary constraints require and force adoption of the online material, and most librarians at this point are willing to drop print. Using this model may result in more satisfied staff, but slow growth of online reference collections.

## One-time Purchases

One tool for growing online collections during slow adoption periods and slow markets is buying products with an outright purchase option for the content and a minimal annual access fee. With a much lower annual commitment, libraries can use grants and gifts to purchase the content, with less worry about how to fund the collection in succeeding years. These purchasing models are especially attractive to academic libraries whose researchers are finding digitized historical collections invaluable to research. Although it is necessary to the mission of the university, a collection of this type might be used only in spurts and will never grow in content like a periodical collection. Some academic libraries are also pursuing local maintenance of the data to guarantee archiving of the content and to avoid annual maintenance fees.

One-time purchases have played a large role in the initial growth of e-book collections in libraries. The transition from print books to e-books may be slow—hampered by less than ideal technology for reading them—but the e-book environment has several characteristics that help librarians bring about the transition at a pace that approximates user adoption. First, the majority of e-book purchases to date have been one-time purchases with minimal or no fees for continued access in succeeding years. Libraries don't have to fear not having the money to relicense their collections annually. TexShare, Texas' statewide consortium for public and academic libraries, has designated one-time money annually for the purchase of e-books, precisely because the financial commitment is finite.

In addition, comparing e-book to print book performance provides the most accurate comparison of online use to print use available today. E-book views resemble print circulations more than any other online use count. Having these counts for both collections allows libraries to track the percentage use by each type of source and make budget adjustments as preferences shift. Turnover rate, a popular performance measure for print collections in public libraries, is easily duplicated in e-book collections. The annual turnover rate for the 26,361 e-books in the Houston Public Library catalog is 1.5 uses per volume, compared to approximately 3 circulations per volume for HPL's circulating print collection. The majority of the e-book collection is part of a consortial purchase that is shared with libraries across the state. On a statewide level the annual turnover rate of the collection is more than 8 uses per volume. Clearly, sharing the collection vastly improves its overall performance.

A disadvantage of one-time purchases of e-books is the tendency for the collections to go stale when funding isn't available. A couple of vendors have addressed this issue by offering collections of high-use ephemeral computer books that are kept up-to-date. But ultimately, libraries will need to consider e-books as a part of the total collection management process. Availability of all formats will need to be announced simultaneously so libraries can make selection decisions for all formats of a title simultaneously. As the market evolves and downloadable e-books become more popular, additional pricing models will surely emerge. For example, a percentage of bestseller purchases might include a number of electronic downloads/circulations available during the first month the book is on the market. Not only would an e-book be available the day the print edition comes out, but also the cost of processing and deleting extra copies when a book's popularity has waned could be avoided.

## Consortial Purchasing

No cost-saving tool has proven more effective in the networked environment or provided more benefit to underfunded libraries than consortial purchasing of collections. Realizing that small rural libraries could be funded in the consortial environment—and could move libraries toward equity of access for all users, no mater where they lived—consortia have formed everywhere. Statewide consortia using state funding exist in many states for this purpose. Many academic libraries are members of several consortia, and the use of consortia to expand e-journal collections of all members is a common purchasing strategy. Purchasing models vary widely, but two principles guarantee the pricing that makes consortial purchasing so worthwhile. First, the buying power of a consortium is greatest when all participants agree to participate in the same purchase. The kind of consortial purchasing that offers a small discount on products that members pick and choose seldom results in significant savings. The vendor cannot be guaranteed enough participants for a large discount. Second, the bigger the consortia, the more buying power it has and the lower the cost to individual libraries. When the funding is in the form of state tax dollars that do not cut into individual libraries' budgets, all members are willing to participate. But a consortial purchase for which members contribute local funding is difficult to accomplish on a large scale. When a library contributes precious local funds to a consortial purchase, it wants a guarantee that what is purchased will support the library's individual mission. The larger the consortium, the more difficult it is to get a consensus about what should be purchased.

In Texas, huge state government deficits in 2002 and 2003 resulted in a significant reduction in funding for state government-funded consortial collections. Several initiatives have developed to lessen the impact of the loss of funding. These projects are testing whether libraries can develop enough consensus to make contributions toward large consortial purchases. TexShare responded to its cuts by forming a committee of librarians to explore assessing supplementary fees to fund existing purchases. Following a survey, a ten-tiered fee schedule was developed for which 316 public libraries—each serving a population less than 12,000—paid nothing, and ARL libraries (the top tier) paid $15,000 (2003, Texas State Library and Archives Commission). Fees were adjusted the second year so that all libraries contributed to the cost of TexShare subscriptions. A few large, well-funded libraries felt that much more money should be collected to increase the benefit; however, there was not enough consensus among member libraries to adopt this strategy. Statewide purchasing beyond the existing TexShare collection will likely require the creation of subgroups that have more consensus about the databases they want, but somewhat less buying power.

At a local level, the five largest public libraries in the Houston area met to determine if any benefits could be gained from purchasing databases as a small consortium. The libraries agreed that any purchases would be made by all participants in order to take full advantage of the group's buying power. The goal for the first purchase became finding a database for which each library either saved money or added a database for a reasonable price. The process of evaluating quotes required sharing cost information about each library's existing database subscriptions. For some products, the relative differences in what libraries pay for databases are significant. These products were eliminated, because the consortial quote from the vendor would have resulted in a price increase for one or more members. In fact, the two databases that were purchased in 2004 were databases for which only one or two of the libraries had subscriptions. For the vendors, added subscriptions from other libraries more than made up for the savings afforded to existing subscribers.

To simplify the discussion, quotes were obtained for each physical building. As the discussion progressed, a few libraries with a single building serving a large population joined the purchase. To add smaller libraries in the future will require changing the pricing model to one based on either population or usage. Although purchases by this group have resulted in meaningful savings, the same purchases on a statewide public library scale would produce even more financial benefit.

## Vendor Negotiations

After participating in the library online marketplace for some time, a librarian understands that as many vendors charge what they can get for their products as those who provide the same pricing schedule to all of their customers. The result is a purchasing climate in which there is little uniformity between what libraries with similar size or user base pay. This climate has developed both from uncertainty on the part of vendors about how to make the transition to a new market and from little discussion among librarians and with vendors about how much information is worth, or what is being purchased with the money spent.

The International Coalition of Library Consortia (ICOLC) laid the groundwork for fair purchasing practices with its "Statement of Current Perspective and Preferred Practices for the Selection and Purchase of Electronic Information," most recently revised in December 2001. It affirms that libraries cannot afford rising costs in both print and its electronic equivalents, and that some libraries are responding by dropping print. The document calls for pricing practices that help libraries make the most of their budgets. ICOLC recommends changing from the common practice of adding online e-journals to print subscriptions to the reverse: adding print subscriptions to online e-journals. A payment-per-use model that the ICOLC calls "pay-by-the-drink" is another suggested purchasing model. (International Coalition of Library Consortia, 2001) Paying an annual rate is ICOLC's alternative to "pay by the drink," but basing the annual rate on the previous year's use is not mentioned, and should be considered. (Note: Chapter 6 provides guidance on the writing of a request for proposal or information from vendors that facilitates the negotiation of vendor agreements.)

Libraries should be advocates for uniform price models that are based on use after the first year. For the first year, a library and vendor can mutually agree on a price based on the library's use of a similar database or another library's use of the same database. Insisting on cost per use negates the need for pricing by simultaneous user, building, number of card holders, FTEs, or population served—pricing models that often have no correlation to a library's actual use of a product.

Searches have always been the most easily defined measure of use in the online environment, but the number of searches can be manipulated by increasing or decreasing the efficiency of the search engine. Furthermore, searches increase many times and become almost meaningless with the implementation of increasingly popular federated search tools. The cost per-use measure of the online collection that has the most meaning is cost per units or record examined, since requests reflect a user's selection of material and resemble a circulation. In the immediacy of the networked environment, most libraries have seen demand for any item that is not full-text drop dramatically. Although tables of contents and abstracts will still have a cost in databases that are not full-text, most libraries are increasingly unwilling to pay for abstract-only databases and prefer to measure use in terms of full-text items.

The Houston Public Library used cost per full-text article for the first time in 2003 as part of pricing negotiations for licensed databases. The library set five dollars per article request as the upper limit of an acceptable average cost for a full-text item. Besides a small amount of monetary savings, this accomplished for the library a comparison of online resources to each other and discussions with vendors about what is fair cost. But isolated instances of these practices will do little to move vendors toward adopting new pricing models. More can be accomplished with a common, concerted approach to vendor negotiations on the part of libraries. Strategies adopted by libraries in this effort should include:

• Requiring vendors to supply usage statistics according to NISO standards. (National Information Standards Organization, 2003) If libraries are going to pay based on use in the second year, products for which statistics aren't available should be purchased with caution and only following detailed discussion with vendors about the library's expectations.

- Refusing to sign a license agreement requiring that the cost of online material be kept confidential. Confidentiality is impossible for libraries governed by open records statutes, but *no* library should agree to this practice.

- Advocate tiered pricing schedules so customers with very high use pay less per use than customers with significantly lower use. The effect of consortial purchasing would be to push the consortia into a higher tier, with the savings that entails.

- Treating formal requests for quotes as an advantage, rather than a burden, to the acquisitions process. When several vendors provide similar products, libraries should regularly evaluate the content, the interface, the cost per use, and the vendor support against a predetermined set of criteria.

- Refusing to accept the practice by bigger vendors of bundling their products and negotiating as a whole when a library mentions dropping a single title. Rather than reduce their income from the previous year, these vendors add a new or marginal database to the package and use the cost of an essential title as leverage in negotiations. This practice undermines per-use pricing, forces libraries to accept inferior and/or low-use products, and thwarts attempts to create high-performing library collections.

- Insisting that a percentage of every renewal include new content. Finding out what new content has been added to a product since the library last renewed and what methods are used for growing content is essential to maintaining value in online collections.

Moving toward this type of purchasing increases the overall fairness of the market, but it comes with responsibilities for libraries as well. Collecting usage statistics is no longer a choice; it is a necessity for a library that uses local funds to buy online content. Libraries will need to work with vendors to promote usage of online products by staff and customers, and they must make an effort to increase use by continually improving their Web presence. Conversely, libraries must provide feedback to vendors about improvements to products that will increase usability, and thus use. The ICOLC includes increasing complete and consistent content, adopting interoperable techniques for linking, and enhancing non-English language content among its usability priorities for vendors (International Coalition of Library Consortia, 2001). Additional guidance on negotiating RFPs is provided in Chapter 6.

The open-access movement on the part of the academic community is strong evidence that library budgets cannot sustain unreasonable annual price increases indefinitely. If pay-per-use models were adopted for electronic content, an almost certain result would be that low-use resources would be dropped by commercial publishers. Universities that fund the research published in these titles would have to find different avenues of publication. Free access to the information could provide a wider audience for the information than was provided by commercial publication. Undoubtedly, new avenues of scholarly communication facilitated by the sharing environment of the Internet will emerge, not only by virtue of the inherent good that results, but also because economic sustainability will foster them.

The transition from print to online collections has only just begun. Periodicals and reference resources are already being followed by books that fill homework needs, genealogical resources, locally developed special collections, and digitized primary source material. The sooner librarians and vendors can agree on pricing practices that are fair, the faster both parties can devote their efforts to increasing content, improving access, and marketing to users. Ultimately, we all want to increase the use of the library collection.

## Services and Staffing Implications

As with infrastructure and collections, libraries have made progress in the area of developing and implementing new networked services. Many traditional library services have successfully been extended to the online environment. Some implementations require minor shifts in service emphases, involve inherent cost savings or minor added expenses, often use existing technology, and serve the user at his or her preferred time and place. For example, in only a short time patron-placed holds with e-mail notification have had a major impact on a library's ability to get books quickly to a reader's preferred pickup point. The service has been part of the development of integrated library systems, so costs have been built into the costs of those systems. Staff spends less time processing holds, and when materials budget cuts are necessary, this service lessens the impact of buying fewer copies of well-reviewed titles. The biggest expenses include training a wide variety of staff to use the system correctly and higher costs associated with moving more items from location to location.

E-mail services—including reference and suggestions—use skills that library staff generally already have, but convenience makes these services more popular in the online environment. Minor shifts in staffing as well the creation of efficient procedures are necessary to handle the increased volume of transactions.

No discussion of library services in the networked environment has received more attention than the discussion of the changes in reference services. Few librarians deny that the Internet brought the reference desk changes in clientele, in research methods, and in the questions asked. The preferences of users for services from home, combined with the loss of the fact-finding role of the traditional reference librarian, make reference *doomsday* discussions popular at conferences and in professional literature.

Many libraries have had losses in reference transactions since the advent of the Internet, indicating a need for reevaluation of services. Houston Public Library's 56 percent drop in reference transactions at its central library and the 11 percent drop at its branches over a ten-year period are not uncommon (Fig. 8-3).

**Figure 8-3**
**Houston Public Library reference transactions, 1991–2003.**

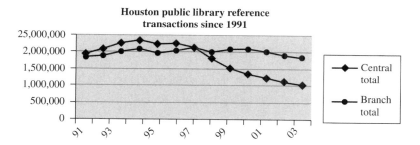

And yet, a look at reference transaction statistics between 1996 and 2002 for 24 more of the largest Texas public libraries shows mixed results (Table 8-2). Changes vary from a yearly annual drop since 1998, like Houston Public's, to ups and downs that amount to minor changes, often with a net increase. In one case, sustained annual increases amount to 313 percent between 1996 and 2002 (Texas State Library, 2003; Public Library Association, 1996 and 1997).

Looking at a library's reference transaction statistics within the context of other statistics, what is most apparent is the complexity of understanding reference changes, due to the number of variables that may affect the changes. Variables for which there are statistics include changes in the number of library locations, population change in service areas, the overall library budget, and the library materials budget. Useful variables that are more difficult to document might also include population demographics of service areas, the focus and location of a library's main branch, changes in counting procedures, and Internet use policy variations. In addition, libraries should begin to collect and report their IT budgets, number of terminals, and amount of staff and customer training, because these factors almost certainly will contribute to the success or failure of networked services.

**Table 8-2**
**Reference transactions: selected large public libraries in Texas.**

| | 1996 | 1997 | 1998 | 1999 | 2000 | 2001 | 2002 | Net Gain/Loss |
|---|---|---|---|---|---|---|---|---|
| San Antonio | 874,949 | 814,531 | 981,566 | 884,716 | 956,848 | 1,236,664 | 1,127,237 | 29% |
| Dallas | 1,740,179 | 1,681,582 | 1,572,643 | 1,493,088 | 1,544,110 | 1,173,516 | 4,661,149 | 168% |
| Harris County | 459,918 | 444,250 | 419,409 | 419,847 | 419,409 | 439,621 | 450,263 | –2% |
| Austin | 483,455 | 436,656 | 396,050 | 396,974 | 409,721 | 440,688 | 427,982 | –11% |
| El Paso | 331,666 | 266,583 | 458,176 | 503,405 | 456,770 | 479,354 | 500,180 | 51% |
| Fort Worth | NA | NA | 1,320,852 | 2,670,333 | 1,777,455 | 1,675,852 | 1,679,483 | 27% |
| Fort Bend | 237,240 | 363,363 | 482,040 | 531,700 | 632,372 | 931,398 | 980,720 | 313% |
| Arlington | 122,179 | 201,760 | 238,979 | 209,872 | 671,151 | 247,845 | 290,979 | 138% |
| Montgomery County | 251,230 | 330,729 | 310,652 | 316,503 | 310,619 | 345,917 | 345,620 | 38% |
| Brazoria County | 48,934 | 54,221 | 45,111 | 48,324 | 40,239 | 38,881 | 45,593 | –7% |
| Lubbock | 263,469 | 266,215 | 239,629 | 131,467 | 206,812 | 289,270 | 227,926 | –13% |
| Plano | 145,241 | 163,867 | 186,598 | 155,303 | 153,063 | 166,117 | 185,591 | 28% |
| Nicholson Memorial | 193,736 | 154,427 | 145,687 | 134,301 | 134,372 | 133,165 | 129,997 | –33% |
| Waco-McLennan | 206,814 | 226,753 | 247,769 | 265,084 | 234,204 | 253,417 | 226,179 | 9% |
| Irving | 163,818 | 164,445 | 145,607 | 164,839 | 182,336 | 199,439 | 197,801 | 21% |
| Amarillo | 753,819 | 785,205 | 740,601 | 700,953 | 721,749 | 825,760 | 902,899 | 20% |

(Continued)

280

**Table 8-2 (Continued)**
**Reference transactions: selected large public libraries in Texas.**

| | 1996 | 1997 | 1998 | 1999 | 2000 | 2001 | 2002 | Net Gain/ Loss |
|---|---|---|---|---|---|---|---|---|
| Bryan/College Station | 29,036 | 31,954 | 30,475 | 27,224 | 24,086 | 28,402 | 27,704 | –5% |
| Pasadena | 38,144 | 35,904 | 37,499 | 29,277 | 33,817 | 31,211 | 26,516 | –30% |
| Mesquite | 100,095 | 105,251 | 127,734 | 143,116 | 170,562 | 172,163 | 150,730 | 51% |
| Ector County | 38,144 | NA | 96,036 | 89,272 | 71,219 | 52,681 | 58,566 | 54% |
| Abilene | 102,663 | 88,948 | 91,966 | 93,123 | 90,401 | 105,049 | 124,929 | 22% |
| Longview | 45,386 | 46,493 | 60,394 | 64,946 | 45,144 | 25,052 | 23,084 | –49% |
| Beaumont | 84,465 | 61,876 | 81,820 | 88,115 | 85,692 | 71,828 | 39,786 | –53% |
| Carrollton | 81,319 | 88,422 | 110,105 | 101,715 | 92,574 | 105,212 | 153,595 | 89% |

While it is difficult to prove that any one factor across all libraries has affected reference transaction statistics since the advent of networked information, it is apparent that some libraries may be making successful transitions to a different kind of reference service. Critical to developing successful reference services into the future is identifying the factors related to success and failure during this initial transition—even if only at an anecdotal, individual library level. Sharing available information with libraries still struggling with the transition is also important.

The most obvious evidence that libraries are reinventing reference services is that thousands of libraries have begun virtual reference services in the last several years. The progress made in this area is significant, considering that the initial setup and training requires more than minor resource adjustments. With IP telephony, telephone and virtual reference can be merged, but most libraries with separate in-person, telephone, and virtual reference services are running three operations. By tracking the use of each type of reference service, libraries can attempt to allocate staff proportionately. However, libraries could do a better job of allocating resources if they had an accurate cost per transaction for each type of reference service. This data could be used to position the best aspects of all three services in such a way that the library provides a convenient and rich reference experience for its users at a reasonable cost for the library. Collecting the data is hampered by a lack of any standards for measuring the cost of any kind of reference services:

> Determining the cost of a digital reference service has many of the same manifold complexities of determining cost of traditional reference. There have been a number of attempts to determine the means of costing reference service, and there have been several estimates of average cost of reference. These estimates have varied widely due to the assumptions under which costs are identified, defined and operationalized. In many cases staff and resources are often utilized by more than one service area within the library and it is difficult to prorate out costs for any one area. (Lankes, Gross, & McClure, 2003)

Even without good cost data, as virtual reference services evolve it is possible to develop strategies that take advantage of the networked environment to decrease costs. The most obvious savings can be gained from collaborating with other libraries to provide the service—another form of consortial resource sharing. Currently, libraries are trying to strike a balance between serving local customers with local staff and partnering with other institutions to take advantage of the benefits of sharing. The cost benefit of sharing staff to cover multiple service areas is important while fledgling services gain popularity. Resource sharing and partial outsourcing of a service also extend service hours and expand the subject expertise available to the service.

Interestingly, the easiest and possibly the most accurate way to measure the cost of virtual reference services is to outsource the entire service. Money spent can be divided by sessions or by questions answered. Both virtual reference and a similar service that provides homework help are being outsourced by libraries. According to Arthur Brady at Tutor.com, a provider of both types of services, online homework help is 100 percent outsourced, but for virtual reference "we have three clients, out of several thousand, that have completely outsourced" (personal communication, December 12, 2003). Since homework help falls outside the usual job description for most library staff, libraries feel comfortable totally outsourcing the homework services. Furthermore, the quality and costs of online homework help are improved when tutors work from home serving multiple clients simultaneously, and the hiring pool is nationwide, rather than local.

With this model in mind, it seems pretty amazing that more libraries don't outsource virtual reference. In fact, separate studies by Tutor.com and the University of Tennessee indicate that most digital reference questions are universal enough to be answered in a collaborative or outsourced environment. Well-developed library Web sites can provide answers to all but a few very specific local questions (Arthur Brady, personal communication, December 12, 2003; Berry, 2003).

## Self-Service

An inherent advantage of the networked environment is that users can help themselves to many of a library's services and collections without ever coming to the library. Although there is little or no staff interaction with the user, a significant amount of ongoing staff time is needed to develop and maintain a functional and effective website. Measuring the success of a website and promoting services that will draw repeated users to the site and into the physical library also increase the staff resources needed for a successful Web presence. There is no existing formula for determining the amount of resources to allocate to web development, but libraries can begin to develop formulas when a significant number of them begin to measure the use of their websites. The first measure should be a count of the number of visits to the website, broken down by users inside and outside the library. If enough libraries collect this one statistic, it can be combined with population data and Web development allocation data to get a sense of the reasonable resources a library should apply to creating and maintaining a website.

Still, measurements of website success do not begin and end with visits. No successful Web business stops at the number of visits to a website, so why should libraries? While libraries should think through the privacy and cost implications of collecting Web statistics for absolutely everything, there is no reason why links to services a library is promoting shouldn't have a clickthrough statistic, or why the library shouldn't keep track of the most frequently visited pages. These statistics can tell the library which pages are being used to get to a service, whether this differs for users inside or outside the library, and whether time is being spent developing pages no one uses. Pages and services that are not being used can be repositioned for another chance at success, or dropped.

Having the resources for a full-blown usability study that includes surveying users and watching them use your website is a nice luxury, but Web usage statistics can provide a lot of useful information with less expense. Information about what statistics to collect and how to collect them can be found in the following references:

- *Statistics and Performance Measures for Public Library Networked Services* (Bertot, McClure, & Ryan, 2001);
- *Data Collection Manual for Academic and Research Library Network Statistics and Performance Measures* (Shim, McClure, Fraser, & Bertot, 2001);
- NISO's *Information Services and Use: Metrics & Statistics for Libraries and Information Providers—Data Dictionary* (National Information Standards Organization, 2003); and
- *Strategies For Measuring and Interpreting E-use* (Breeding, 2002b).

Finally, having staff devoted to Web development should be a goal for every library. Small libraries that can't afford a dedicated Web development position should share a staff person with several other libraries. Besides writing HTML, this person should be able to manage data on the Web, collect Web statistics, and understand the concept of mission-driven Web development. WebJunction (www.webjunction.org), the online community of libraries that OCLC built with the help of the Bill and Melinda Gates Foundation, is a fabulous free resource for learning more about implementing library technology. The site provides classes on a variety of levels, offers tips for saving money, and disseminates news of interest to the library technology community.

## Staffing Reallocations

Ultimately, a commitment to Web-based services requires more than minor shifts in resources—especially in the case of staff resources. Direct costs include keeping the services running and staff and users sufficiently trained to administer them. Indirect staff costs involve marketing the services to the community, advocating for and explaining the services to funding sources, and working for cost-saving standards of all kinds within the library service provider community. Implementing these types of services without additional funding will mean discontinuing a service or increasing the cost efficiency of an existing service. Either option usually requires some amount of staff reallocation.

Networked infrastructure can provide some staffing solutions. For example, a low-use library location might be staffed by paraprofessionals, with the library's virtual reference service supplementing the in-person public service. Web-based bibliographic utilities make it possible to complete collection development assignments from any location. Libraries will ultimately have to find out what each member of its staff does and determine whether other staff can do it as effectively at a lower cost. Instead of being tied to a service desk for thirty hours a week, reference librarians might be *on call* for in-depth transactions, while paraprofessionals and library assistants manage procedural research, technology queues, and troubleshooting. Ideally, a reference librarian might spend half of her or his time on call and the other half in a management activity. Management activities related to the networked environment include managing the services; outreach to users and funding sources; fundraising; training related to networked services; and development of online collections, including website development, search and retrieval improvement, and the creation of digital content.

## Performance Indicators

The Internet is the ultimate tool for resource sharing. Whether extending resources and services to all the locations of a single library or facilitating partnerships among libraries, the opportunities for cost savings and service enhancements seem limitless. The challenge—especially in times of limited budgets—is to resist the inclination to halt innovative projects that may bring about these savings and services. Meeting the challenge requires a commitment on the part of library administrators to evaluate services continually. Evaluating every service the library offers against performance and cost standards ensures that library resources are allocated to provide the most service to the most customers. Realizing that the virtual environment may make sharing or outsourcing of some services more effective and/or less expensive should be part of this evaluation.

In addition, committing to any new project demands establishing performance measures for the project that include not only the number of customers served, but also the cost of serving them. Networked services for which cost formulas might be applied include cost per use of the online collection, cost per visit to the library website, cost per person to train a customer to use technology, cost per use of a public workstation, and cost per use of the library catalog. When a networked service has a non-networked counterpart, corresponding cost formulas for the non-networked services should be developed. Side-by-side comparison of both use and cost can determine the speed at which a transition from non-networked to networked services should move.

To develop these formulas, a library must collect networked statistics. As part of a project to educate public librarians to collect these statistics, the Information Use Management and Policy Institute (Information Institute) conducted a study to develop a core set of e-metrics through surveys and discussions with public librarians, state library agency staff, and consortia staff. The results of this study yielded the following core e-metrics that libraries should collect (Bertot, Subramaniam, McClure, & Davis, 2003):

• Sessions, Searches, and Units/Records examined for databases;

• Virtual Reference Transactions;

• Public Access Work Stations;

• Public Access Workstation Users;

• Virtual Visits;

• Formal User Information Technology Training;

• Electronic Access Expenditures; and

• Electronic Materials Expenditures.

The Information Institute, through a grant from the Institute of Museum and Library Services, developed an online instructional system (the E-metrics Instructional System–EMIS) that provides instruction, guidance, and various other information regarding the collection of these e-metrics (see http://www.ii.fsu.edu/emis). Training modules for instructing libraries about how to collect these statistics are currently available on this site.

Factoring staff costs into these formulas is more difficult. Since few libraries allocate staff to single functions, estimating staffing costs for many services is complicated. Still, occasionally asking staff to account for time spent in established service categories could provide enough information for a cost assessment of services at a local level. Much could be done in the way of standardizing methods for collecting this information.

While many performance measures may be project- or library-specific, adopting a few nationwide measures will allow comparison between similar libraries, a popular assessment tool. Over the past five years, efforts in two areas have been critical to making comparative data sets possible. First, advocacy by the ICOLC and COUNTER for uniformity of database usage definitions across vendor platforms is making database usage statistics a more realistic expectation. (International Coalition of Library Consortia, 2001; COUNTER, 2001) Second, the participation of the Information Institute with the National Information Standards Organization (NISO) and the International Standards Organization (ISO) to revise and enhance library standards—NISO's Z39.7 and ISO 2789 and 11620— for the networked environment is providing libraries with network statistics and performance measures to test and adopt. What remains is collection of the statistics by enough libraries to convince data clearinghouses such as state libraries, the Federal-State Cooperative System, the Public Library Data Service, and the Association of Research Libraries to add a few of the statistics to their standard data sets. With time and a commitment on the part of individual libraries, nationwide data about networked services and collections will be a reality.

## Conclusion

In the history of modern libraries, few advances have had more impact on the way libraries serve customers than the arrival of networked information and services. None has required major service adjustments at so accelerated a rate. Libraries have responded to the change with overwhelming success in the first 10 years of the transition. Taking advantage of further savings and services provided by the networked environment requires continuing to reallocate infrastructure, collections, and staff resources. The result is an evolving suite of networked and non-networked services to provide traditional and new library users with the services they want.

The reallocation effort can be a logical progression. The networked environment itself provides more tools and data for running libraries well than have ever been available. All segments of the library community are helping libraries make infrastructure changes, develop new collections and services, and identify data and performance measures to assess projects and determine the rate of adoption by users. Participation in the process and discussions of the results with other libraries, vendors, and funding agencies furthers the goal of libraries to work better in the networked environment. A continued commitment by libraries to be a part of the cooperative effort makes a difference in the ability of all libraries to serve customers' needs wherever and whenever they choose.

## Acknowledgments

The authors are grateful to several colleagues who provided expertise and information that made this article possible. Mary Beth Thomson at the University of Houston read several drafts and offered invaluable input about academic library issues. Sue Phillips (University of Texas), Toni Lambert, Jeff Robin, George Eggleston, and Brian Carusella (Houston Public Library) also contributed facts, figures, and editorial input that kept us on the right track.

## References

Association of Research Libraries. (2003). *ARL supplementary statistics.* Retrieved from the ARL Statistics and Measurement Program Home at http://www.arl.org/stats/sup/index.html.

Berry, T. U. (2003, Fall). The local nature of digital reference. *The Southeastern Librarian,* 51(3): 8–15.

Bertot, J., McClure, C. and Ryan, J. (2001) *Statistics and performance measures for public library networked services.* Chicago: American Library Association.

Bertot, J., Subramaniam, M., McClure, C., & Davis, D. (2003) *Librarian education for the collection, analysis, and use of library networked services and resources statistics: Interim report* II. Retrieved from the Information Use Management & Policy Institute website at http://www.ii.fsu.edu/projects/2003/imls_training/interim.report2.09_17_2003.pdf.

Breeding, M. (2002a, Summer). A hard look at wireless networks. *Net Connect: Supplement to Library Journal,* 48(8): 14–17.

Breeding, M. (2002b, May-June). Strategies for measuring and interpreting e-use. *Library Technology Reports,* 38(3).

COUNTER (2002, December 1). Counter Code of Practice. Retrieved from http://www.projectcounter.org/code_practice.html.

Elsevier. (2003, October 8*). Elsevier launches THE LANCET backfiles on ScienceDirect* [Press Release]. Retrieved from http://www.elsevier.com/homepage/newhpgnews/production/lancet/links/link1.htm.

Hedges, S. (2003, October 20). Nelsonville Public Library: Questions and answers about open source. *Webjunction.* Retrieved 12 November 2003 from http://www.webjunction.org/do/DisplayContent?id=3941.

Holt, G. (2003, November 1). Starting a revolution: Placing a limit on collection size. *The Bottom Line: Managing library finances.* Retrieved from the Emerald website at http://ariel.emeraldinsight.com/vl=1810003/cl=106/nw=1/rpsv/index.htm.

Hulsey, R. (2003, June 1). Purchase on demand a better customer service model. *Library Journal* [electronic version]. Retrieved from http://www.libraryjournal.com/index.asp?layout=articlePrint&articleID=CA300101.

International Coalition of Library Consortia (2001). *Guidelines for statistical measures of usage of Web-based information resources.* Retrieved from the ICOLC website at http://www.library.yale.edu/consortia/2001webstats.htm.

International Coalition of Library Consortia (2001). *Statement of current perspective and preferred practices for the selection and purchase of electronic information. Update no. 1: New developments in e-journal licensing.* Retrieved from the ICOLC website at http://www.library.yale.edu/consortia/2001currentpractices.htm.

Lankes, R., Gross, M. and McClure, C. (2003, Winter). Cost, statistics, measures and standards for digital reference services: A preliminary view. *Library Trends,* 51(3): 401–413.

Murdock, C. (2003, October 20). Open-source software in the Meadville Public Library. *Webjunction.* Retrieved 12 November 2003 from http://www.webjunction.org/do/DisplayContent?id=3973.

National Information Standards Organization. (2003). *NISO Z39.7-2002 [Draft Standard for Trial Use]: Information services and use: Metrics & statistics for libraries and information providers–Data dictionary, Version 2002a.* Retrieved from the National Information Standards Organization website at http://www.niso.org/emetrics/current/complete.html.

Nelson, S. (2003, February 21). *Managing for tomorrow: Leadership for results.* Workshop presented for the Houston Area Library System, Houston, TX.

Public Library Association (1996). *Statistical Report '96.* Chicago: American Library Association.

Public Library Association. (1997). *Statistical Report '97.* Chicago: American Library Association.

Scilken, M. (1976). Solving space and performance problems in a public library. In Daniel Gore (Ed.), *Farewell to Alexandria: solutions to space, growth, and performance problems of libraries* (pp. 62–71). Westport, CT: Greenwood.

Shim, W., McClure, C., Fraser, B., & Bertot, J. (2001) *Data collection manual for academic and research library network statistics and performance measures* [electronic version]. Retrieved from http://www.arl.org/stats/newmeas/emetrics/phase3/ARL_Emetrics_Data_Collection_Manual.pdf.

Texas State Library and Archives Commission (2003, October 8). *TexShare database fees FY2004 (for July 1, 2004–June 30, 2005).* Retrieved from the Texas State Library & Archives Commission website at http://www.texshare.edu/programs/academicdb/texsharefees.2004.html.

Texas State Library and Archives Commision. *Public Library Directory and Statistics.* Retrieved from the Texas State Library and Archives Commision website at http://www.tsl.state.tx.us/ld/pubs/pls/index.html.

University of California (2003, September 2). Preliminary findings from the journal use and user preference studies. *Collection Management Initiative.* Retrieved from the University of California website at http://www.ucop.edu/cmi/docs/cmi_prelim_findings_072103.doc.

Wolf, G. (2003, October 23). The great library of Amazonia. *Wired News.* Retrieved from http://www.wired.com/news/business/0,1367,60948,00.html.

# CHAPTER 9

# Getting the Most out of Vendor-Supplied Usage Data

Wonsik Shim

## Introduction

This chapter is primarily concerned with the academic library environment. However, the author believes that academic libraries and public libraries have more in common, rather than less, when it comes to dealing with usage data from database vendors. Therefore, most of the arguments and examples made in this chapter should also apply to libraries beyond the academic environment. One result of the networked information provision environment is that libraries are increasingly depending on external providers of information content and services. This is a phenomenon that is happening across all types of libraries-academic, public, and special libraries. Much of the content available as electronic resources have existed in the library in the form of subscription print journals and magazines, print indexes and abstracts, books, etc. However, there is a significant difference between traditional information content and digital information content in terms of their ownership and control of contents.

With physical media, the library owns the objects and controls their use. For example, the library catalog-be it card catalog or online catalog-represents what the library owns and could make available to its users.

With electronic media, however, the library often does not own the content and acts only as one of many access points to the information resources. As a result, the library has much less control over the use of these resources. It is possible that users may not even realize that the content is provided through the library because most electronic databases validate user logins based on originating Internet protocol (IP) addresses. Users can bypass the library website when they access external electronic databases as long as they use the computers carrying a legitimate IP address. Furthermore, the library catalog might include pointers to external information sources that, in some cases, may no longer exist when the user tries to access them.

In the traditional library, most information contents were housed in physical library buildings. Users typically needed to go to the library to use those library materials and services. Availability is an important concern for any library because of the physical characteristics of the materials. In the networked library, however, library materials and services increasingly reside outside of the physical library building. Libraries now depend, in large measure, on the publishers of electronic journals (e.g., Elsevier's ScienceDirect and Cambridge Journals Online), electronic content aggregators (e.g., EBSCO and Gale), and other electronic information providers to meet user demands for resources and services.[1] Availability has become less an issue in the networked library environment because the electronic medium allows many people to use the same material at the same time.

The rapid transition from the traditional paper-based information environment to a networked, electronic environment in libraries has significantly altered the ways in which libraries gather and use data to make a range of decisions to provide efficient and quality services to their users. As library materials and services increasingly reside outside the physical library buildings, so do the data that can describe the collection and its use. Consequently, libraries find themselves dealing with inconsistent and incomparable data from external vendors who follow their own conventions to report usage statistics.

Librarians need reliable and accurate statistics that will allow them to make good resource allocation decisions, in areas such as cost/benefit analysis, contract negotiation, and justification of expenditures. These statistics also help identify barriers of access and aid in understanding user behaviors. In addition, they provide information used in planning strategies for user education, peer comparison, and the development and operation of electronic services and resources.

While there has been some progress over the last several years, most notably in the guidelines produced by the International Coalition of Library Consortia (ICOLC),[2] the provision of usage statistics by electronic content providers has been considered by many librarians as problematic at best.

This chapter explains the current status of usage statistics offered by database vendors and suggests ways in which libraries could better utilize the data for decision making and improving performance. The need for and use of usage statistics will inevitably vary according to institutional operating environments and organizational culture relative to assessment. On the other hand, there is much overlap in terms of activities required to collect and analyze usage statistics of electronic materials.

## Why Vendor Data?

Just a few years ago, many librarians lamented the lack of usage data from electronic content providers. As a result, they were unable to make resource allocation decisions that would have required usage data. However, at the present time many vendors appear to provide such usage data in one form or another. Several important initiatives from the library, vendor, and standards communities have all contributed to the availability of usage statistics for libraries and library consortia. See Chapter 4 for a discussion of these initiatives.

The Association of Research Libraries (ARL) e-metrics project was an attempt by the academic research library community in North America to investigate various problems related to collecting and using data regarding electronic materials and services.[3] The project, which began in April 2000 and was completed in December 2001, was funded by a group of 24 ARL libraries. This e-metrics project aimed to:

- Develop, test, and refine selected statistics and performance measures to describe electronic services and resources in ARL libraries;

- Engage in a collaborative effort with selected database vendors to establish an ongoing means to produce selected descriptive statistics on database use, users, and services; and

- Develop a model to describe possible relationships between library activities and library/institutional outcomes.

Librarians who participated in the ARL e-metrics field testing saw usage reports as a necessary and valuable indication of the extent to which subscription-based services are being used. They liked the fact that the vendor-generated data are straightforward and easy to use. In some cases, reported statistics from some vendors are quite extensive and include not only aggregate user activity indicators (e.g., number of searches or number of full-text units requested), but also information about detailed user activities and behaviors within services and products. When collected, analyzed, and interpreted, vendor-supplied usage data can aid in library decision making, can answer service-related questions, and can provide materials for internal and external reports. The general availability of vendor usage reports is likely to prompt librarians to begin using usage statistics.

## Advantages of Vendor Data

Generally speaking, data that are collected by a library have the distinct advantage of being under control of the library. Like gate counters that measure attendance, tools are available (e.g., *WebTrends, Analog*) that can tell librarians how many users come to the website. These front-end methods for the collection of vendor-based data are often impractical, costly, and beyond the capability of most libraries.

Some libraries have set up a pass-through page by which they track user access to subscription-based materials that occur within the library websites. This way libraries can collect the so called *attempted* logons broken down into IP address domains that belong to different departments, schools, branch libraries, and modem pools. The result is an approximate picture of where the requests for licensed databases are made.

This *attempted logon* measure has several advantages. First, it is available locally and thus gives the library some independence from database vendors. Second, since the numbers are collected by the library across vendors using the same rules, libraries could compare results across vendors and over time. However, there are also shortcomings. Although consistent, the measure is very limited in that it represents only the number of requests for a database, in essence the number of times the pass-through link is clicked. Furthermore, this measure fails to count user access to the databases that bypasses the pass-through counter (for example, going to vendor websites by using bookmark links for easy access).

The advantages of usage statistics from vendors are obvious. First and foremost, libraries do not have to invest significant amounts of time and resources to set up and collect the data. Second, data from vendors are comprehensive, covering all user access regardless of the means (e.g., in-library vs. remote).

Third, vendor-supplied usage data are much more detailed than the data that can be gathered locally. For example, when there are limitations such as simultaneous login limits, vendors report the number of user requests denied due to that limit (turnaways). The vendor also reports the number of full-text article requests, by journal title. This information has been difficult to collect in the print journal collection environment.[4]

The biggest drawback of vendor-supplied data is that since the data do not conform to a standard, the data are not yet comparable across vendors. Because of this limitation, libraries cannot and should not attempt to use vendor statistics to benchmark performance across libraries and across different products. Another shortcoming of vendor data derives from the fact that typical libraries (especially large academic libraries) deal with so many vendors, and that collecting the data from vendors' websites takes an enormous amount of time and effort.

An interesting endeavor would be a comparison of the aforementioned attempted logon figures and the number of session data supplied by vendors, in order to assess the degree to which these numbers correspond. There is no published report yet, but some anecdotal evidence suggests that there is a significant discrepancy between these two streams of data.

### Reporting Requirements

One important reason why librarians start using vendor-supplied usage data is because of the institutional reporting requirements. Also, many library and standards organizations have now included network statistics in their data compilations, and vendor-supplied data are an integral part of these data sources. To be able to meet these reporting responsibilities, libraries need to organize themselves and be systematic in collecting and analyzing data from database vendors.

## The Use of Vendor Usage Data

Libraries have been increasing their acquisition of electronic resources for some time now. For example, during 2000-2001, research libraries spent (on average) 16.3% of their materials budget on electronic resources, a sharp increase from a mere 4% in 1992–1993.[5] More telling is the fact that in 85 out of 118 ARL libraries, the dollar amount spent for electronic resources surpassed $1 million annually. Given the significant costs associated with these products, library managers are seeking ways to measure the use of these digital services and resources. Accordingly, usage statistics have become increasingly important because of their role in supporting analysis, reporting, and decision making.

However, reports about how usage statistics are being used to evaluate electronic resources are hard to find. Not too long ago, the author of this chapter came across a posting in the liblicense listserv by a well-known electronic resources librarian. She made a request to the listserv participants to send stories about how they evaluate electronic materials, and she promised to compile the stories and post a summary. However, the plea came up empty handed, and she reported that "so far, I haven't got any other than messages like yours expressing interest and hoping to see or hear about results."

This result is in sharp contrast to voluminous exchanges on the same listserv on other topics such as licensing agreements, copyright law, and market developments. It is not that the episode is not indicative of what is going on in many libraries. However, the author recognizes that many libraries have just begun collecting and using vendor usage data, and they must feel that they are still experimenting with different ideas and strategies.

The following sections describe how usage statistics, especially those supplied by electronic database vendors, could enhance library evaluation and decision making. The hope in presenting them is to encourage the active sharing of specific cases and best practices.

## Analysis

Usage statistics of electronic resources and services are important to a wide variety of methods of analysis that enable libraries to gain an understanding of the usefulness and effectiveness of library systems, resources, and services. Examples include:

- **User behavior and demand:** Usage statistics that track the way patrons use library online systems and electronic resources can provide insights into user information? seeking behavior and user demand for information. For example, the number of searches conducted over time can serve as a general indicator of demand for certain electronic resources. Further, examining the number of searches in relation to other usage statistics, such as login time and articles downloaded, can help to assess patrons' success or failure in finding the information they need.

- **Electronic resource efficiency and limitations:** Statistics about electronic resource use can help identify strengths and weaknesses of different electronic resources. Usage statistics, for example, that reflect long connect times with relatively few pages or articles downloaded might suggest, among other things, that a particular online product is difficult or confusing to use, or contains few useful resources, or that there is a connectivity problem.

- **System design and configuration:** As libraries struggle to make more resources available electronically, they need to deal with issues related to system design and configuration. These include developing user interfaces, designing paths and linkages among resources, and configuring computer systems and telecommunications links. Electronic resource usage statistics, therefore, are an important tool in assessing system requirements, identifying over/underutilization, and designing efficient systems capabilities.

## Report Generation

Libraries produce a myriad of reports for various purposes. These purposes include: accountability and record keeping; support and justification for funding requests, strategic planning; and managerial decision-making. Usage statistics can help fulfill or enhance the library's need to supply faculty and/or administration with useful information relating budget allocations to actual electronic resource use. For instance, journal use can be tracked and documented along with cost information to give an idea of the cost/benefit of particular resources. Reports that can document the use of electronic resources, and the demand for them, can be used to support and justify resource allocation decisions. Examples of such reports include:

- **Cost analysis reports:** These reports are useful to management in assessing the effectiveness and efficiency of a product or service and its cost effectiveness.

- **Trend analysis reports and interpretation:** Viewing electronic use over time and in comparison with other variables can help identify changes or shifts in patron information needs and demand for resources.

- **Management reports:** The results of local analyses of electronic resources and user demand can be incorporated into various types of reports prepared for library management, thereby help to inform managerial decision-making.

- **Faculty-administration liaison:** Allocating scarce funding for library information resources must rest on a rational and functional basis, a basis which can be communicated effectively to various library user groups and administrative entities.

## Decision Support

Underlying the analysis and reporting functions described above is the frequent need for information in support of a decision or decisions of some sort. Guided by the information provided through analysis of electronic resource use, libraries can make more informed decisions relating to the management of library resources and services. Such decisions include:

- **Resource allocation:** Decisions relating to collection development and the allocation of scarce funding increasingly involve a balancing of traditional print resources with electronic resources. Striking an optimal balance among resources requires an understanding of library user demand and how patrons are using the resources available. Circulation and reshelving statistics, along with the observations of reference staff, provide a general indication of the level of print resource use. Declining print resource use, coupled with high use of the electronic version of a given resource, may suggest a preference for and migration to the electronic resource. In these situations, the library may choose to cancel the print equivalent of the particular resource. Usage statistics therefore become an important tool in making decisions related to materials/resource selection or deselection; purchasing versus licensing of resources (owning vs. leasing); outsourcing library resources and services; document delivery versus electronic delivery; and identifying the best electronic resource products.

- **Systems design and configuration:** The integration of electronic resources into the entire mix of resources available to library users has resulted in an intertwining of library systems design, library instruction, and resource selection. The challenge of making available the expanding universe of information resources from a single integrated source (e.g., online catalog, scholar's portal, library Web pages, etc.) requires a coordination of design elements and resource allocation decisions. Usage statistics therefore supply important information as libraries struggle to develop new user interfaces, bibliographic instruction methods, and reference services.

- **Funding and support:** One of the biggest challenges and frustrations for library administrators is answering the question posed by key library funders: "If circulation, reference transactions, in-house material use, and gate count are all going down, why should we continue to invest in the library?" Librarians know that they are busier than ever, that the library is providing more and better resources and services than ever before, and that the need for adequate funding is as acute as ever. However, the traditional measures of library resources and services are not reflecting the increased activity and use that is indeed occurring. Electronic usage statistics therefore become vital to convincing potential funders and supporters groups (e.g., university administration, local community, state legislature) of the continuing demand for library services and the need for adequate funding.

- **Consortia and resource sharing:** Usage data from database vendors can also be used to evaluate the efficacy of consortium relationships or other resource-sharing arrangements. Most vendors allow consortium participants to view usage statistics of other members. By looking at electronic resource use across several consortium participants, it may be apparent that the cost of a particular electronic resource, or package of resources, is justifiable when shared among several participants. These costs can also be evaluated in relation to the use of other shared electronic resources. For example, a low-use resource at one institution may be a high-use resource by another participant. By packaging this resource with another for which the reverse is true, the institutions can even out and share the cost of these products.

## Issues and Challenges

Although electronic usage statistics have many current and potential applications, libraries must exercise caution in interpreting and drawing conclusions from them. Issues for libraries to consider include:

- **Quantity not quality:** First and foremost among the limitations of purely numerical data on electronic resource use is that they measure activity and not results, or the quality of those results. It could be that a very high number of searches per session for a particular resource means that the product is being heavily and successfully used. It could mean that users are having trouble finding what they need due to a poor user interface, search engine, or limited content.

- **Cost vs. benefit:** One must be very careful with usage statistics that attempt to assess quality, value, or benefit from data on costs and activity. The problem here is really no different from what collection development librarians have faced over the years with print material. Any given resource, whether print or electronic, may be of tremendous value and importance to a particular group of users, yet that use is relatively small and limited. If those users, for example, are using the resource in support of leading-edge research, and/or in a line of research deemed a high priority by the institution, then the high cost relative to use and relative to other electronic resources may not be the deciding factor as to its ultimate value.

- **Misleading ratios:** Also potentially misleading are usage statistics that are, in effect, *ratios*, such as cost per search or cost per session. For most licensed electronic resources, the cost is, in accounting terms, a *sunk* cost, and the cost must be paid up-front regardless of how much or how little the resource is used. Therefore to conclude, for example, that a product with per-search cost of 2 cents is *cheaper* than one that costs 50 cents per search would be misleading. The cost-per-search ratio actually says more about *use* than it does about cost. The more the resource is used, the lower the per-search cost.

- **Lack of standardization:** Probably the greatest limitation of usage statistics at present is the inconsistency in how data are counted across vendors and which data are provided. Even with some basic guidelines, like those of ICOLC, librarians feel that data are not comparable among products or among libraries. This creates an *apples versus oranges* problem that further limits the usefulness of the statistics and the conclusions that can be drawn from them. Librarians feel that they cannot give credence to the statistics because they are not comparable, and therefore are not useful for decision making.

- **Vendor disincentives:** Vendors stand to gain much (e.g., improved customer service, product evaluation) by standardizing and supplying electronic resource statistics, but libraries also must understand that the development of these statistical capabilities is not without cost. Furthermore, vendors may fear that oversimplified analyses of the statistics reported by them and their competitors may result in their product being viewed, correctly or incorrectly, in a less favorable light by comparison.

## Collection and Use Strategies

Even with the best intentions, collecting and making use of vendor-supplied data is not an easy task. The timing, the format, and the form of usage reports from vendors all conspire to create a massive data management problem and can quickly overwhelm many librarians who are not prepared and not systematic about this endeavor. In this section we address several areas that need to be considered in the planning stage. First, we encourage people to begin by giving thought to the kinds of questions that need to be answered and the kinds of data that can answer those questions, instead of jumping right into the data collection. We discuss a different organizational setup to support data collection and sharing of intelligence from data analysis, followed by a detailed description of steps essential for getting organized. We hope that by using these guidelines, libraries can formulate appropriate strategies to facilitate data collection and analysis. Chapters 1, 3, and 4 present additional library strategies for the collection, reporting, and use of e-metrics data in the larger context of evaluating network services and resources.

### Start by Asking Crucial Questions

In thinking about different strategies to collect and analyze vendor-supplied usage statistics, a good starting point is to ask what kinds of questions the data will answer or bring to resolution. For example, a big question that many libraries have regarding electronic resources is: How is this being used? Though the question sounds quite simple, once librarians begin to gather data and formulate different queries, more probing questions will surely ensue.

Even if it appears that the available data are limited or far from desirable, beginning with questions-instead of with available data-will help libraries set the goals of this exercise. When data collection is the main driver, it is more than likely that data collection becomes the goal in and of itself, possibly obscuring the main goals of data collection. Too much focus on data collection can be a serious threat in the case of vendor-supplied usage data, because it becomes too easy to get bogged down by the difficulty and complexity of data collection.

On the other hand, we are not suggesting that all of the goals need to be established from the beginning. What we are advocating is the fact that questions to be answered should be taken into consideration before libraries start collecting data. The questions or the goals of data collection can be reexamined and reevaluated after actual data collection and analysis.

We propose three steps toward making data collection useful. First, establish the value-added uses of the collected data. This could be accomplished by asking such questions as: What could we do (or what questions could we answer) if we had these data? Second, the library identifies and rationalizes certain data for current and future use. For example, Fig. 9-1 shows a generic, but useful, rationale for the usage measure "queries (searches) in electronic databases" taken from the ARL E-Metrics Project manual. Third, the library develops specific procedures and work flow patterns that support data collection and analysis. The remainder of this section deals specifically with this third step.

**Figure 9-1**
**Sample rationale for a usage measure.**

> **Rationale:** This statistic provides libraries with an indication of the databases that are most heavily used, areas of user interest, database popularity, and a level of usage detail that goes beyond an initial session. It also can provide important information for billing purposes, as some vendors charge for database usage by number of searches. This statistic can complement the number of electronic reference transactions, as more user requests bypass staff mediation. Some portion of this statistic is also analogous to in-library use of reference sources.

## Organizational Configuration

The dispersed nature of vendor usage statistics in the networked environment makes it difficult to consolidate and manage statistics. This is a growing source of frustration for many librarians who deal with electronic resources. Related to the issue of the dispersed nature of usage statistics is the organizational structure needed to manage electronic resources and services, particularly the configuration of personnel and workflow to support the collection of statistics and measures. Two types of organizational setups are typically observed in carrying out data collection:

- A single person making requests to other librarians and staff members for data needs and processing and summarizing collected data. This person is most likely the electronic resource librarian, head of collections, or someone who is responsible for overall library statistical matters. For this kind of organizational structure to work, the library needs to understand that what this person is doing is critical, and to see the benefits of sharing information. A drawback to this arrangement is that there is a lack overlapping expertise and broad sharing of information.
- A team structure that coordinates the entire aspect of electronic resource management, including acquisition, access, and evaluation. For example, the team might consist of representatives from various library departments such as reference, collection management, systems, and administration. This team will then oversee the management of electronic services through monthly and yearly reviews. Collection and review of usage statistics concerning licensed resources will be an integral part of the team (or committee's) activities. While the amount of staff time and coordination can be substantial, it gives various internal stakeholders an opportunity to participate in the decision making process. In addition, it promotes the sharing of expertise in the library.

## Getting Organized

Libraries need to determine how much data they want to collect and from which database vendors. Not all electronic resources should receive the same attention, because the expenditure and importance will vary. The amount of time it takes to collect necessary information will depend on the number of vendors the library deals with and the complexity of usage reports being provided. A typical work process can be divided into the following three steps.

Step 1: Sort out which publishers and vendors provide statistics.

Step 2: Receive those statistics.

Step 3: Compile these statistics into a report.

The amount of time it takes to complete all three steps will vary, according to (among other things) the number of vendors from which each library collects data and the level of skill and experience of the person doing the collecting. Figure 9-2 demonstrates the experience at one library. Libraries should plan enough staff time for the initial setup, but once necessary preparation is done, steps 1 and 2 will not take as much time. Libraries can then allocate resources for analyzing data and drawing interpretations. The following sections review each step in more detail.

**Figure 9-2**
**Case study of library effort related to vendor data.**

---

### Case Study

Arizona State University compiled its first electronic usage data in July, 1999. One librarian took nearly 180 hours to 1) find out which vendors provided statistics, 2) download those statistics, and 3) compile those statistics into a report.

Three years later, one librarian and a staff member put the report together in 40 hours. Some interesting observations about this report include:

- 70% of indexing and abstracting services supplied usage data;

- Most of these vendors said they were ICOLC-compliant;

- Major e-journal publishers produced some data; and

- Distribution formats still varied, including e-mail in html and ASCII formats, self-administered website access, and print mailings.

---

### Tracking Information About Vendor's Statistics

Unfortunately, there is not at present a central place from which libraries can gather data about what statistics vendors report and the manner in which the reports are furnished (e.g., report formats and delivery mechanisms). Therefore, individual libraries need to compile data on their own. At a minimum, libraries need to prepare two sets of tables to organize relevant information. One is a detailed summary of usage report contents and delivery methods, organized by each vendor. Figure 9-3 shows one such example.

**Figure 9-3**
**Sample vendor report summary.**

| Vendor Name: | XXX |
|---|---|
| Data Available at: | http://www.companyname.com/stats/login.asp (Login name: xxx, Password: xxx) |
| Report Access: | • Log-in required<br>• Same log-in is used to manage subscription |
| Time Period: | • Can set time range (month and year) |
| Data Elements (tables): | • Session Usage (total only)<br>  • Number of log-ins, Number of searches, Number of hits<br>  • Number of abstracts, Number of e-mails, Number of full-text articles, Number of full-text pages, Number of PDFs viewed<br>• Database Usage (by database)<br>  • Same as the Session Usage report, with the exception of log-ins<br>• Title Usage Report (by specific title)<br>  • Number of abstracts, Number of E-mails, Number of full? text articles, Number of full-text pages, Number of PDFs viewed<br>• IP Address Usage Report (log-ins by IP address)<br>• Interface Usage Report (total, Web vs. Z39.50)<br>  • Same as the Session Usage report |
| Data Formats: | • HTML and text |
| Delivery: | • Display and e-mail |
| Documentation: | • Reports and statistics menu<br>• Running reports<br>• Setting e-mail options for reports<br>• Viewing and editing scheduled reports |

\* The figure is for the purpose of illustration only.

**Figure 9-4**
**Common data elements from vendors.**

| | Sessions (Log-ins) | Queries (Searches) | Menu Selections | Full-Content Units Accessed | Turnaways | Reporting Frequency |
|---|---|---|---|---|---|---|
| Vendor A | ✓ | ✓ | ✓ | ✓ | n/a | Monthly |
| Vendor B | | ✓ | ✓ | ✓ | ✓ | Quarterly |
| Vendor C | | | | ✓ | ✓ | Monthly |
| Vendor D | ✓ | ✓ | ✓ | ✓ | n/a | Custom |

✓ = available; n/a = not applicable

Another table that helps organize information is a matrix that shows common data elements from vendors. Figure 9-4 shows one example based on the recommended measures in the ICOLC Guidelines. Individual libraries can choose which data elements they want to collect across vendors.

### Retrieving Statistics From Vendors

The good news is that since most vendors make statistics available at their websites, libraries will only need a web browser to retrieve usage reports. The bad news is that since the report generation interfaces are not standardized, librarians will need to deal with different system interfaces. In some cases, librarians or staff members might need training to use some of these systems. Figure 9-5 shows a fairly typical user interface from one database vendor. Since the process appears to be very difficult (or nearly impossible) to automate, libraries will not enjoy dramatic savings of time, even after repeated retrieval of usage data.

**Figure 9-5**
**Sample usage statistics retrieval interface.**

Generate and e-mail **LIBRARY** Usage and Retrievals Report

**Period**

|  | Day: | Month: | Year: |
| --- | --- | --- | --- |
| Begin Date: | 1 | July | 2003 |

|  | Day: | Month: | Year: |
| --- | --- | --- | --- |
| End Date : | 31 | July | 2003 |

**Report Type***
- ☑ Usage Summary
- ☑ Usage by Database
- ☑ Time-of-Day / Day-of-Week
- ☑ Retrievals by Citation
- ☑ Retrievals by Alphabetic Journal List

**Format**
  ○ ASCII  ● Comma Separated Values  ○ PostScript

**Compression**
  ● None  ○ ZIP  ○ PKZIP

**Attachment**
  ● Yes ○ No

**Recipient***
  E-mail address

As of this writing, usage reports are usually available in at least two formats: HTML tables and text files. HTML tables are easy to view in a browser, but they are more difficult to process in a standard database, or in spreadsheet programs such as Microsoft Access, Excel, or FileMaker Pro. Figure 9-6 illustrates an HTML table view of a usage statistics report from a journal publisher. If the library intends to store raw data files on a local server, it might want to download usage reports in HTML format so that local users can access them easily. If the library wants to process usage reports in one way or another, it should consider downloading reports in a text format, as shown in Fig. 9-7.

**Figure 9-6**
**HTML table view of usage report.**

3. Number of Successful Item Requests and Turnaways by Month, Journal and Page Type (Journal Report 3 - Turnaways not applicable)

| Journal Name | Print ISSN | Online ISSN | Page Type | Jan-2003 | Feb-2003 | Mar-2003 | Apr-2003 | May-2003 | Jun-2003 |
|---|---|---|---|---|---|---|---|---|---|
| Astronomy and Geophysics | 1366-8781 | 1468-4004 | List of Issues | 1 | 0 | 2 | 2 | 0 | 1 |
| | 1366-8781 | 1468-4004 | Tables of Contents | 1 | 0 | 4 | 6 | 0 | 3 |
| | 1366-8781 | 1468-4004 | Abstracts | 1 | 0 | 1 | 4 | 0 | 0 |
| | 1366-8781 | 1468-4004 | Full-text HTML Requests | 0 | 0 | 2 | 1 | 0 | 1 |
| | 1366-8781 | 1468-4004 | Full-text PDF Requests | 0 | 0 | 8 | 0 | 0 | 0 |
| | 1366-8781 | 1468-4004 | Full-text Total Requests | 0 | 0 | 10 | 1 | 0 | 1 |
| | 1366-8781 | 1468-4004 | Supplementary Materials | 0 | 0 | 0 | 0 | 0 | 0 |
| Autonomic & Autacoid Pharmacology | 1474-8665 | 1474-8673 | List of Issues | 0 | 1 | 0 | 0 | 2 | 1 |
| | 1474-8665 | 1474-8673 | Tables of Contents | 0 | 0 | 0 | 0 | 3 | 0 |
| | 1474-8665 | 1474-8673 | Abstracts | 0 | 0 | 0 | 0 | 0 | 0 |
| | 1474-8665 | 1474-8673 | Full-text HTML Requests | 0 | 0 | 0 | 0 | 0 | 1 |
| | 1474-8665 | 1474-8673 | Full-text PDF Requests | 0 | 0 | 0 | 0 | 3 | 0 |
| | 1474-8665 | 1474-8673 | Full-text Total Requests | 0 | 0 | 0 | 0 | 3 | 1 |
| | 1474-8665 | 1474-8673 | Supplementary Materials | 0 | 0 | 0 | 0 | 0 | 0 |

Text formats usually are identified by the kind of character or mark that separates data records. The most commonly used separators are tab, comma, and colon. Regardless of what separator is being used, programs such as Excel or Access can read them and convert them into database or spreadsheet files (Fig. 9-8). Most libraries studied in the ARL E-Metrics Project were using Microsoft Excel because of its data manipulation and graphics capabilities (for drawing charts).

**Figure 9-7**
**Sample text format view of usage statistics.**

```
Number of Successful Full-Text article Requests by Month and Journal (Journal Report 1) (Counter Compliant)
     Print ISSN       Online ISSN     Jan-2003      Feb-2003       Mar-2003     Apr-2003       May
Total for all journals              693     1625   1116  1165   805  1076  1103   271   785
Astronomy and Geophysics       1366-8781     1468-4004    0       0     10     1     0     1
Autonomic & Autacoid Pharmacology    1474-8665     1474-8673    0     0     0     0     3
Acta Anaesthesiologica Scandinavica   0001-5172    1399-6576     0     8     0     0     8
Abacus  0001-3072      1467-6281      0     0      0     7    1     0     0     8
Aging Cell    1474-9718    1474-9728    0     0      0     0    3     0     0     0
Accounting and Finance   0810-5391    1467-629X     0     0      0     0    3     0     0
Ambulatory Child Health  1355-5626    1467-0658     1     0      4     0    0     0     0
Acta Neuropsychiatrica   0924-2708    1601-5215     0     0      0     0    3     1     1
Acta Psychiatrica Scandinavica  0001-690X    1600-0447    10     4      6    17    5     9
Addiction    0965-2140    1360-0443     8    21     16    22   33    14    29    21
Austral Ecology 1442-9985    1442-9993     0     2      7     3    0     0     0     0
Australian Journal of Entomology  1326-6756    1440-6055     0     0      1     0    0
Asia Pacific Family Medicine     1444-1683    1447-056X     0     0      0     0    1     0
Anzeiger fur Schädlingskunde     1436-5693    1439-0280     0     0      1     0    1     0
Animal Genetics 0268-9146    1365-2052     0    20      1     1    0     1     0     0
Anatomia, Histologia, Embryologia: Journal of Veterinary Medicine Series C    0340-2096    1439-0264
Annals of Human Genetics         0003-4800    1469-1809     0     0      1     2    1     0
Art History     0141-6790    1467-8365     0     1      0     0    0     0     0
The Australian Journal of Agricultural and Resource Economics   1364-985X    1467-8489     0     0
Asia Pacific Journal of Clinical Nutrition   0964-7058    1440-6047     0     3      1     2
Australasian Journal of Dermatology     0004-8380    1440-0960     0     1      0     0     0
African Journal of Ecology       0141-6707    1365-2028     0     1      0     0     3
American Journal of Reproductive Immunology     8755-8920    1600-0897     2     0      0     3
The Australian and New Zealand Journal of Obstetrics and Gynaecology   0004-8666    1479-828X     0     2
American Journal of Political Science   0092-5853    1540-5907     0     0      0     0     2
Australian Journal of Rural Health      1038-5282    1440-1584     2     6      5     2     0
Asian Journal Of Social Psychology      1367-2223    1467-839X     0     0      2     0     0
American Journal of Transplantation     1600-6135    1600-6143     3     1      3     1     0
Allergy 0105-4538    1398-9995     5    15      3    32    7     3    14     0    79
Acta Medica Austriaca    0303-8173    1563-2571     0     0      1     0    0     1     0
Anaesthesia     0003-2409    1365-2044     9     7     11     6    1     3     4     0
```

Many vendors provide usage reports on a monthly basis, or they provide an option to set the time range (in some cases down to a specific date). Libraries need to determine how frequently they will go to vendors' websites to collect usage data.

Another important decision to make is how much data libraries want to collect. Some libraries want to collect aggregate data only, whereas other libraries will collect title-level information, be it database product or journal or book title. Also, libraries need to decide whether they want to collect a common subset of reported statistics or all statistics reported from vendors.

Libraries also need to consider the storage of collected data, as well as retrieval options. Varying degrees of effort are required for this process. One simple option is to store raw data files from vendors in the library intranet (or file server). However, these raw data may not get used because of the amount of effort needed to process them. On the other hand, some libraries will take the so-called *data warehousing* approach and convert raw data into structured files. In this case, each library will have to decide on an approach to normalize data in such a way that collected data acquire some level of uniformity.

One important issue to think about is that of access: Who will have access to the data and how will that access be provided (e.g., password protection)? This is necessary because of security, privacy, management practice, and various other issues that the library should consider.

**Figure 9-8**
**Converting a tab-delimited file in MS Excel.**

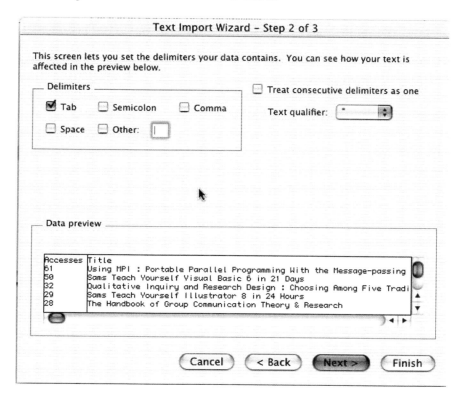

## Generating Reports and Analysis

To make the effort of collecting and storing usage data a worthwhile activity, some form of report generation facility needs to be established. A simple solution is to incorporate formulas to generate use ratios such as cost per search, cost per session, cost per full-text unit requested, searches per session, etc. A more complex solution would involve creating custom report generation, so that the requester can set different parameters and retrieve only the data he or she wants to examine. However, the cost of developing such an interface can be significant.

Eventually, libraries may need to develop a management information system that houses usage statistics and related library performance data. The goal of the management information database is to allow librarians responsible for a particular product or service to extract useful reports. Librarians not only need to understand and be able to assess product performance, but they also need a system that does not overwhelm them with meaningless numbers.

Reports may not necessarily have to be complex. In some cases, publishing the top 15 electronic journals or journal articles may fully satisfy the reporting needs of some readers of the report. It is important to underscore the fact that data alone provide little information. Data need to be processed, analyzed, and converted into a form that users can relate to and understand. Even elementary analysis, such as the formulas mentioned earlier, can help librarians perform basic and/or elaborate ratio analyses. Such exercises will help librarians gain a more complete understanding of product use.

Being able to work with the data is of paramount importance. Assuming libraries receive good and timely data from database vendors, they must be able to make sense of the data and incorporate it into the process of developing library collections and marketing these collections to users, as well as to funding sources.

## Recent Developments

It is necessary to note two significant developments since the ARL E-Metrics Project: Project COUNTER and NISO Z39.7 Library Statistics.[6] Although it is difficult to estimate the exact impact of these initiatives because of their evolving nature, it is clear even now that they will have an important role in shaping the collection and reporting of usage statistics from database vendors. This chapter will not review these initiatives because they are covered in Chapters 3, 4, and 10.

## Conclusions

The last several years saw noticeable improvement in the provision of usage statistics. This is largely thanks to the combined efforts of the library and vendor communities. It is important that the library and vendor communities continue to work together and continue to develop those sets of data that can be of use to the library community at large.

For the vendors, efforts at standardizing reports and providing training for librarians are areas that will continue to need attention and development. While vendors are faced with the problem of providing usage statistics to a wide variety of libraries and organizations, they are able to furnish more or less uniform reporting to satisfy most, if not all, clients. They need to realize that typical libraries deal with several dozen vendors, and thus deal with many different kinds of usage reports. To the extent possible, vendors need to work together to standardize not only usage report delivery formats, but also the terminologies and their definitions. The ICOLC Guidelines and the new Project COUNTER initiatives have laid important foundations in this regard, and they need to be strengthened.

As was mentioned earlier, many libraries lack the kinds of resources and training necessary to collect vendor-supplied usage statistics. Lack of documentation, training, and other forms of assistance burdens not only libraries in their effort to collect data, but also vendors in their efforts to provide support for usage-related queries and troubleshooting. The issue of training is intertwined with standardization of reports. The more standardized the reports, the less time and money the vendors will have to spend in the development of training.

For the libraries, we recommend two things: start using data now, and start sharing expertise to avoid duplication of efforts. Librarians have yearned for reliable and useful usage data from vendors. Although the system is far from perfect, that data is currently being supplied. Granted that vendor-supplied usage data are not yet complete, verifiable, and comparable, they nonetheless provide crucial information that can be put to use *now.* Libraries should not wait until all the problems associated with usage statistics have been resolved; it may take years. Improvement comes in small steps, and as we have witnessed, technologies and other developments will continue to complicate the issue. Some librarians might believe that initiatives such as COUNTER or the ICOLC Guidelines will eventually solve most of the problems, but this is wishful thinking at best. For example, through COUNTER, publishers of scholarly journals, aggregators, and other types of database vendors will use a standardized format, and librarians might get third-party opinions regarding the comparability of measures from different companies. Still, COUNTER represents only a fraction of the vendors, and availability of data is only one aspect of the equation. Libraries need to realize that usage data, however imperfect, contain clues to many of the important questions they are trying to answer. In addition, unless libraries begin to use vendor-supplied data, potential problems in the data may go unnoticed and affect libraries' ability to make relevant decisions.

The amount of work required to collect usage data in a consistent and systematic manner is significant. On the other hand, libraries of different sizes and types go through more or less the same processes to retrieve usage data from database vendors. This duplication of efforts can be avoided if libraries work together to streamline the data collection process and begin sharing how they utilize usage statistics. For example, a clearinghouse that organizes information about usage statistics, data elements, access methods, and documentation can dramatically cut down data collection efforts by libraries. Various reporting requirements set by organizations such as ARL and NISO will help. However, these requirements primarily address external reporting, not local data requirements.[7]

In an increasingly networked environment, libraries are striving to become an information portal—a 24-hour-a-day access point through which users obtain information services and resources on their terms, including when they want such services. However, the requirements of supporting this unprecedented user access are significant, forcing libraries to reexamine their operations at many levels. In this context, the ability to gather data from multiple sources, both internal and external, will be a key competency for many libraries. We hope that libraries find the suggestions made in this chapter useful in attaining that competency.

## Notes

1. There is a large and diverse number of electronic content providers in the market, and it is difficult to describe them collectively. The term *database vendors* is used in this chapter to denote various content providers, including traditional journal publishers, aggregators of full-text journals and reference databases, electronic book providers, and so on.

2. International Coalition of Library Consortia, 'Guidelines for Statistical Measures of Usage of Web-Based Information Resources' (ICOLC, 2001) [revised December 2001]. Available on line at http://www.library.yale.edu/consortia/2001webstats.htm.

3. Detailed ARL E-Metrics Project information and final reports can be found at http://www.arl.org/stats/newmeas/emetrics/index.html.

4. Libraries are using sampling techniques to measure the use of journal articles. But the measure is approximate at best, and the cost of implementing the technique cannot be ignored.

5. Association of Research Libraries, ARL Supplementary Statistics 1999-2000 (ARL, Washington, D. C., 2001). Available at http://www.arl.org/stats/sup/sup00.pdf.

6. Counting Online Usage of Networked Electronic Resources (COUNTER). See http://www.projectcounter.org/. Last accessed March 11, 2004.

   National Information Standards Organization (NISO). (2003). *NISO Z39.7-200X Draft. Information services and use: Metrics & statistics for libraries and information providers-Data Dictionary.* Bethesda, MD: National Information Standards Organization. Available at http://www.niso.org/emetrics/. Last accessed March 11, 2004.

7. A notable exception to this is Z39.7, which is designed to inform those who develop survey instruments to define the items measured and provide guidance on methods of measurement.

## References

Association of Research Libraries. (2002a). ARL *supplementary statistics 2000-2001*. Washington, DC: Association of Research Libraries. Retrieved 15 March 2004 from http://www.arl.org/stats/pubpdf/sup01.pdf.

Association of Research Libraries. (2002b). *ARL statistics 2000-2001*. Washington, DC: Association of Research Libraries. Retrieved 15 March 2004 from http://www.arl.org/stats/pubpdf/arlstat01.pdf.

Counting Online Usage of Networked Electronic Resources (COUNTER). See http://www.projectcounter.org/. Last accessed March 11, 2004.

International Coalition of Library Consortia. "Guidelines for Statistical Measures of Usage of Web-Based Information Resources" (ICOLC, 2001). [revised December 2001]. Available at http://www.library.yale.edu/consortia/2001webstats.htm.

National Information Standards Organization (NISO). (2003). *NISO Z39.7-200X Draft. Information services and use: Metrics & statistics for libraries and information providers-Data Dictionary*. Bethesda, MD: National Information Standards Organization. Available at http://www.niso.org/emetrics. Last accessed March 11, 2004.

Shim, Wonsik, McClure, Charles R., Fraser, Bruce T., & Bertot, John Carlo. (2001). *Data collection manual for academic and research library network statistics and performance measures*. Washington, DC: Association of Research Libraries.

# CHAPTER 10

# Usage Statistics from the Vendor's Perspective

**Oliver Pesch**

## Introduction

The vendors that operate the various online services to which libraries subscribe have the responsibility of collecting, processing, storing and presenting the usage statistics needed by the market. Vendors have the challenge of creating statistical reports that meet the varied demands of the different libraries they serve. Many vendors are also obliged to provide detailed statistical reporting for other constituents as well, such as the publishers of the information they may host.

This chapter examines the following vendor-related issues:

- **Types of vendors.** The term *vendor*, when used in the context of online information, covers a fairly broad range of service providers. The nature of the service provider will often dictate the type of statistics that must be captured, as well as determine to whom the statistics are being provided.

- **The parties involved.** The parties interested in the usage statistics captured by vendors will vary somewhat with the type of vendor. Many vendors have to provide statistics for more than one audience. Each party involved has a different motivation for wanting statistical information, and thus the nature of the statistics, or at least their presentation, varies.

- **Capturing and processing statistics.** Providing statistical reports does not come without first creating the systems to capture and process the transactions on the vendor's service. The nature of the data to be captured and the needs for organizing and presenting the data will dictate the systems to be built.
- **The impact of standards initiatives and the challenges they bring.** Recent standards initiatives are beginning to impact the vendors. While these initiatives bring some uniformity to the business of statistics, they also bring some additional challenges.

## Definitions and Issues

When talking about vendors of online information, it is worth taking a couple of minutes to review the different kinds of vendors that are part of a library's information landscape. Each plays a role in providing information to the end user. Each has its own unique requirements when it comes to providing usage statistics to their stakeholders. Table 10-1 presents an alphabetical list of the types of vendors.

Most of the vendors defined in Table 10-1 serve more than one master when it comes to providing usage statistics. Full-text aggregators, secondary database providers, online hosting services for e-journals, and e-journal gateways are normally in the business of providing the library community with access to information that is owned or provided by someone else. When it comes to usage statistics, both the information consumers (the libraries) and the information providers (the publishers) want to have reports on usage. In addition, the vendors themselves have a need for statistical data to help them manage the service. The motivation for the statistics—and thus the nature of the statistics themselves—varies among the three parties.

### Information Consumer (the Library)

Libraries often need to provide statistical information to funding bodies to show how their money is being spent. To effectively manage their collections, libraries must understand what it consists of, how the collection meets the institution's charter, and how effectively the collection is being used. Some institutions use statistical data to help guide purchasing decisions, to drive bibliographic instruction needs, and to analyze how their collection is being presented and used.

The typical statistics that are relevant to libraries are found in the following list (Chapter 4 presents a number of these statistics in the form of standards-based e-metrics).

- **Number of databases.** A count of databases, possibly with a breakdown by subject discipline. Libraries generally compile these figures themselves.
- **Number of titles.** A count of journal titles under subscription. A breakdown by subject is also desired.

**Table 10-1**
**Types of vendors.**

| Type of Vendor | Definition |
| --- | --- |
| A-to-Z list | An A-to-Z list is a library-controlled service that is designed to provide the library's users with a relatively complete directory of journals and other e-resources available online through the various services the library makes available to its patrons. |
| | The A-to-Z list provides access to the resources through links to the actual service. Much like a link resolver, the A-to-Z service cannot provide detailed usage of actual content; it is essentially a pass-through. However, it can provide statistics on the frequency of linking to journals and other e-resources. As a library controlled service, the statistics are usually solely for the use of the library. |
| E-journal gateway | A service that provides access to e-journal content. Typically these services are associated with subscription agents. An E-journal gateway normally will not host the actual full text; however, it will provide a cross-publisher service for locating information and linking the end user to it. Examples of E-journal gateways are EBSCOhost Electronic Journals Service from EBSCO Information Services and SwetsWise from Swets Information Services. |
| | Gateways are services that know where e-journal content is and what a user's institution subscribes to. While they don't directly provide access to the full text, they can track what is being searched and which journals the users are linking to. |
| | From a statistics point of view, the e-journal gateway is similar to the A-to-Z list, in that it can track the frequency of linking to journal content. Statistics are provided for the libraries and often for participating publishers. |
| E-journal online host | Very few publishers have their own Web-based services. Most contract with outside services, such as Project Muse, MetaPress, Ingenta, and Extenza, to provide the Web-based hosting and searching. |
| | For most e-journals, it is the responsibility of the online hosting service to track usage and provide these reports to the libraries and participating publishers. |

(Continued)

**Table 10-1 (Continued)**
**Types of vendors.**

| Type of Vendor | Definition |
| --- | --- |
| Full-text aggregator | Full-text aggregators are services that create extensive full-text collections that are accessed as a complete database, rather than as individual e-journals. Although aggregations could be viewed as collections of articles, they can provide statistical information broken down by the journals and other resources that make up the aggregation.

Similar to the E-journal online host, the aggregator needs to compile statistical information for the publishers they work with as well as for the institutions they sell to. |
| Link resolver | Link resolvers, such as SFX, LinkSource, and LinkFinderPlus, are library-controlled services that facilitate and expand item-level linking between the various online services an institution may subscribe to. With link resolvers, a user finding an item or article of interest on one service can be linked to the library's link resolver, where the library can control which services are appropriate for the user to see, thus helping address the Appropriate Copy Problem.

Link resolvers are library-controlled services; therefore, the statistical reporting is generally targeted only to the library. Similar to e-journal gateways, the link resolvers typically redirect the user to another service, and although they cannot track actual full-text usage, they can, for example, track where a user came from and what the user was linked to. |
| Metasearch engine | A metasearch engine is another library-controlled service designed to provide a uniform search interface for most, if not all, of a library's online services. The service is often referred to as providing federated or broadcast searching of a number of services. In its most typical application, the metasearch engine does not actually store or index any content of its own. Instead, it acts on the user's behalf to search the content stored on the other online services, and then it brings back the results and presents them to the user in a uniform way. When a user wants to access an item, such as the full text of an article, the user is normally directed to the content provider.

Like e-journal gateways and link resolvers, the metasearch engine will not be able to provide statistics on full-text usage. It is, however, a good source of information on user sessions and searches performed. Like the link resolver, the metasearch engine is the library's tool; therefore, the statistical reporting is generally targeted only to the library. |

(Continued)

**Table 10-1 (Continued)**
**Types of vendors.**

| Type of Vendor | Definition |
| --- | --- |
| Publisher | Some publishers host their online content on their own websites, and therefore are required to provide usage information to subscribing institutions. They also may take usage into consideration when evaluating the performance of their various journals. |
| | Commercial publishers often provide services to societies, such as publishing journals for them. In such cases, regardless of where the content is hosted, publishers are often obliged to provide their society customers with information on usage. |
| Secondary database provider | A secondary database acts as a directory service, facilitating users in discovering where certain subject-specific information can be found. For example, a secondary database will provide subject-oriented access to journal article citations and abstracts, but will not provide the articles themselves (note that some secondary databases do include some full text.) Most secondary database providers include linking capabilities to help the user move from the discovered citation to the item itself. |
| | Through various usage statistics, secondary databases can provide libraries with an interesting perspective on what their users are searching for and which journal citations are being viewed most frequently. |
| | Normally, secondary database providers do not have formal agreements with the publishers of the journals that are covered in their database. Thus, statistics are typically produced for the library customers and not for the publishers. |

- **Session count.** The number of logins to the various services. Sometimes referred to as *virtual visits* to the library, this figure is used to measure how frequently an end user initiates usage of a particular service.
- **Number of turnaways.** This statistic measures the number of times users are not able to access a database or journal that is licensed on a simultaneous-user basis, due to simultaneous use capacity being reached.
- **Search count.** The number of queries performed against databases or online resources. This figure is sometimes roughly correlated with "reference questions asked."
- **Number of items examined.** A count of full-text articles and other items accessed through the service. Similar to the circulation count for a print collection, this figure provides similar use figures for online collections.
- **Number of abstract records examined.** When a database provides access to citations and abstracts rather than direct access to the full text, this count is useful for tracking use of the secondary materials.

- **Number of links followed.** When an online service provides links to other services, as is often the case with secondary databases, tracking the number of links followed from a given resource is an indicator of the usefulness of that resource in helping guide the end users to the answers they seek.

Statistics from the foregoing list are presented in the following types of reports:

- **Collection analysis**. A list and/or count of journals that are part of a database or package, with an optional breakdown by subject or discipline;
- **Session reports.** To determine the overall use of the various services, a session report tracks of the number of sessions and possibly the average length of sessions;
- **Turnaway report.** Tracking the number of times user sessions were rejected due to the simultaneous-user limit being exceeded. The primary breakdown of the report will be by the database or resource licensed. A monthly summary is useful in determining if excessive turnaways are being encountered, but an hourly analysis is often needed to understand how frequently and severely license limits are being reached;
- **Database activity.** A count of sessions, searches, and full-text retrievals by database;
- **Title usage.** A count of activity (normally items examined) by journal. Breakdowns of the numbers are by title, by year of publication, and by subject;
- **Link-out reports.** These reports provide information on the number of times users followed a link. Typical breakdowns for these reports would be by title (the title of the resource the user was viewing when the link was clicked); by target type (e.g., full text, ILL, link resolver, etc.); or by actual target. In the case of link resolvers, link reports may also provide details on the sources of the link and the genre of item for which the links are being requested.

Consortium customers will desire usage reports showing the breakdown of usage by institution, and individual institutions often want to see figures by department (or IP range) to facilitate charging back the cost of the service to those who use it.

### Information Provider (the Publisher)

The information provider, particularly in the case of publishers, will need usage data from the vendors who host or resell their data. In some cases the need for the data relates to the payment of royalties to authors. Most often, however, the publisher wants to see which of its content is available for access and which is being used.

Some publishers are starting to measure the success of on-line journal editors on the basis of usage. With many e-journals being sold as part of bundles and packages, it is no longer simply a matter of measuring the success of a journal by subscription revenue. In the electronic world, impact factors take time to build. Therefore, the only available measure of a journal's worth is tied to its readership. If the journal is being read, the usage statistics will tell the story.

Likewise, many commercial publishers publish journals on behalf of societies. A publisher's success with e-journals will hinge on its ability to encourage readership of the content. Aggregations, third-party, link-in, and a number of other technologies come into play as means of stimulating access and use of the content. Publishers need to employ all of these tools, and they need the statistics to measure the level of success of their efforts. Publishers are interested in a smaller set of statistics than libraries are, and the number of articles available for access and the number of items examined are of prime interest. The following list includes the typical reports requested.

- **Content-hosted reports.** These reports, which are often required of database aggregators, usually provide a publisher with a list of their journals included on the service, with the number of articles for each journal. Frequently the article counts are broken down by year.
- **Usage by journal.** This report will provide the total number of full-text retrievals, by journal. A breakdown by year of publication is also helpful in determining the importance of the back-file data.
- **Usage by article.** Required for determining royalty payments to authors. However, some publishers are interested in this level of detail so that they can perform a more detailed analysis of their service, for example:
  - Ranking authors based on usage;
  - Analyzing use by section of the journal;
  - Analyzing use by volume and issue (e.g., which issues receive the most activity).

These serve as the major reports used by publishers to measure the success of their online content.

## Internal Needs

The vendor who is also the provider of the online service needs access to statistical data to effectively manage the service. Statistics are the cornerstone to capacity planning, performance monitoring, and the future development of the service.

Most vendors serving the academic market will see peak periods during the beginning of the work week, with the highest peaks coming in spring and fall to coincide with an academic schedule. The response time of an online service is impacted by the number of simultaneous users on the system (being logged in takes up some resources), as well as by the level of activity. For many systems, the acts of logging in (establishing a session) and performing searches are the major consumers of computing power. Conversely, the amount of network bandwidth used is often determined by the number (and size) of items retrieved (e.g., PDF files).

To monitor performance and predict future growth, the vendor must capture the following data:

- Number of logins;
- Number of searches;
- Nature of the searches;
- Number of items retrieved; and
- Which content is being accessed.

Monitoring how system features are being used requires access to and analysis of data that typically are not made available to external groups (e.g., libraries or publishers, in the case of a full-text aggregator). Some systems have been built with special logging that is analogous to Web logs that one might see from a standard Web server. Others rely on the Web logs themselves. Typically a vendor is interested in capturing which pages are being accessed (each page would represent a type of activity or usage of a specific feature) as well as the options that are selected on each page. The amount of data captured can be daunting for a large and complex system. The architecture of the online service typically is such that there are multiple tiers of computing, and each tier can be counted on to contribute data that might be analyzed for usage—either for the health of the system or for the analysis of end-user activity.

Some vendors provide administrative tools that allow libraries to customize their users' experiences. The settings chosen can also be a source of data to be analyzed, although strictly speaking this is not usage data in the traditional sense.

It is worth noting that the library often serves as its own vendor in some ways. The library often promotes access to the various services that it subscribes to, from its own website. Users of this website can be tracked, counted, and reported, in ways similar to the ways in which users of A-to-Z lists can.

## Collection and Providing Access

When it comes to collecting the usage data a vendor has choices to make. The simplest option is to take advantage of the Web logging facilities built into most Web server software (Web logs). Another choice is for the vendor to write its own key-event logging system.

Using Web logs is common for many smaller online services. Typically, Web logs will capture all activity on the Web server. An entry is written to the log each time a link is clicked or anything is sent to the browser, whether that is a page of a PDF file, a stream of HTML, or an icon appearing on the screen. The advantage of using the built-in logging service is that it is easy to set up, and a number of commercial products are available to help with the analysis and report generation.

For high-volume online services, using Web logs can be problematic. The sheer amount of data gathered can exceed the tool's ability to analyze this data. Analysis can be further complicated when an online service is operating in a stateless mode, using a farm of Web services. In such a stateless environment, a user's session may be served by many Web servers, and thus activity from a single session can be scattered in many logs.

To avoid the complication of merging and processing the huge mountain of data that is recorded by web logs, many larger online services have chosen to create their own key-event logging system. For content providers, key-event logging involves writing software so that their system only writes transactions when an event occurs that they want to track (e.g., the start of a user session, a search, or the retrieval of full text). They do not record each link clicked or icon displayed to the screen. With key-event logging, far less data is being harvested and this data is generally directed to a central data warehouse for processing. The fact that a user session may be handled by more than one server is no longer an issue, because the transactions are merged at the data warehouse.

Even with key-event logging in place, the volume of transactions can still run into the millions per day. Providing a customer with a three-year analysis of full-text requests by journal may require summarizing information from hundreds of millions—or billions—of transactions in the data warehouse. Most libraries expect vendors to provide the usage reports in real time. To avoid the expensive operations of performing real-time queries on the raw data, many vendors perform a procedure known as *rolling up the data* and just store summary-level data. For example, if the usage reports require a count of searches by database on a monthly basis, then rather than recording the thousands of unique searches performed on a given database, these individual searches would be summarized and a single record with a count of searches for the month stored for the database. The advantage of rolling up the data is that much less storage is required and report delivery is many times faster. The downside comes when reporting needs change and a different level of summarization is needed—without the raw data the vendor has lost this ability.

Customers are generally provided access to the usage statistics through a Web-based reporting module, often bundled with other administrative tools. The typical reporting module is password-protected and allows a customer to generate reports only from activity on their own account.

Reporting modules will vary in sophistication, but most will offer a variety of reports, each with multiple choices for refining the report. The following are examples of criteria that can be used to tailor reports:

- Limit by institution (when report is for a consortium);
- Limit by user group or IP range;
- Limit by database;
- Limit by date range; and
- Select fields to show.

Collecting, maintaining and providing timely access to usage statistics is a complex task. This can be a costly endeavor for vendors who, for the most part, provide this service at no additional charge to their customers.

## Impact of Standards

A number of standards initiatives exist to promote uniformity in the handling of usage statistics. From the vendor's perspective, the two initiatives that have the greatest impact are ICOLC and COUNTER. These two initiatives set out specific guidelines for the elements to capture and the types of reports that are needed. Behind both of these standards is NISO Z39.7 (NISO, 2003), the library statistics standard that is designed "to assist the information community in the identification, definition, collection, and interpretation of statistical data used to describe the current status and condition of libraries in the United States" (NISO, 2003, Introduction). Chapter 9 contains additional discussions of ICOLC, COUNTER, and NISO Z39.7.

ICOLC's *Guidelines for Statistical Measures of Usage of Web-based Information Resources* (ICOLC, 2001) identifies the elements that are to be provided, as well setting out the minimum requirements for the subdivisions used to delineate the reports (see Table 10-2).

**Table 10-2**
**ICOLC requirements.**

| Elements to Capture | Report Subdivisions | Example Reports |
|---|---|---|
| Number of Sessions | Database | Consortium |
| Number of Queries | Institution | member report |
| Number of Menu | (consortium member) | Journal title usage |
| Selections | Overall consortium | report |
| Number of | Time periods | Institutional |
| Full-Content Units | – Month as primary | database report |
| – by journal | coverage unit | Consortium |
| – by database | – Annual | database report |
| Number of Turnaways | aggregation | |
| | – Ranges of months | |
| | – Usage summary | |
| | by hour of day | |

ICOLC provides examples of reports for reference only, and these are not intended to be required reports. ICOLC does address some of the common issues in processing the statistics by stating, "Immediately repeated duplicate searches, double clicks, or other evidence indicating unintended user behavior should not be counted."

The *COUNTER Code of Practice* (http://www.projectcounter.org/code_practice.html) takes the ICOLC guidelines to the next level by introducing a more formal notion of compliance (see Table 10-3). The code of practice not only lays out the elements to be captured, it is also explicit on how the data is to be processed. It also dictates the exact report formats to be offered by vendors.

Vendors need to meet the COUNTER requirements as described in Table 10-3 in order to be listed as compliant. In 2005 a formal audit of the vendor's statistical output will be required to obtain certification of compliance.

NISO Z39.7 is another important initiative. As the only *official* standard of the three, it serves as a centerpiece for normalizing definitions of terms. The definitions also provide insight into how the various statistics are to be processed. Table 10-4 compares the elements presented by these three standards initiatives, and more detailed comparisons of these e-metrics are available in Appendices 4-A and 4-B of this book.

Standards initiatives such as NISO Z39.7, ICOLC, and COUNTER are, without a doubt, good for the library. These initiatives promote uniformity in the statistics gathered from different vendors. Uniformity allows the statistics of different vendors and institutions to be accumulated, compared, and contrasted.

For the vendor, being able to reference standards and best practices is a real benefit when developing and enhancing statistical reporting systems. Virtually all vendors are interested in providing functionality that is useful to their customers. This interest becomes even more pronounced when compliance becomes embodied in contracts.

Having these standards to follow removes some of the guesswork from development. This should translate to lower development costs as the basic requirements are formally documented by these initiatives.

## Issues Faced by Vendors

The standards initiatives mentioned have, by necessity, taken a pragmatic approach of addressing only the most common elements. In order to encourage wide adoption by both the library and vendor communities, these initiatives focused on only the most generally accepted elements and reporting needs. However, organizations for which vendors provide statistics will frequently have more detailed requirements. Additionally, as the electronic information landscape evolves, so do the statistical requirements.

**Table 10-3**
**COUNTER requirements.**

| Elements to Capture | Processing | Report Subdivisions | Required Reports |
|---|---|---|---|
| Sessions<br>Searches Run | –Remove double-clicks of same HTML link within 10 seconds. | Institution<br>Department within institution | –Journal Report 1<br>(Full-text requests by journal) |
| Full-text Requests<br>– by journal<br>– by databaseTurnaways | –Remove double-clicks of same PDF link within 30 seconds.<br>–Use session inactivity time limit of 30 minutes.<br>– Count only transactions with accepted return codes in Web logs | Overall consortium<br>Time periods<br>– monthly accumulation<br>– calendar year orientation | –Journal Report 2<br>(Turnaways by journal)<br>–Database Report 1<br>(Sessions and searches by database)<br>–Database Report 2<br>(Turnaways by database) |
| | | | – Database Report 3 (Total sessions and searches for service)<br>– Format as Excel spreadsheet of comma-separated format that can be imported into Excel. |

**Table 10-4**
**Comparisons of data elements in standards.**

| ICOLC Term | COUNTER Term | NISO Z39.7 Equivalent | NISO Selected Notes |
|---|---|---|---|
| Sessions | Sessions | 7.9.1.3 Sessions | Vendors to report if time-out is other than 30 minutes. |
| Queries | Searches Run | 7.9.1.2 Searches/Menu Selections (Queries) | Do not count mistyped searches or activity from crawlers. |
| Menu Selections | | | Include menu selections under searches. |
| Full-Content Units | Full-Text Requests | 7.9.1.1.2 Commercial Services Full-Content Units Examined | Definition is derived from ICOLC. |
| Turnaways | Turnaways | 7.9.1.4 Rejected Sessions (Turnaways) | Failure of login because of wrong passwords is excluded. |

The standards initiatives only address the very basic needs of the library community. This leaves vendors needing to fulfill the additional requirements of their customer base. Frequently large customers, particularly consortiums, will frequently have some very specific needs that the vendor will agree to in order to secure the business. The net result is that the vendor will create systems for capturing and presenting statistics that meet this more detailed need.

## Standards Often Mean Additional Development

On the positive side, some of the standards initiatives prescribe how statistics are to be processed, and these documented requirements can be applied to all of the vendor's statistics. This means less work for the vendor.

However, there are instances in which new standards mean additional work, and there are two examples of this. The first is the obvious case of new standards defining new reports, e-metrics, and/or mechanisms. This is not avoidable (*new* implies *undone*), and should be recognized as a cost associated with late-breaking work in the standards area. Also, the fact that it takes work to create a momentum for change should not be overlooked. This is one reason human nature resists change—it takes work.

A more tangible example is the COUNTER reports. These reports have a specific format and tend to be much simpler than those offered by most vendors. They also have some idiosyncrasies, such as providing only a calendar-year view of results that are more restrictive than the vendor's current reports. As a result, vendors must create these new reports, in some cases having to modify the way they capture or store data. Since these reports provide less functionality (for some uses) than existing reports, the COUNTER reports will appear as additional options and will not replace existing reports.

## Standards Do Not Address Publisher Needs

Most of the standards initiatives are either driven by libraries or have been created to address the needs of libraries. Many vendors that host content provided by others are also obliged to provide statistics reports to the publishers of the information they host.

Many vendors create a separate report generation system to meet the needs of their publisher partners. Not only are the reports somewhat different from those they provide for libraries, the way the data is accumulated is also different. For instance, a library is interested in the activity of all titles they subscribe to regardless of the publisher, whereas the publisher is interested in seeing (or restricted to seeing) only the activity on their own titles from all customers.

Frequently, individual publishers will require special reports to meet some specific need. For the vendor this means the added expense of custom reporting, on top of the cost of building the separate reporting system for publishers.

## Conflicting Definitions Can Be a Problem

NISO Z39.7 states that mistyped queries should not be counted. COUNTER mentions that searches with zero hits should be included (descriptive text for Journal Report 4). The ICOLC guidelines are silent on this issue.

The zero-hit situation is an excellent example of how something simple can impact not only the results, but the cost of processing. To step back for a moment, there is more than one school of thought when it comes to zero-hit queries. If a researcher is doing advanced work and is validating a dissertation topic, then a zero-hit query is a good thing. However, if an undergraduate is trying to find information, a zero-hit query may be due to bad spelling—or it may be just a badly structured query. An online service that performs natural language searches will have far fewer zero-hit queries (because hits are often returned if any of the words match) than another online service using strict Boolean syntax, yet the effectiveness of both systems could be equal.

Furthermore, the notion of eliminating "mistyped query," as suggested by NISO, is an extremely subjective and possibly expensive proposition for the vendor. Many online services provide access to complex materials, often in more than one language. Determining what is mistyped becomes a challenge. One could surmise that a mistyped query is simply one that gets zero hits, or perhaps a mistyped query is one containing words that are not in the dictionary. If so, the question is *which* dictionary—and what about acronyms and technical terms?

For the vendor, the inconsistency of the standards in areas such as zero-hit queries leaves room for interpretation and room for discrepancies when comparing results between vendors. For some online services the percentage of queries yielding zero hits can be 25% or greater. This situation is bad for the libraries, and it may also increase the cost to the vendor who chooses to provide a flexible solution. For example, in order to address the zero-hit query situation, a vendor may choose to store a count of zero-hit queries separately from the count of queries that generated hits, and then introduce an option by which the library can choose if these should be included or not.

## Are Information Needs Outpacing Standards?

At the beginning of this chapter the author listed a number of vendors who are involved in providing information services to libraries. The standards initiatives tend to focus on only a few types of vendors, namely the full-text aggregator, the publisher, and e-journal hosting sites. Standards for the other vendor types are incomplete, even at the most basic level.

E-journal gateways have been offering libraries a single site for cross-publisher access for a number of years. These gateways may not deliver the full text directly, but may instead link the end user to the content. As a central access point for what may be a considerable portion of the library's electronic holdings, the gateway can offer some interesting insight into journal usage. However, the standards initiatives do not address how this activity should be measured.

Link resolvers are a technology that puts the library in the driver's seat when it comes to directing the end user to the correct information. As the middleman that sits between most of the library's online services, the link resolver is uniquely positioned to provide statistical information on collection use and end-user access patterns. The standards initiatives have yet to begin to address this type of activity.

A-to-Z lists, like their link-resolver and E-journal gateway cousins, facilitate access by end users to a library's holdings. Although the search and session counts that may occur within an A-to-Z application are addressed by standards initiatives, it is the resource-level activity that is of most interest.

Another technology that is starting to take root is that of the metasearch (federated) engine. This technology is logically inserted above many of the library's online services and searches many services and databases simultaneously. The nature of metasearch engines is such that a single user query on the metasearch interface can result in dozens of sessions and searches being invoked on the underlying online services, creating an overall inflation of search and session counts. Standards initiatives have not yet begun to address this phenomenon.

Although standards do provide vendors with some direction for the basic statistical services, the vendors are required to address the immediate needs of the market as new services are being offered.

## Future Visions May Stress Standards and Vendors

Recently there have been discussions of future trends in standards and codes of practice. Some of these trends will address needs of the libraries and others will address the needs of the publisher. All of these trends will affect the vendor as they work to create systems that are and continue to be *compliant*. Table 10-5 lists just some of the trends and the issues they may cause for vendors.

**Table 10-5**
**Vendor issues due to future trends in usage statistics.**

| Trend | Primary Audience | Needs Addressed | Issues for Vendors |
|---|---|---|---|
| Breakdown of usage by section of journal | Publisher | *Development of content* by being able to better analyze which sections of a publication draw readers and which do not. | Vendors such as aggregators may not have sufficient metadata to identify journal sections. Journal sections may be handled differently from publisher to publisher and journal to journal. |
| Breakdown of usage by subscribed or nonsubscribed | Publisher/Library | *Collection management tool* that can be used to demonstrate to libraries how packaged journal sets are being used. High usage of nonsubscribed content indicates the value of the extra content made available through the deal. | This can only really apply to publishers and their online hosting sites. Aggregators and gateways may not know what is under subscription and what is not. |
| Breakdown of usage by year of publication | Publisher/Library | *Collection management tool* that can help determine the importance of back files of content. | The vendor must at least store the year published along with the transaction. This may increase the amount of information stored, with a resulting increase in cost for storage and processing. |
| Article-level statistics | Publisher | *Ranking of authors* based on the use that an author's writings see. If publishers can relate an article to additional information, such as subject category, they can use this information as another *product development tool* by looking for trends in the usage, not only by journal but also by subject. This information can be used to adapt journals to better meet the needs of their readership. | The level of detail that must be stored to retain a history for article-level activity can increase storage/processing requirements by as much as 50 times. This results in higher costs for the vendor. |

## Providing Consistent Breakdowns for Statistics

Both the COUNTER and ICOLC guidelines reference IP range as a means of providing a breakdown of statistics by institution, group, or department. Unfortunately, IP address is not a constant. Many organizations use proxy servers or firewalls to protect the site. In these organizations, all users share the same IP address, so IP range is not a valid measure. Other institutions provide their users with remote access without using proxy servers. In these cases the user's IP address could reflect their Internet service provider or even a computer at another site, and not that of the institution. In still other situations, two or more sites (usually within the same organization) may share the same set of dynamically assigned IP ranges. In all of these cases, IP is neither an accurate nor a reasonable method of providing statistical breakdowns.

For the vendor, who wants to provide solutions for most—if not all—customers, this issue presents a problem. Some customers will insist on IP breakdown, while others will need some other method of achieving the desired results. The normal answer is to introduce the notion of user groups or access profiles into the account structure and to track usage statistics by these subdivisions. The customer must be given a mechanism to allow the appropriate subdivision to be specified on login.

ICOLC and COUNTER both stipulate the need for reports to be summarized to the consortium level. Given that IP address ranges are unreliable, the vendor's system will need to store relationships between institutions and consortium so that the roll-up of statistics can occur. This scenario is made much more complicated to achieve because institutions are often members of multiple consortia, and for a given vendor it is possible that the institution may receive access to different resources from the same vendor, but through different consortia.

## Different Markets Have Different Needs

Needs for statistics vary by market and, to a certain extent, by geography. Corporate customers may want very detailed reporting of activity by end user to allow charge-back of the service to the user's department. Such reports often include a listing of articles and journals accessed. Public institutions, on the other hand, often require that no connection is made or retained between individual users and the information they access—their motivation being the protection of individual freedoms. The vendor who serves multiple markets must create a system which retains the detailed user information for one customer while protecting user anonymity for another.

## Summary

The success of a vendor is often determined by their ability to provide services that meet the needs of their customers. The provision of usage statistics is no exception–a vendor must meet the needs of the customers or partners to gain or retain their business.

Standards initiatives help pave the way to meeting market-specific needs by providing a frame of reference upon which to base systems development. In this regard, standards have a positive impact for vendors by providing the yardstick necessary for measuring success. But standards provide only partial answers–or partial guidance, if you like. The needs of libraries, publishers, and the vendors themselves are varied and complex. Add to this the sheer volume of information gathered and stored, and the underlying systems quickly become very sophisticated. This sophistication is reflected in the cost to create and maintain the required solution. Ultimately the customer is the one to pay.

In the future we will see even more of a library's collection available online. The techniques and technologies used to provide access to this content will continue to evolve. Linking technologies, which have taken root in recent years, will become an even greater asset. Metasearch engines will improve and become more prevalent. Libraries will demand more statistical feedback to better understand their content, their users, and their systems, so that all three can be managed more effectively. For the vendor of these solutions, the new challenges in providing user access will be joined by equal challenges in presenting effective usage information. Ideally, standards initiatives will keep pace with the changing times, not only to promote consistency for the library community, but also to help the vendor control the escalating costs of providing the service.

## References

Counting Online Usage of Networked Electronic Resources (COUNTER). See http://www.projectcounter.org/. Last accessed March 11, 2004.

International Coalition of Library Consortia (ICOLC). (2001). Guidelines for statistical measures of usage of Web-based information resources. Available at http://www.library.yale.edu/consortia/2001webstats.htm. Last accessed March 11, 2004.

National Information Standards Organization (NISO). (2003). *NISO Z39.7-200X Draft. Information Services and Use: Metrics & statistics for libraries and information providers–Data Dictionary.* Bethesda, MD: National Information Standards Organization. Available at http://www.niso.org/emetrics/. Last accessed March 11, 2004.

# CHAPTER 11

# Key Issues, Themes, and Future Directions for Evaluating Networked Services

## Charles R. McClure

## Introduction

Evaluating networked services continues to be an important topic for libraries planning, implementing, and managing the provision of network services and resources. This networked environment may rely on the Internet, a regional or statewide network, a local library or library system network—or increasingly, a combination of all of the above. Nevertheless, a significant shift in attention and resources is occurring as libraries attempt to better exploit the networked environment to meet user information needs and provide a range of innovative services.

E-metrics are indictors that describe the amount, frequency, type, or other aspects of a service, program, or resources available electronically. The importance of e-metrics for library and information services continues to expand as additional services, resources, and programs are made available in a networked environment. Libraries depend increasingly on such services to supplement traditional services—or in some cases, to replace some traditional services—as users become more familiar with and dependent on the Internet and the Web.

Libraries have maintained a host of traditional statistics that describe their activities and use, both in the print environment and from a library building. Statistics from the networked environment (e-metrics) also are essential to:

- Describe the *total* range of services use and other activities taking place over the network through the library;
- Justify the provision and costs of these networked services;
- Determine which networked services are *most important* to maintain or augment, and which might be eliminated;
- Assess the degree to which the costs of these services and resources are acceptable, given their use and impact;
- Ensure that the information needs of users of these networked services are being met;
- Determine if the information technology infrastructure of the library adequately supports the provision of these networked services; and
- Plan for the next generation of networked services.

For these and additional reasons, e-metrics require careful attention from libraries and information centers as they evaluate existing services and plan for new ones.

This book begins with an assumption stated by Bertot and Davis in their Preface:

> Libraries in general do not assess their network services and resources, incorporate network service and resource assessment into larger organizational evaluation efforts, or report the actual use, uses, and value of libraries in an increasingly networked society. This leads to two significant problems for library managers and staff: (1) They do not have access to critical data that can assist them in making key decisions regarding services and resources, and (2) They do not have data that can demonstrate to the communities that they serve the true nature of library use and value, one that reflects both building-based and network services and resources.

The book offers a range of information, strategies, methods, metrics, analyses, and insights that may help to remedy this situation.

The chapters in this book all demonstrate the importance and need for evaluating network services and resources, and the use of e-metrics. But more than this, the chapters also identify a range of practices, issues, challenges, and opportunities that together paint an important state-of-the-art view of e-metrics and their application. Drawing on both the content in this book and the experience of the author, the purpose of this final chapter is to highlight these practices, issues, challenges, and opportunities and offer an integrated perspective and set of recommendations for future work in this area. Given the range of material covered in previous chapters, some themes, issues, and future directions clearly are significant.

## Themes

An overall theme throughout the book is that we currently have "exciting times" in the evaluation of network services and the development and application of e-metrics. This excitement, however, borders on the excitement of going 180 miles per hour with no brakes. Nevertheless, the following sections identify and discuss key themes and issues.

### We're Making Progress

Even with the premise of the book that much work still needs to be done in the evaluation of network services, one can also suggest that much progress has been made and is being made in evaluation methodologies, practical strategies, metrics, standards, and coordinated efforts among various stakeholder groups. In short, the state of the art for evaluation of network services in 2004 is considerably better than in 2000. The comparative list of e-metrics and indicators in the appendix for Chapter 3 simply could not have been written in 2000.

The first three chapters of the book offer a range of new ideas and approaches that demonstrate the strides that have been made in the area of new and improved methods. The various tools to support the evaluation effort described in Chapter 3 also demonstrate a number of approaches that libraries can integrate into the day-to-day practice. Indeed, the evolution of a set of tools and validated e-metrics for the evaluation of networked services–in both academic and public libraries– bodes well for library staff to actually *do* evaluation.

Progress is also evident in developing a better conceptual understanding of evaluation in a networked environment and how this process is similar to and different from evaluation in a print-based environment. The model offered in Bertot's "Complexity of Access to Network Services and Resources" (Fig. 3-8) demonstrates that a range of considerations affect the evaluation of networked services. For example, the impact on technology and the type of information infrastructure in a specific library can have a huge effect on the types of methods that are appropriate for evaluation, the type of data that will be generated, and the manner in which users access networked information.

## We're All in This Together

Some years ago an academic library director commented to this writer that evaluation of network services in his library was much more complicated than in smaller libraries or public libraries. The more the director tried to make this point the better he made the case that "a full text download" is, in fact, a full text download, regardless of whether it occurs in an academic, school, public, or special library. Moreover, the method to compute a full text download also stays the same in every setting. In recent years there has been a growing realization that evaluation methods and metrics for the networked environment have more commonalities than differences among types and sizes of libraries.

Database vendors have also recognized the need to work more closely with the broader library community in terms of the development of networked services. Pesch (Chapter 10) outlines a range of issues and strategies that EBSCO has considered as it has moved to work more closely with the library community. The establishment of the COUNTER group—also noted by Pesch—indicates that the vendor-publisher community is actively involved in working with the library community to improve the process by which data and procedures for their collection can be improved.

Another encouraging aspect of recognizing the importance of all stakeholder groups' involvement with network evaluation is the increased involvement of various vendors in this process. For the last five years an informal group of database vendors; state, academic, public and consortia librarians; researchers; and government officials have met in conjunction with the American Library Association's mid-year conference. At these meetings, participants update each other on new developments, key issues, strategies, projects, and other information broadly related to evaluation and metrics in the networked environment. This sharing of information and ideas has demonstrated that solutions for evaluation issues are best when they include the views from a range of stakeholder groups.

## We Have Tools and Methods

No longer can the library community dismiss the evaluation of network services because we do not have evaluation tools or evaluation methods, nor because we lack either basic or conceptual knowledge about evaluation of network services and the use of e-metrics. The chapters by Bertot (1, 3, 4), Bertot and Snead (2), and Pesch (10) make clear that these tools are available. Indeed, work that is summarized in this book, as well as additional work done by others and referenced throughout the book, clearly shows that the tools, methods, models, and e-metrics are available, have been tested, and work.

In addition, a number of *specialty* guides, manuals, and workbooks have been developed within the broad area of evaluation of networked services. For example, Matthews (2002) offered *The Bottom Line: Determining and Communicating the Value of the Special Library* with an appendix presenting a range of performance measures, many of which deal with network services, as well as his 2004 work, *Measuring for Results: The Dimensions of Public Library Effectiveness.* McClure et al. (2002) produced *Statistics, Measures, and Quality Standards for Assessing Digital Reference Library Services: Guidelines and Procedures.* As of 2004, NISO is developing a standard for networked reference services and has a draft standard under review for Library Statistics, Z39.7 (http://www.niso.org/emetrics). These and other sources provide plenty of metrics for evaluating networked services.

The advancements described in this book and noted in the various references also suggest that new tools and methods will continue to evolve over time. For example, Moen et al. (2004) are developing tools that can analyze online database usage statistics produced by different vendors. In addition, new research related to using server log files to assess Web use (Sterne, 2002) suggests that software programs such as WebTrends, Webtracker, and others will become increasingly sophisticated and useful in the future. The concern is *not* that there are adequate tools available, but rather that librarians will take advantage of using these tools!

## We Need More Research

Virtually all of the chapters in this book either directly or indirectly conclude with a range of questions, issues, and concerns about how best to conduct network service and resource assessment, implement and organize network assessment strategies within the library, select appropriate and *useful* e-metrics and indicators for library assessment needs, and use vendor data successfully, as well as how network assessment can improve the overall quality of networked services and resources. These are but a few of the research topics identified throughout the book.

At present, only a handful of researchers are addressing these and related research questions. If we are to continue making progress in how to assess network services successfully, there is a need for more research, more support for research, and more researchers engaging in such activities.

## Issues

The book raises numerous issues that will require attention if the evaluation of network services and the development of e-metrics are to continue to evolve. All of these issues cannot be summarized in this chapter, but a number of the issues raised cut across two or more chapters.

## Do You Believe?

This writer's beginning experience with performance indicators and library evaluation dates back to doctoral work at Rutgers University with Ernie DeProspo in the mid-1970s. At that time—and since—evaluation oftentimes remains as a "hard sell." Many of us who studied with DeProspo recall his oft-stated quip that library evaluation was a concept in search of a practice. On this score, however, there is little apparent change. This writer's view is that while much lip service is given to evaluation, there continues to be a struggle to implement ongoing programmatic library evaluation on a regular basis—regardless of the type of library and regardless of the importance and potential positive impacts of such evaluation.

There are a number of approaches to consider in the process of increasing the practice of evaluation and the belief that evaluation is an important management component essential for the successful development and operation of the library. One approach is through *persuasion,* in which the evidence of evaluation is so self-evident that library staff clearly see the importance and impact of the effort. Another approach is the *fascist* approach, in which funding agencies require some type of ongoing evaluation on a regular basis—no evaluation, then no funding. Still another approach, best described as a *facilitative* approach, would provide incentives, training, and clear rewards to those that evaluate services successfully.

Thus, the issue is: How can the evaluation of network services evolve into an ongoing practice in the library community? The chapters in this book suggest that *conceptual* advances in the testing of specific e-metrics and the use of various methodologies have surpassed the *actual* use of these concepts, metrics, and methods. To some degree, those who believe in the importance and use of ongoing evaluation have yet to convince those in the field that evaluation is, in fact, worth their time and effort.

## Reliance on Vendor Statistics

While it is clear that there are improved working relationships among vendors, librarians, aggregators, and software developers, the library community relies on vendor-supplied data to evaluate network services and resources. Shim (Chapter 9) points out that there is still a significant range of effort required by librarians to use these data supplied by various vendors. Further, the extent, quality, and comparability of the vendor-based data vary widely from vendor to vendor. Libraries that hope to be able to provide comprehensive, integrated, and accurate statistical use summaries of online databases simply cannot do so at this time—or they cannot do so without making a number of estimates, assumptions, and extrapolations.

So while we applaud the improved communication and working environment among the members of the library and vendor communities, much work needs to be done. Pesch outlines some of this work, but the key issues here are:

- How can vendors better coordinate and standardize the data that they provide to the library community?

- To what degree can vendors improve their management modules on their various products to assist in evaluation?

- Is it possible to develop software that can better integrate data across vendors to produce summaries of use and users that are accurate and timely?

- How can the library community better articulate its needs in terms of the collection and presentation of data from the vendors?

The library community must recognize that vendors cannot provide customized datasets for each library on demand, or spend significant consulting time assisting each library in using and understanding their datasets. And as Davis points out in Chapter 6, the licensing agreements and negotiations for such services can be complex. On the other hand, the vendors must recognize that better use of existing standards (e.g., NISO) and better software to manage and manipulate data can improve evaluation efforts significantly.

## Costs and Use as Drivers of Services

For many libraries, the recent years have produced relatively stagnant budgets that may have increased marginally, may have generally stayed the same, or may have declined somewhat. Given the range of pressures on libraries for staffing, resources, programs, facilities, and so forth, careful scrutiny of the purchase of network resources and services will likely continue. Yet against this backdrop, prices for many networked services and products have increased; information technology, when considered system-wide, has increased; and maintenance and repair of the physical facility continues to increase.

As Hoitt and Zerkow point out in Chapter 8, innovative–and perhaps some nontraditional–means to determine what network services and resources are most important, receive the most use, and cost the least will likely receive more attention in the future. At issue here is how best to balance the costs of electronic services (and their supporting infrastructure) against other library costs in light of the use of these products and services. Also at issue is how to negotiate good agreements with vendors and others in the business of providing network services and resources.

To some degree, then, the library community needs data from vendors as a basis to make purchase decisions. Such decisions may require a granularity or detail in the data that vendors either cannot or might be unwilling to provide. Further, some vendors may be reticent to provide such data if analysis of the data results in reduction of purchases. How vendors and the library community might find common ground on what data are needed to *best* assess collections and use will be an interesting process over the next few years. Nevertheless, it is clear that costs and use (however defined) will drive the purchase of electronic services and products in the near term.

## Comparative Data

The quest for comparative national data among libraries continues to be a complex issue, despite the good work on NISO and ISO standards and guidelines from ICOLC (http://www.library.yale.edu/consortia/) and COUNTER (http://www.projectcounter.org/index.html). In addition to the national and international policy issues described by Bertot and Davis, policy issues related to the responsibility for collecting, analyzing, and reporting networked information are still unclear. Key players in this area in the United States are the National Commission on Libraries and Information Science (NCLIS), the Institute for Museum and Library Services (IMLS), the National Center for Educational Statistics, and the various library professional organizations such as the American Library Association and the Association of Research Libraries.

Comparative data cannot be collected to describe network services and resources until there is agreement as to whom or what has responsibility for collecting what data, and when. Currently, the patchwork of organizations and agencies involved in this issue results in inadequate and untimely data that describes network services and resources in the library community. Resolving the issue of responsibility for collecting national and comparable data to describe network services and resources is only part of the problem. Yet to be addressed is the issue of augmenting existing national data collection efforts so that a meaningful range of statistics that describe networked services is accomplished. Without such national data the library community is unable to effectively contend with various policy debates at both the state and the national level.

Comparative data also depend on the development and acceptance of standards. Simply stated, the measure "units/records examined," (as an example) has to be defined the same—and the method employed to produce the statistic has to be same—every time it is used. The only standard currently available is the NISO Z39.7 standard on Library Statistics

(NISO, 2003). This standard, while currently under development, will need to be constantly updated and expanded– which will take considerable time and effort. But we also need to recognize that guidelines that have been offered by COUNTER (Project COUNTER, 2003) and by ICOLC (ICOLC, 2001) are not national or international standards with the status of Z39.7 and ISO 2789. Thus, an issue in this area is the need to evolve and expand data collection and measurement standards at the same time as the development of new methods and measures continues.

# Future Directions

As the library community continues its work and experimentation regarding the measurement and evaluation of networked services, a number of future directions still require attention. This section offers some recommendations for which future directions might be most useful to pursue in the immediate years ahead.

## Quick and Clean Core Metrics, Measures, and Statistics

One might suggest that currently, the problem is not the lack of metrics, measures, and statistics, but rather the assessment of *which* measures, metrics, and statistics are *most useful* and provide the *best insights* in evaluating network services and resources. Library managers simply do not have the time and resources to collect a broad range of data to assess network services. They need methods that are quick, clean, and valid; they need to determine which metrics would best assist them in planning and services development at their library; and they need metrics that are possible to collect automatically and unobtrusively–an example being log file analysis.

Research into this topic needs to better understand contingencies, or the factors unique to a specific library and its provision of network services, as a decision factor for which metrics are most important for that library (see Chapters 1 through 4). Experience by this author, and other authors in this book, in working with a range of libraries to evaluate network services and resources is that one size does not fit all when it comes to selecting measures for use in a particular library environment. Moreover, factors that should affect the selection and use of metrics need to consider the library's political environment and the importance of determining in advance the metrics that "sell" or make sense to external constituencies.

## Understanding Evaluation Data

Consider the following questions:

1. If the average cost per search is $0.49, is that *good* or *bad?*

2. If, on average, there is one search per resident per year, is that *good* or *bad*?

Ultimately, library decision makers will need to place a value judgment on what constitutes *good* or *bad* usage data in light of ongoing longitudinal data and trends in that data; benchmarking the data compared to other similar libraries or consortia; consideration of usage statistics with data coming from focus groups and individual interviews (among other techniques) that explore satisfaction and use; and in consideration of target goals and objectives and *expectations* for desired levels of use of these various networked services and resources.

One should also note that because X number of searches, sessions, or downloads occurred, it is still not possible to say that these activities satisfied a user's information need, if he or she found the information helpful, or if the information obtained was accurate, for example. In short, usage data provided are *indicators* of use and not necessarily of satisfaction or other factors related to the quality or impact of the networked services or resources. A better understanding of how- and why-related questions having to do with networked services evaluation should be a top research priority in the years ahead. Understanding evaluation data in a particular library context will require multimethod evaluation approaches, with multiple metrics. We must move beyond *how much* of something occurred and concentrate on why did it occur, what was the impact/outcome of that use, and to what degree did such use satisfy user information needs (see Chapters 1 through 4).

## Managing Networked Evaluation Data

In the future, much more attention needs to be given to managing and integrating library evaluation data. Again, the author's experience is that the vast majority of libraries need to:

• Maintain evaluation data in a systematic management information system or decision support system;

• Collect e-metrics longitudinally with standard definitions;

• Collect data other than that required by an external governing or national reporting agency;

- Integrate evaluation data into other descriptive data from the library's OPAC, from community information and community demographics, etc.;

- Establish a formal organizational mechanism with a regular budget for evaluation and assign specific responsibilities for the evaluation effort; and

- Produce regular and timely reports on evaluation results that are targeted at specific audiences, such as governing boards, users, trustees, policy makers, etc.

These are but a few of the recommendations that need to be considered in the management of evaluation data. Sadly, evaluation of any type—to say nothing of network evaluation—is often a one-shot effort conducted to meet a pressing need, and then forgotten.

Development of manuals to assist libraries in the management of evaluation data may be as important as the development of manuals on how to collect and analyze the evaluation data. The best practices in how this is being done now (if in fact there are best practices) need to be described and distributed so that everyone does not have to reinvent the wheel when managing and integrating evaluation data into a coherent process.

## The Changing Environment of Evaluating Network Services

In the past, library statistics were relatively static. Volume and title counts (and a range of other statistics) could be computed with the same method year after year. Such is not the case in the networked environment. Evaluation of networked services will require ongoing changes in method and measurement for the following reasons:

- Technology innovations and advancements are likely to continue;
- In-house applications of that technology and the degree to which that technology is interoperable with other technologies will change;
- Measures that may have once seemed especially useful (sessions) may not be useful as the technology changes (in this case due to authentication, fire walls, and emerging federated search engines); and
- New network services and products that we cannot imagine now will be developed (i.e., the capability to search multiple databases simultaneously) and will require methods and measures for assessment.

Some implications of this situation are that (1) ongoing research will be necessary to accommodate these changes and produce valid methods and measures to assess network services and resources, and (2) measures may have a very short life span, making longitudinal assessments quite difficult.

Thus, the key questions are:

- How well can the library community adapt to these changes and develop new methods and measures?
- Are there adequate researchers and support for research related to assessing networked services and resources on an ongoing basis?
- How quickly can the library community respond to and implement the new technologies and applications?
- To what degree is the library community willing to stay up-to-date with the development of new methods and measures?

The much-mentioned term *change management* may take on a whole new meaning as libraries continue to move services into the networked environment.

## Training, Training, and More Training

Learning how to implement a formal, ongoing process of evaluation of networked services requires learning new information, obtaining additional skills, and supporting an attitude that evaluation is important and necessary for the long-term success of any library. Education and skills development can occur through:

- National conferences and workshops;
- Online instructional modules such as those developed at the Information Institute of Florida State University for the Florida State Library, in the areas of outcomes assessment (see http://www.lstatoolkit.com) and e-metrics instruction (see http://www.ii.fsu.edu/emis) (Bertot, et al., 2004);
- On-site staff training and development;
- Formal coursework at institutions of higher education; and
- One-on-one, on-the-job skills development and education as a normal part of professional staff development.

The venue for training related to assessing networked services may be less important than that some training is made available and supported by library administration. New topics that may require staff training related to network services assessment include (but are not limited to):

- Statistics uses and applications;
- Focus groups;
- Online and traditional surveys;
- Interviews;
- Log file analysis;
- Unobtrusive data collection strategies and techniques;
- Report writing; and
- Data management.

Indeed, a key to successful staff training is the degree to which library administration supports such training efforts, rewards those who participate in training and education, and integrates that training into the ongoing management and development of networked services.

## Improving Library Network Services and Resources

As libraries continue to depend increasingly on delivering services and resources in the networked environment, so too must they determine the overall cost, effectiveness, quality, and impact of these services. Perhaps the most striking example of this dependence is the reliance on library Web sites that now provide access to full-text online databases, chat-based reference services, the capability to check one's circulation records, placing a hold on an item that someone wants to check out, and completing an interlibrary loan request. While these and other services may be available in a traditional service context, they increasingly are network-based.

To *not* know what web pages are most often hit, to *not* know where 404 errors are generated, to *not* know if the quality of the chat-based reference is the same or better than the on-site reference service, or to *not* know what pages of the website are opened rarely is to invite disaster. Ignorance is not bliss when it comes to the effectiveness, cost, impact, or benefit of library services—regardless of whether they are delivered in a networked or a traditional environment. Thus, libraries will need to become better organized to conduct network evaluations, better trained, and better able to take evaluation results and integrate them into the decision making process.

The risk to libraries is that they may become marginalized. Becoming marginalized means that the services that libraries provide are better provided by other services and organizations, at less cost and with greater impact. Why, for example, do most Web users go directly to a search engine such as Google rather than to the homepage of their local academic or public library? Addressing questions such as this one will be critical to the long-term success of libraries in the networked environment. Ongoing assessment of how well libraries provide these services, as a basis for improving them and for developing new and innovative services that compete with other providers in the networked environment, will be essential.

The challenges to the library community are to continue research and development in assessing network services and resources; to improve the working relationships among vendors, librarians, and policy makers to coordinate our work in this area; to continue to demonstrate the importance of assessing networked services, regardless of library type; and to use the assessment process as a means to the greater end of improving the quality and usefulness of networked services to library users. As libraries rely more on the provision of services and resources in the networked environment, these challenges will take on increased importance. The day of the electronic *networked* library (one that is *only* electronic and networked) may not be too far away!

This book draws attention to these and other issues. The various chapters accomplish the following:

- Provide the context for the evaluation of library network services and resources;
- Identify e-metrics and performance indicators that enable the assessment of network services and resources;
- Offer guidance on the selection, methods, analysis, and use of various e-metrics and performance indicators for decision making and other purposes that *best* meet the needs of various library situational factors;
- Suggest additional forms of evaluation besides e-metrics and performance indicators to derive service quality and outcomes, and others to assess satisfaction with, quality of, and change in users due to library-provided network services and resources;
- Identify the potential impact of emerging technologies, standards development, and other initiatives; and
- Point to the skills, training, and other needs of library professionals as libraries increase their offering of network services and resources.

These and related topics provide an important compendium of basic information related to measuring networked services and resources. But there is additional research and development work still to be done, additional issues that are likely to be identified, and advances in technology that will require new approaches for measurement. Let us hope that in three years there is another comprehensive overview and update as to the research progress made and new knowledge that is available on this topic.

## References

Bertot, J.C, McClure, C.R., Davis, D.M., and Ryan, J. (2004). E-metrics: Get the numbers you need. *Library Journal*, 129 (May 1, 2004): 30–32.

Counting Online Usage of Networked Electronic Resources (COUNTER). See http://www.projectcounter.org/. Last accessed April 10, 2004.

International Coalition of Library Consortia (ICOLC), (1998). Guidelines for statistical measures of usage of web-based indexed, abstracted, and full text resources. *Information Technology and Libraries*, 17(4): 219–221. See also http://www.library.yale.edu/consortia/webstats.html. Additional ICOLC documents are available at http://www.library.yale.edu/consortia/statementsanddocuments.html. Last accessed April 11, 2004.

Matthews, J.R. (2002). *The bottom line: Determining and communicating the value of the special library.* Westport, CT: Libraries Unlimited.

Matthews, J.R. (2004). *Measuring for results: The dimensions of public library effectiveness.* Westport, CT: Libraries Unlimited.

McClure, C.R., Lankes, R.D., Gross, M., and Choltco-Devlin, B. (2002). *Statistics, measures, and quality standards for assessing digital reference library services: Guidelines and procedures.* Syracuse, NY: The Information Institute. Available at http://quartz.syr.edu/quality/quality.pdf.

Moen, W.E., Orguz, F., and McClure, C.R. (2004). *TexShare database usage: A longitudinal analysis.* Denton, TX: Texas Center for Digital Knowledge.

National Information Standards Organization (NISO). (2003). *NISO Z39.7-200X Draft. Information Services and Use: Metrics and statistics for libraries and information providers–Data Dictionary.* Bethesda, MD: National Information Standards Organization. Available at http://www.niso.org/emetrics/. Last accessed March 11, 2004.

National Information Standards Organization (NISO). (2004). Standard for networked reference services. Bethesda, MD: National Information Standards Organization. Available at http://www.loc.gov/standards/netref/. Last accessed April 19, 2004.

Sterne, J. (2002). *Web metrics: Proven methods for measuring Web site Success.* New York: Wiley Publishing Company.

# Index

# About the Editors and Contributors

**JOHN CARLO BERTOT** is Professor in the School of Information Studies at Florida State University. He serves as the Chair of the International Standards Organizations (ISO) Working Group 4 which develops library performance indicator standards; is a member of ISO Working Group 2 which develops library statistics; and serves on the National Information Standards Organizations (NISO) library statistics committee. Bertot serves as editor of *Government Information Quarterly*, an international journal of policy, practice, and management, and co-editor of *Library Quarterly*, the longest running information science journal in the United States.

**DENISE M. DAVIS** has held management positions in technical services, reference and electronic collection development in academic, public and special libraries. From 1995 to 1997 she facilitated the collection development teams of Sailor, Maryland's Online Public Information Network. Denise has graduate-level information studies teaching experience at Syracuse University (NY) and the Catholic University of America, Washington, DC. She is a frequent speaker at local, state and national library conferences.

**JUDITH HIOTT** is the Assistant Coordinator of Materials Selection at the Houston Public Library where she manages the library's electronic collections. Her areas of expertise include collecting networked statistics, federated searching, and electronic books collections. Her MLS is from the University of South Carolina.

**CHARLES R. MCCLURE** is the Francis Eppes Professor and Director of the Information Use Management and Policy Institute in the School of Information Studies at Florida State University. He conducts research, publishes widely, and teaches courses in the areas of library planning and evaluation, library e-metrics and performance indicators, and federal information policy. McClure serves as the associate editor for *Government Information Quarterly.*

**OLIVER PESCH** is the chief architect of EBSCO Publishing. He oversees the technical direction for the EBSCOhost service and has been intimately involved in the development and implementation of multiple generations of the service's comprehensive usage statistics features. Playing an active role in the area of standards, Oliver's numerous committee memberships include NISO committees on OpenURL and Library Statistics, Project COUNTER's Executive Committee and Audit Task Groups, as well as PCC Task Groups 1 and 3 for Journals in Aggregator databases.

**WONSIK "JEFF" SHIM** is assistant professor in the School of Information Studies at Florida State University. Jeff's research focuses on vendor database usage statistics and how libraries can use such statistics for decision-making purposes. Jeff served as the co-principal investigator for the Association of Research Libraries (ARL) e-metrics project, which resulted in the publication of *Data Collection Manual for Academic and Research Library Network Statistics and Performance Measures*, a manual for the collection of e-metrics within academic libraries.

**JOHN "TOMMY" SNEAD** is a doctoral student and research associate for the Information Use Management and Policy Institute at Florida State University. Tommy conducts research and teaches in the areas of planning and evaluation of digital library services and usability.

**SYMA ZERKOW** is the Coordinator of Materials Selection at the Houston Public Library. In this capacity, she guides the development and management of all the library's collections. She is the current chair of TexShare's Electronic Information Working Group. Her MLS is from Columbia University.